The SUFFICIENCY of SCRIPTURE

The
SUFFICIENCY
of
SCRIPTURE

The

Key to

Revival

JOSEPH STEPHEN

The Sufficiency of Scripture
Joseph Stephen

Copyright © 2009-2015 Joseph Stephen
All rights reserved.

Faithful Generations
Orlando, Florida
South Australia, Australia

Library of Congress Catalog Card Number: 2014904766

ISBN-13:978-1-940243-32-0
ISBN-10:1-9402-4332-7

No part of this book may be reproduced without written permission from the publisher or copyright holder, except in the case of brief quotations embodied in critical articles and reviews. No part of this book may be transmitted in any form or by any means—electronic, mechanical, photocopy, recording, or other—without prior written permission from the publisher or copyright holder.

All Scriptures are taken from The *King James Version* of the Holy Bible.

CONTENTS

Foreword xi

Dedication xv
   In memory of my grandmother, Irma Naughton. xv
   To my precious children, grandchildren, and great
      grandchildren. xv

Acknowledgments xvii

Introduction xix

Chapter 1: The Sufficiency of Scripture 1
  1.1 What Is the Sufficiency of Scripture? 2
  1.2 Is the Sufficiency of Scripture a Biblical Doctrine? 7
     1.2.1 God Magnifies His Word Even Above His Name 7
     1.2.2 God Warns Us Not to Add to or Subtract from
           His Word 7
     1.2.3 He Declares That His Written Word Is His Revelation,
           Word for Word, Even to the Last Jot and Tittle (Stroke
           of the Hebrew Pen) 8
     1.2.4 He Declares That His Word Is Not Open to Private
           Interpretation. 8

      1.2.5 He Declares His Word to Be Powerful, Piercing, and Precise 9
      1.2.6 He Declares His Word to Be Perfect and Forever Settled 9
      1.2.7 He Has Declared It Sufficient to Fully Equip the Man of God for Every Good Work 9
      1.2.8 He Declares That His Word Shall Be Accomplished .. 10
      1.2.9 Times of Apostasy Will be Marked by Men Burdened by Their Own Word Rather than God's Word 10
  1.3 Why Is the Sufficiency of Scripture Important? 10
  1.4 What Happens When the Sufficiency of Scripture Is Forsaken? 11
  1.5 Man Is Commanded to Live by Every Word That Proceedeth from the Mouth of God 24
  1.6 Summary of the Doctrine of the Sufficiency of Scripture ... 26

Chapter 2: Personal Revival 27
  2.1 We Must Examine Ourselves to See If We Are in the Faith ... 32
  2.2 We Must Renew Our Mind 33
  2.3 We Must Study God's Character, Titles, and Attributes 35
  2.4 We Must Understand What It Means to Love God with All of Our Hearts, Minds, Souls, and Strength 38
  2.5 We Must Keep God in All Our Thoughts with a Constant Prayerful Attitude 48
  2.6 We Must Constantly Consider the Works of God Both in Creation and History 49
  2.7 We Must Humbly Submit to His Lordship 53
  2.8 We Must Present Our Bodies as Living Sacrifices 54
  2.9 Summary of Eight Necessary Prerequisites to Personal Revival 54

Chapter 3: Revival in the Home **56**
  3.1 Marriage (Poem) 56
  3.2 The Father's Role 62
      3.2.1 Head of the Family. 62
      3.2.2 Physical and Spiritual Protector of the Family 63
      3.2.3 Provider for the Family. 65
      3.2.4 Shepherd and Teacher of the Family 65
  3.3 The Mother's Role 69
      3.3.1 Helpmeet to Her Own Husband 69
      3.3.2 Home Keeper 69
      3.3.3 Instructor and Bearer/Main Nurturer of Children . . . 71
      3.3.4 Minister of Practical Help 71
      3.3.5 Who Bears a Double Curse Today?. 71
      3.3.6 A Word to Single Mothers 73
  3.4 What the Bible Says About Children. 73
      3.4.1 What About Large Families Contributing to
            Global Warming?. 77
      3.4.2 The Foundation and Purpose of Marriage 78
      3.4.3 Children (Poem) 85
  3.5 The Biblical Pattern for the Education and
      Training of Our Children 87
      3.5.1 What Is Education? 90
      3.5.2 The Rewriting Of History 92
      3.5.3 True Discipleship 95
      3.5.4 The Foundation of Biblical Education 98
      3.5.5 Teach Your Children the Sufficiency of Scripture . . . 105
      3.5.6 Discipline. 106
      3.5.7 Requiting Parents. 109
      3.5.8 Summary of Education and Discipline. 109
  3.6 The Family Economy 111
      3.6.1 The Two Extreme Views of Wealth. 112
      3.6.2 The Ability To Get Wealth Is From God 114

  3.6.3 The Idolatry and Snares of Riches 116
  3.6.4 God Commands Us To Live By Faith. 122
  3.6.5 The Pursuit of Wisdom Ahead of Riches 123
  3.6.6 Communism or "Commonism?" 125
  3.6.7 The parable of the Nobleman 126
  3.6.8 Debt. 129
  3.6.9 Inheritance. 132
  3.6.10 Summary 136
 3.7 Final Thoughts on the Biblical Pattern for the Family 137

Chapter 4: Revival in the Church 140
 4.1 What Is the Church?. 141
 4.2 What Is the Church's Role?. 144
 4.3 What Is the Local Church's Biblical Structure? 146
 4.4 What Is the Biblical Pattern for the Public Meeting
   of the Local Church?. 152
  4.4.1 Open Worship 152
  4.4.2 A Note on the Spiritual Song and Music in Worship. . 161
  4.4.3 Headship and Creation Order 166
 4.5 Tithing vs Freewill Offering 172
 4.6 Hospitality 176
 4.7 How Is the Church to Be Kept Pure?. 179
 4.8 What Is the Local Church's Jurisdiction?. 183
 4.9 The Sabbath vs The Lord's Day. 184
  4.9.1 The Sabbath Declared 184
  4.9.2 The Sabbath Codified in the Mosaic Law 184
  4.9.3 The Principle of Rest and Delight in the Lord 185
  4.9.4 Paul's Teaching on the Sabbath. 186
  4.9.5 The Early Church Met On The First Day of
    the Week 188
  4.9.6 Principles for the Church 188
 4.10 He That Hath an Ear, Let Him Hear What the Spirit
   Saith unto the Churches 189

Chapter 5: Reviving Christian Influence in the Governing of the Nation **195**
  5.1 The Role of Civil Government 198
  5.2 Temporary Dual Citizenship...................... 199
  5.3 Imposing Morality on the Unbeliever 200
  5.4 The Lord Jesus' Teaching in Context.............. 201
  5.5 Today's Battles: Socialism, Islam and Environmentalism .. 204
  5.6 The Wise Master Builder......................... 208
  5.7 Concluding Thoughts on Christians in the Civil Sphere .. 209

Chapter 6: The Role of Prayer in Revival. **210**
  6.1 The Attributes of Biblical Prayer 210
  6.2 God Will Not Do For Us What He Has Commanded Us To Do 211
  6.3 Pray With Humble Expectation 211
  6.4 Fasting May Be Appropriate 213
  6.5 Comprehend The Meaning of Praying In the Name of The Lord Jesus 213
  6.6 Prayer Is Not An Excuse For Inaction 214

Chapter 7: The Spiritual Battle **216**
  7.1 Not "If" But "When" 216
  7.2 The Eternal Perspective.......................... 217
  7.3 The Enemy and the Armour 218
  7.4 Are We Ignorant Of His Devices? 219
  7.5 The Spiritual Realm 221

Chapter 8: Complacency **224**
  8.1 The Dangers of Complacency.................... 225
      8.1.1 Our View of God Is Diminished 225
      8.1.2 Our Respect of Authority Is Diminished 228
      8.1.3 Weak Leaders Bow to the People's Whims 228
      8.1.4 We Become Distracted..................... 229
      8.1.5 We Must Be Chastened 229

  8.1.6 We Are Eventually Blinded to the Truth 229
  8.1.7 We Become Unteachable 229
 8.2 How Can We Recognize Complacency? 230
 8.3 Antidote to Complacency 231
  8.3.1 Diligent Observation 231
  8.3.2 Prayer. 232
  8.3.3 Diligent and Earnest Heed to God's Word 232
 8.4 Final Thoughts on Complacency. 233

Chapter 9: Conclusion. 234

Endnotes 239

FOREWORD

"I have read through your work in *The Sufficiency of Scripture* and must say what an enormous amount of good work you have put into it. I commend you for your commitment and detailed effort. If only more of us all would work at a personal pilgrimage in the Word of God, we would have much peace and joy in believing."

—J. A. Short, Australian missionary to
China region for 50 years
Christian Book Room, Hong Kong

"I have just now read in particular the sections on the church. As an overall opinion, I would say that it is a very sound biblical approach to the topics and points that you raised. Of particular note, the opening remarks on what defines a healthy church is a very good summary, along with the points you make a little later as to the role of the church; also, the explanation between what constitutes the universal and local church is clear and important, as is the difference between the elder and the pastor. You also noted the very important point of a biblical pattern for the local church meeting, and the need to turn to the Scriptures to know how God would have us conduct ourselves in the church of God.

THE SUFFICIENCY OF SCRIPTURE

These and other points you raise are timely and necessary, as you point out, to revival in the church.

"You cover a vast array of topics and points that are rarely tackled by modern authors, and this is a good thing as people need to think and be challenged outside the box that most modern material determines that they should be placed in."

—J. Ayoub, Elder
Unley Christian Assembly, South Australia

I have found Joseph's books eminently satisfying; they are packed with things modern Christians need to understand.

This excellent book serves two purposes. It asserts the sufficiency of Scripture for all Christian faith and life, and shows how Scripture is the key to revival in our time. Both are important issues. On the one hand while Christians usually affirm the infallibility, inerrancy and authority of Scripture many doubt that Scripture is sufficient for all Christian life and faith. Christians who rely on unbiblical methods and pragmatic solutions rather than relying on the Scripture as sufficient for all aspects of Christian ministry, prove the point.

By asserting the sufficiency of scripture, Joseph presents a corrective to a serious flaw in much contemporary evangelical thought. However, this is no dry academic treatise. The correlation between Scripture's sufficiency for all life and spiritual revival is then fleshed out. His method is thoroughly Biblical. Revival is not the result of Christians attempting to manipulate God, nor the result of a fervent pietism. It is the result of true Christian obedience and this starts with the individual believer, and it starts in the home. Personal revival is emphasized, then revival in the home, in the church and in the disciplines of prayer both personal, family and corporate. His treatment is eminently practical and thorough. It is also searching. If men are not living Biblically as the spiritual leaders in their home and family, there is a problem. This is well addressed. And if men fail in their life at home so they will in the local church. It

FOREWORD

can be confidently said, that here is "meat for men", and of course for godly women.

—Dallas Clarnette
Presbyterian Minister,
Journalist and former College lecturer, author of
The Blessedness of Death and 50 Years On Fire For God,
Victoria Australia

DEDICATION

In memory of my grandmother, Irma Naughton.

As I ponder the subject of revival, I can't help thinking of my late grandmother Irma Naughton, a Jewess who recognized and came under the lordship of her Messiah, the Lord Jesus Christ. She prayed daily for the salvation and growth of her grandchildren for as long as I can remember. I know beyond a shadow of a doubt that it was her fervent and faithful prayer that had a direct bearing on my life. Her faithfulness in fervent prayer has always challenged and convicted me of my need to pray for my own descendants and others whom the Lord brings to mind (see Col. 1:9; 1 Thess. 5:25; 2 Thess. 1:11, 3:1; Heb. 13:18; James 5:14, 5:16; 1 John 5:16). It is not that we "twist God's arm" by our prayer; He loves us more than any human can and He would have all men to be saved and to come to a knowledge of the truth (see 1 Tim. 2:4). Fervent prayer, I'm convinced, is at least partially for our sake, to prove our dedication and commitment to a course of action that God in turn blesses when He sees our utter surrender to His will and our total dependence on Him to accomplish it.

To my precious children, grandchildren, and great grandchildren.

I have spent my life studying God's Word to learn how to apply it to all areas of my life. No doubt I have blind spots and have not applied

THE SUFFICIENCY OF SCRIPTURE

it consistently as I should have. I confess that this book just scratches the surface of what we can know about God and His Word and there is much still to be learned. I pray that each of you would take this book as a foundation and build on it. Do not be complacent just because I've given you this foundation. Rather, begin with this, and write the next volumes as you fine-tune and discover more gold, silver, and precious stones in the greatest mine of all treasure. Take heed to its warnings and do your best to apply the principles herein. I pray by God's grace and mercy that each of you may see the revival spoken of in these pages in your own lives, in the lives of your families, and in the local church to which you contribute. I pray each son will plant a local church or contribute to the ministry of a local church according to the biblical model described in these pages. I pray that each daughter will contribute to a local church as described in these pages through practical help, and by standing beside your godly husband in such an assembly. May God richly bless your progeny as you submit to His Lordship.

Having spent hours writing this book, I am terribly conscious of my own need for constant revival and reformation. I am deeply aware of my own frailty as a husband and father, and humbly say with the apostle Paul, "I keep under my body, and bring it into subjection: lest that by any means, when I have preached to others, I myself should be a castaway" (1 Cor. 9:27). I, as much as any reader, need to constantly assess and reassess my first love, my application of the Scriptures; my effectiveness as a shepherd and teacher, and the teachableness of my own heart. For if my progeny or I fail to keep God's Word as the apple of our eye, then indeed I have become a castaway. One thing is sure, however: Though I do fail constantly, my keeping His Word has no bearing on its absolute truth, inerrancy, or sufficiency. If we fail to understand it or keep it, it is we who are in error, not God.

"O God, thou hast taught me from my youth: and hitherto have I declared thy wondrous works. Now also when I am old and greyheaded, O God, forsake me not; until I have shewed thy strength unto this generation, and thy power to every one that is to come" (Ps. 71:17-18).

ACKNOWLEDGMENTS

I AM INDEBTED to many men who have dedicated their lives to the study of God's Word and who have faithfully and often patiently preached into my life through word and testimony, sometimes knowingly and sometimes unknowingly. Some of these men and their wives opened their hearts and homes to me at crucial times in my journey. This hospitality will not go unnoticed by the Righteous Judge, and often spoke louder to me than the sermons of those difficult years. I wish to express my deepest gratitude and respect to the following people: Frank and Pam Revink, Steve and Mandy Anson, Reg and Gwen Row, Kingsley and Glenda Congdon, John and Sheryle Ford, Colin and Phyllis Stock, Morrie and Florence Munyard, Guy and Pat Howell, Ian and Ruth Tonkin, Hubert Kimber, Greg and Sue Dalton, Greg and Leanne McPherson, David D'Lima, Fred Nile, Vishal Mangalwadi, John Mackay, Scott and Debra Brown, Geoff Botkin, Kevin Swanson and Paul Washer.

I also wish to thank John Short, Jon Ayoub and Dr. Dallas Clarnette who contributed to the foreword of this edition of the book.

I thank Jim and Elva Schroeder, Merv Harris, Mark Swaim, Colin Devine, David Compton, Derek Blacker, George Tucker, Lance Box,

THE SUFFICIENCY OF SCRIPTURE

Andrew and David Craig, Terry Arnold, Mathew and Rachel Green, Don and Janet Milway, Anthony and Christie Moore, Ninel Lazar, and Andrew, Gary and Debbie Higginbotham, as well as many acknowledged earlier, for help with proofreading and providing valuable feedback on the three editions of this book, often from a very different background and perspective. Iron indeed sharpeneth iron. (Prov. 27:17)

I thank my precious bride, Mary Florence, who constantly challenges me to walk the talk and disciple my own family. Thank you for the hours spent helping to edit this work amidst marking math, English, science, and history; and housework, being my eyes, and remaining my best friend despite many pressures and difficulties raising a large family.

I thank my children, who are often the motivation and vehicle for learning and growing in grace.

Most of all I thank with eternal gratitude my Lord Jesus Christ, to whom be glory forever. Amen!

INTRODUCTION

REVIVAL IS A topic near and dear to every parent, pastor, and elder who deals with the mediocrity of a family or congregation drowning in a culture of humanism, feminism, hedonism, apathy, complacency, and blasting noise from every quarter. Much has been written about revival. Many books look at methods, philosophies, and psychology. This book takes God's Word itself as the basis for determining the keys to personal, family, church and even national revival through the recognition of the doctrine of the sufficiency of Scripture, a doctrine largely unknown in today's modern church. I take this approach because any work of God must begin with His own Word and standard or it is a work of man and doomed to fail.

This book may not be what you want to hear. This is not a quick fix to our spiritual problems—there is no such thing. This is not a formula for success but a summary of the doctrines that are plainly revealed in God's Word and which have been obscured or deeply entombed under the rubble of man's traditions and pragmatism. We are warned that "the time will come when they will not endure sound doctrine; but after their own lusts shall they heap to themselves teachers, having itching ears" (2 Tim. 4:3). This means that as time goes on, the process of discipling mature believers will only become more difficult. This doesn't mean we should give up, but that we must understand the times in which we live and what we ought to do (see 1 Chron. 12:32). Indeed some think we shouldn't even discuss revival since the Scriptures teach that in the last days there will be a great falling away (2 Tim. 3:1; 2 Pet. 3:3). Though this may be the case, this does not preclude local revivals, nor does it mean we don't set in order that which is sorely lacking in Christendom today.

In spite of the free access to printed and electronic Bible study aids, Christians today are relatively Bible illiterate compared to our forefathers. This is partly due to an incredible number of other distractions, but also because of an unhealthy reliance on these study aids and devotional programs. The use of commentaries can be very useful indeed, however a daily devotion based on another man's writings, and not on God's Word itself, has led to the stunted growth of many children of God. We almost feel we "need" an explanation of every verse we read rather than allowing the Holy Spirit to be our teacher first, and consulting the commentary only to compare notes.

Going to the commentary before we have diligently studied a subject can often lead to a biased interpretation of a passage. The habit of Baptists to only read Baptist authors, Brethren to only read Brethren authors, and Presbyterians to only read Presbyterian authors, etc., only adds to this problem. No one denomination has every point of doctrine perfect, as man is fallible. We are also so used to sermons containing lots of commentary on only a few verses that we almost feel cheated to have someone simply stand up and read the Scriptures, the living Word of the Almighty God, without comment. In this book I have tried to let the Scriptures speak for themselves, and only offer commentary to link ideas and emphasize things the Scriptures teach that are contrary to popular practice today.

In this book, after first discussing the foundation of the Sufficiency of Scripture, I look at four areas of revival—personal, family, church and national—and summarize the Scriptural commands, patterns and precepts, which if obeyed and applied, will create an environment ripe

INTRODUCTION

for such revival. I then discuss several hindrances to revival in the areas of prayer, spiritual warfare and complacency.

This book is a summary of a 35 year learning journey, which began when I was born again at the age of seven. As well as engaging in much personal Bible study, I have sat under the diverse teaching of most of the major denominations as well as having been a member of several non-denominational meetings. It should be an obvious conclusion that none of man's movements, resulting in today's denominations, has a monopoly on the truth. Each has blind spots and shortcomings and each has wonderful strengths.

Revival, however, will not come by simply taking the great teachings of a man and repeating them. Luther, Calvin, Knox, Darby, Wesley, and Spurgeon were all great yet imperfect men of God who contributed much to reformation. To do them justice we must not stop at repeating the great truths and sometimes the errors they taught, but go forward rediscovering more hidden treasure in the greatest mine of truth (Prov. 2:3-5). Even if your church repudiates the reformation, and claims an unbroken history right back to the New Testament, such as the Anabaptists or other such groups, traditions of men still cloud the pure Word of God over time necessitating reformation. No church is immune to such man-made traditions gradually creeping in. Revival will only come, as has been demonstrated by many a godly man throughout history, by returning to God's own Word as the all-sufficient guide to life with a repentant and humble heart. As Sir Robert Anderson once said so aptly, "Christians fail to distinguish between what the Scriptures teach, and what men teach about the Scriptures."[1] Am I a Calvinist? An Arminian? A Baptist? A Brethren? No, I'm a student of God's Word who, I pray, will continue to learn until the day of my calling home. May we all be like the Bereans, who received the Word with all readiness of mind, and searched the Scriptures daily, whether those things were so (see Acts 17:11).

Chapter 1

THE SUFFICIENCY OF SCRIPTURE

THIS BOOK IS about a doctrine for which many were martyred during the reformation. It is a doctrine that has largely been forgotten by the modern church, but may well be the most fundamental doctrine after the doctrine of God, and the doctrine of His gospel, and its denial has all but destroyed Christianity in the West and rendered even fundamental Bible-believing churches utterly ineffective. It is a doctrine that has been under attack since the serpent asked the woman, "Yea, hath God said?" (Gen. 3:1). This doctrine is the sufficiency of Scripture. Many Christians acknowledge that the Scriptures are inerrant—that is, that God's Word is infallible—but few truly demonstrate recognition of the sufficiency of God's Word in every area of their lives.

In this section I discuss the following points:

- What is the sufficiency of Scripture?
- Is the sufficiency of Scripture a biblical doctrine?
- Why is the sufficiency of Scripture important?
- What happens when the sufficiency of Scripture is forsaken?
- Man is commanded to live by every Word that proceeds from God.

THE SUFFICIENCY OF SCRIPTURE

1.1 What Is the Sufficiency of Scripture?

By definition, to be a Christian is to rest in, and rely entirely on, the atoning power of Christ's propitiatory sacrifice for our personal salvation. It is to take literally the warnings and promises of a holy God, as conveyed in His Word, regarding the position of our souls in relation to Him. It is to willingly submit to His Lordship, and to embrace every Word revealed to us by Him in the holy Scriptures as necessary wisdom for our earthly sojourn. Just as we fully trust that Word in relation to our salvation, we must also trust it for that process we call sanctification, the application of that Word to our lives which results in us becoming more like our Lord, and thinking His thoughts in our daily experience. The Bible is not silent regarding the manner in which we ought to live, and it speaks to every area of our existence. God's Word is entirely sufficient to instruct us—either by direct commandment, principle, or pattern—in every issue and situation we may encounter. This is the sufficiency of Scripture.

The Scriptures speak to our origin, fall, destiny (salvation or judgment), marriage, family life, economics, aesthetics, music, dress, speech, government, business, church operations, stewardship—literally everything. Christianity is thus more than a religion for spirituality for one day of the week—it is an entire worldview. That is, it provides the only firm foundation for every aspect of life. If we have taken that first step of faith and obedience in receiving the gospel, and if we confess that God's Word is true, we must be prepared to trust in its utter reliability as it relates to our daily Christian walk. There should be no secular and sacred distinction but the Christian should stand firmly on God's Word and glean wisdom for every decision, practice, and habit of life. (1 Cor. 10:31, Col. 3:17)

Even beauty is not in the eye of the beholder, contrary to popular belief. God defined it by declaring that His creation is good. God defines the words *wonderful, love, excellent, wisdom,* and *truth* in His very character, attributes, and titles, as we will see.

It is clear from studying the Scriptures that God cares that we take notice of every word He utters. We live in a culture where words have

THE SUFFICIENCY OF SCRIPTURE

become arbitrary and close enough is good enough. When God gave commands, precepts and principles to His people throughout history, there were grave consequences when these commands were disobeyed, patterns changed or principles ignored. While many commands are well known, other patterns and principles are less familiar to many Christians today. It takes careful diligence to search the Scriptures and serious prayer for wisdom as to how to apply Biblical principles to any given situation in life. One thing is clear, God is Holy and it is our responsibility to find out what the Almighty, holy, omnipotent God has said before claiming that it doesn't matter how we live. Let us consider some examples where God's people failed to take His every Word seriously.

> *And Nadab and Abihu, the sons of Aaron, took either of them his censer, and put fire therein, and put incense thereon, and offered strange fire before the LORD, which he commanded them not. And there went out fire from the LORD, and devoured them, and they died before the LORD. Then Moses said unto Aaron, This is it that the LORD spake, saying, I will be sanctified in them that come nigh me, and before all the people I will be glorified. And Aaron held his peace.*
> (Lev. 10:1-3)

The key to understanding this is that Aaron's sons offered what God had not authorized on His holy altar, something foreign and out of place. It literally polluted His holy altar and He destroyed them for it. Note what He says to Moses in verse 3: "I will be sanctified in them that come nigh me, and before all the people I will be glorified." Those who identify with God's name and draw near to Him as Christians must sanctify or set Him apart in their lives so God may be glorified in other people's eyes. In other words, we must do God's work on God's terms using God's methods declared in God's Word that God may be glorified.

Another example of God's severe judgment on someone who failed to follow specific instructions is found in 1 Chronicles 13:9-10, where Uzza put out his hand to steady the ark of God and was struck dead.

THE SUFFICIENCY OF SCRIPTURE

This was because David failed to carry the ark in God's appointed way (see Deut. 10:8).

If you think that somehow God changed in the New Testament and that He no longer cares that we live by every word that proceedeth out of His mouth, consider the words of Jude 4-11, where Jude by the Holy Spirit warned of those with liberal theology who had crept into the church and lead the flock astray. He writes, "Woe unto them! for they have gone in the way of Cain, and ran greedily after the error of Balaam for reward, and perished in the gainsaying of Core." (Jude 1:11). The way of Cain was through his own works, attempting to please God on his terms rather than God's terms (Gen. 4:1-8). The error of Balaam was to cause God's people to sin through compromise and syncretism (Num. 22:5-24:25, 25:1-3, 31:7-16; Rev 2:14), and the gainsaying of Korah was the despising of God's order and authority and profaning the holy as we have already seen in Lev. 10:1-3. All three are summed up as doing things man's way rather than God's way – proud pragmatism rather than humble obedience. (Also see Acts 20:29-31.)

There are four common misconceptions in the church that contradict the sufficiency of Scripture:

1. The red letters (Christ's words) are the only relevant instruction for today.

The Lord through the apostle Paul's letter to Timothy said the Old Testament is inspired by God and thus is as important as Christ's words (see 2 Tim. 3:16-17 and 1 Cor. 10:1-11).

> *Now all these things happened unto them for examples: and they are written for our admonition, upon whom the ends of the world are come.*
> *(1 Cor. 10:11)*

This verse authorizes four types of Bible study:

- "Now all these things happened"— We should study the Bible as literal history because these things actually happened

- "unto them for examples" (Greek: *tupos*; *types*)—We can study the Bible for types and shadows
- "and they are written for our admonition"—We should study the Bible to apply it to our everyday lives through obeying relevant commandments, and gleaning wisdom from patterns, precepts, and principles
- "upon whom the ends of the world [ages] are come"—We can study the Bible to distinguish the ages or dispensations

2. If it is not mentioned in the Bible then it is automatically lawful.

Many Christians claim if the Scripture doesn't mention something then they are free to do it. For example, somebody might claim that as the Scripture doesn't mention particular illegal substances, they are free to partake of them. The Scripture does, however, lay down many principles that would indeed disallow any illegal substance abuse. We are the temple of the Holy Spirit and must maintain a sober and alert mind (see 1 Cor. 6:19-20; 1 Peter 4:7, 5:8; Titus 2:6; 1 Thess. 5:8; Eph. 5:18, etc.), something one can't do when abusing illegal substances.

3. If there is no explicit command then it is not required.

This is not necessarily true. God often speaks to something via a pattern or principle, and these are as valid for demonstrating God's will as a direct command, especially when we note that the pattern holds true throughout the Scriptures. An example of such a pattern would be the manner in which daughters are given in marriage, and until they are given, they are to be under their father's protection and provision and in his house (see Gen. 34:9, 38:11; Lev. 22:13; Num. 30:3, 30:16; Deut. 22:21; Judg. 21:7; Ezra 9:12; Neh. 10:30; Ps. 78:63; Jer. 29:6; Luke 17:27, 20:34). A son, on the other hand, is to prepare his fields, build his house, and then find a wife and begin a new jurisdiction (see Gen. 24, 28:1-2, 34:9; Deut. 24:1; Ezra 9:12; Neh. 10:30; Prov. 24:27; Jer. 29:6; 1 Cor. 7:27).

THE SUFFICIENCY OF SCRIPTURE

4. Any Old Testament statement is void unless specifically mentioned in the New Testament.

This is simply false. The New Testament builds on the Old and doesn't repeat all of the Old Testament's foundational teaching. It is indeed true that we must rightly divide and discern the audience of some Scriptures (see 2 Tim. 2:15), however, even when a promise is made to Israel, often we can learn a principle that we can apply to our own lives even though the promise itself is not to us (see number one above).

Consider the following verses carefully:

Behold, I have taught you statutes and judgments, even as the LORD my God commanded me, that ye should do so in the land whither ye go to possess it. Keep therefore and do them; for this is your wisdom and your understanding in the sight of the nations, which shall hear all these statutes, and say, Surely this great nation is a wise and understanding people. For what nation is there so great, who hath God so nigh unto them, as the LORD our God is in all things that we call upon him for? And what nation is there so great, that hath statutes and judgments so righteous as all this law, which I set before you this day?

(Deut. 4:5-8)

Note again what Moses wanted them to show the Gentile nations: "What nation is there so great, that hath statutes and judgments so righteous as all this law?" In other words, the Jews were instructed to be a light to the nations demonstrating the goodness and sensibility of God's laws, precepts, and principles (also confirmed in Isa. 42:5-6, 49:6 and Acts 13:47). I am not talking about bringing Christians saved by grace under the Jewish law. We are free from the ceremonial law, though we are never free from God's moral law. We are saved by grace, but our faith's outworking or demonstration is in obedience to every command, precept, or pattern that God calls good, perfect, or wise and that was not superseded under the new covenant. Today, some Christians will glean wisdom from the Proverbs yet fail to search the great volumes of wisdom declared in other Old Testament books.

THE SUFFICIENCY OF SCRIPTURE

1.2 Is the Sufficiency of Scripture a Biblical Doctrine?

1.2.1 God Magnifies His Word Even Above His Name

God has placed great emphasis on the importance of His Word, magnifying His Word even above His most holy and awesome name, which is a name above every name (see Eph. 1:21).

> *I will worship toward thy holy temple, and praise thy name for thy lovingkindness and for thy truth: for thou hast magnified thy word above all thy name.*
>
> *(Ps. 138:2)*

1.2.2 God Warns Us Not to Add to or Subtract from His Word

We add to His Word by teaching for doctrine the traditions of men (see Mark 7:7)—that is, making up our own rules. We subtract from it by denying or disobeying clear commands, patterns or precepts (see Mark 7:9). We also subtract from it when we make any of man's philosophies or dogma equal or above God's Holy Word. For example, we subtract from it when we argue away the first eleven chapters of Genesis because they do not support the currently popular theory of evolution. Theories and philosophies rise and fall throughout the generations, but God's Word "liveth and abideth for ever" (1 Peter 1:23).

> *Ye shall not add unto the word which I command you, neither shall ye diminish ought from it, that ye may keep the commandments of the LORD your God which I command you.*
>
> *(Deut. 4:2)*

> *Every word of God is pure: he is a shield unto them that put their trust in him. Add thou not unto his words, lest he reprove thee, and thou be found a liar.*
>
> *(Prov. 30:5-6)*

THE SUFFICIENCY OF SCRIPTURE

For I testify unto every man that heareth the words of the prophecy of this book, If any man shall add unto these things, God shall add unto him the plagues that are written in this book: And if any man shall take away from the words of the book of this prophecy, God shall take away his part out of the book of life, and out of the holy city, and from the things which are written in this book.

(Rev. 22:18-19)

These three passages make it clear that those who add to God's Word or those who subtract from it will be reproved. Revelation makes the nature of this reproval abundantly clear, a reproval that no Christian would desire.

1.2.3 HE DECLARES THAT HIS WRITTEN WORD IS HIS REVELATION, WORD FOR WORD, EVEN TO THE LAST JOT AND TITTLE (STROKE OF THE HEBREW PEN)

For verily I say unto you, Till heaven and earth pass, one jot or one tittle shall in no wise pass from the law, till all be fulfilled.

(Matt. 5:18)

1.2.4 HE DECLARES THAT HIS WORD IS NOT OPEN TO PRIVATE INTERPRETATION

God not only told man precisely what to write, He also defined the exact meaning of His Word, something very opposed to the postmodernist approach to textual interpretation, which says that a text's interpretation is defined by the reader and not the writer.

Knowing this first, that no prophecy of the Scripture is of any private interpretation. For the prophecy came not in old time by the will of man: but holy men of God spake as they were moved by the Holy Ghost.

(2 Peter 1:20-21)

Also see Exod. 34:27; 2 Chron. 26:22; Isa. 8:1, 30:8; Jer. 30:2, 36:2, 36:28; Rev. 1:11, 1:19, 2:1, 2:8, 2:12, 2:18, 3:1, 3:7, 3:14, 10:4, 14:13, 19:9, 21:5.

THE SUFFICIENCY OF SCRIPTURE

1.2.5 He Declares His Word to Be Powerful, Piercing, and Precise

For the word of God is quick, and powerful, and sharper than any twoedged sword, piercing even to the dividing asunder of soul and spirit, and of the joints and marrow, and is a discerner of the thoughts and intents of the heart.

(Hebrews 4:12)

This verse means His Word is living, powerful, sharper than any two-edged sword, and extremely precise in its meaning and application, making plain the depravity of the intents of man's heart with brutal clarity.

1.2.6 He Declares His Word to Be Perfect and Forever Settled

The law of the LORD is perfect, converting the soul: the testimony of the LORD is sure, making wise the simple.

(Ps. 19:7)

The words of the LORD are pure words: as silver tried in a furnace of earth, purified seven times.

(Ps. 12:6)

For ever, O LORD, thy word is settled in heaven.

(Ps. 119:89)

Thy word is true from the beginning: and every one of thy righteous judgments endureth for ever.

(Ps. 119:160)

1.2.7 He Has Declared It Sufficient to Fully Equip the Man of God for Every Good Work

All Scripture is given by inspiration of God, and is profitable for doctrine, for reproof, for correction, for instruction in righteousness: That the man of God may be perfect, thoroughly furnished unto all good works.

(2 Tim. 3:16-17)

THE SUFFICIENCY OF SCRIPTURE

1.2.8 He Declares That His Word Shall Be Accomplished

For as the rain cometh down, and the snow from heaven, and returneth not thither, but watereth the earth, and maketh it bring forth and bud, that it may give seed to the sower, and bread to the eater: So shall my word be that goeth forth out of my mouth: it shall not return unto me void, but it shall accomplish that which I please, and it shall prosper in the thing whereto I sent it.

(Isa. 55:10-11)

1.2.9 Times of Apostasy Will be Marked by Men Burdened by Their Own Word Rather than God's Word

Jeremiah prophesied that in the time of Israel's great apostasy, men would be more burdened by their own word rather than God's Word. This appears to be a mark of apostasy throughout history—a denial of the sufficiency of Scripture in favour of man's wisdom.

And the burden of the LORD shall ye mention no more: for every man's word shall be his burden; for ye have perverted the words of the living God, of the LORD of hosts our God.

(Jer. 23:36)

The other side of the coin to preachers not preaching the Word of God, as pointed out in the introduction, is that their hearers will also not tolerate the Scriptures as Timothy warned us.

For the time will come when they will not endure sound doctrine; but after their own lusts shall they heap to themselves teachers, having itching ears; (2 Tim. 4:3).

Eventually, with preachers preaching their own wisdom and the hearers desiring the same, we find the Lord of Glory standing outside His church knocking, waiting patiently to come in (Rev. 3:20).

1.3 Why Is the Sufficiency of Scripture Important?

When we deny the sufficiency of Scripture, we are saying that man's wisdom is equal to God's Word. If we favor man's wisdom over

God's Word, we blaspheme, literally taking the name of the Lord our God in vain. Since His Word is magnified even above His name (see Ps. 138:2), devaluing His Word profanes God's very name. This is a most grievous sin.

The apostle Paul writes to Timothy that man's traditions passed down as profane and old wives' fables must be refused (see 1 Tim. 4:7). Old wives' fables, or traditions of man, are not equal to God's Word, and they detract from the process of exercising ourselves unto godliness, which can only be accomplished by giving the counsels of the Almighty God pre-eminence above all of foolish man's wisdom.

> *But refuse profane and old wives' fables, and exercise thyself rather unto godliness.*
>
> *(1 Tim. 4:7)*

Our cultural traditions and philosophies, whether in our personal lives, educational model, family tradition, or church practices, if not rooted in biblical principles, are profane, and equating them with God's Word is blasphemy against His holy name.

1.4 What Happens When the Sufficiency of Scripture Is Forsaken?

When Christians say their indecision on the issue of origins is inconsequential, and that some kind of a marriage between evolutionary theory and biblical creationism can be conceived—allowing the world to have been formed in some way by God, yet have an age of billions of years—they undermine the very Gospel. If the world is billions of years old, then death and suffering must have predated Adam to allow for the evolutionary struggle of our species. If death predated Adam, then death did not come by sin, making God and his apostle Paul a liar (see Rom. 5:12). The creation God called "good" must then have contained suffering and death, which is clearly not "good." To do away with a literal Adam and Eve, and original sin, is also to make the Lord Jesus, the Last

THE SUFFICIENCY OF SCRIPTURE

Adam (see 1 Cor. 15:45), a liar, since He referred to the beginning of creation several times (see Matt. 19:8 and Mark 10:6, 13:19).

The Lord Jesus gave a crucial answer to the Jews who wanted to kill Him, which is just as relevant today to those who would undermine the authority of any of the Scripture to which He referred. He said, "For had ye believed Moses, ye would have believed me: for he wrote of me. But if ye believe not his writings, how shall ye believe my words?" (John 5:46-47). The books of Genesis through Deuteronomy are accepted as Moses' writings. So the Lord Himself declared that those who will not believe Moses (who, incidentally, wrote of the Lord Jesus prophetically) cannot believe His words either, because the two are inseparably linked.

The following table presents just a few instances where Moses writes about the Lord Jesus, either directly as prophesy, or through types and shadows which Christ fulfilled.

	Prophesy/ Type/Shadow	**Fulfillment**
Prophesy of incarnation/ crushing of Satan	Gen. 3:15	Col. 2:15
Prophesy of incarnation	Gen. 49:10; Deut. 18:15	John 1:1-17, 5:39, 7:40-42; Acts 3:20-23, 10:43
The lamb of God promised/ Isaac picture of Christ	Gen. 22:7-8	John 1:29, 1:36
Christ prefigured in the Passover	Exod. 12:5-14	1 Cor. 5:7-8
The living water	Exod. 17:6; Num. 20:11	1 Cor. 10:4; John 6:35
The living bread	Exod. 16:15	John 6:31-32
Brazen serpent a picture of Christ crucified	Num. 21:9	John 3:14-15

THE SUFFICIENCY OF SCRIPTURE

The Lord Jesus literally authenticates all of the prophets, the A-Z of them, from Abel to Zacharias (Luke 11:51). Abel is a literal person, the son of a literal person, Adam. Thus, those who allegorize away Genesis not only invalidate Moses' writings, they shred the Gospels. Not only do they shred the Gospels but also the epistles (see Rom. 5:12-14; 1 Cor. 15:22, 15:45; Eph. 3:9; 1 Tim. 2:13-14; 2 Peter 3:4-6; Jude 1:14). Once Genesis' foundation has been undermined, the Gospels and epistles shredded, the prophets allegorized away, and the rest relegated to the land of doubtful integrity, all we have left is an empty shell, an ornamental cover, a powerless and harmless piece of sentimental and irrelevant historical literary babble from a forgotten culture—which is exactly what Satan wants us to believe. The truth is that the eternal Word of our almighty God is quick, powerful, and sharper than any two-edged sword, piercing even to the dividing of soul and spirit, and of the joints and marrow, and is a discerner of the thoughts and intents of the heart (see Heb. 4:12).

A Note on the Days of Creation

Since many have argued that the word "day" in Genesis can be interpreted as a longer period of time than 24 hours, it is fitting to take a moment to consider the definition of the word used in the Genesis account, as it has great bearing on the foundation of all of Scripture. The word *day* comes from the Hebrew word *yome*:

> Strong's Definition 03117 יוֹם yowm yome from an unused root meaning to be hot; n m; AV-day 2008, time 64, chronicles + 01697 37, daily 44, ever 18, year 14, continually 10, when 10, as 10, while 8, full 8 always 4, whole 4, always 4, misc. 44; 2287
>
> 1. Day, time, year
>   1a. Day (as opposed to night) {#Gen. 7:4, 12, 8:22, 31:39, 40; Ex. 24:18, 34:28; Num. 11:32; Josh. 10:13; Deut. 9:9, 11, 18, 25, 10:10; Gen. 1:5, 14, 16, 18; 1 Sam. 30:12;

THE SUFFICIENCY OF SCRIPTURE

    Judges 19:8, 9, 11; Amos 5:8; 1 Kings 8:29, 19:8; Neh. 4:22; Eccl. 8:16; 2 Sam. 3:35}
1a1. The heat of the day {#Gen. 18:1; 1 Sam. 11:11; 2 Sam. 4:5}
1a2. The day is still high {#Gen. 29:7}
1a3. Cool of the day {#Gen. 3:8}
1a4. From dawn until midday {#Neh. 8:3}
1a5. Growing lighter and lighter until the full day {#Prov. 4:18}
1a6. Until the declining of the day {#Judges 19:8}
1a7. The day has sunk down and become evening {#Judges 19:9}
1b. Day (24-hour period)
1b1. As defined by evening and morning in Genesis 1
1b2. As a division of time
1b2a. A working day, a day's journey
1c. Days, lifetime (pl.)
1d. Time, period (general)
1e. Year
1f. Temporal references
1f1. Today
1f2. Yesterday
1f3. Tomorrow

While it is true that the word *yome* may at times mean a period other than twenty-four hours, the context is always unambiguous. In Genesis, in the record of creation, the words *evening* and *morning* define the period and Hebrew scholars have no disagreement that this means a literal twenty-four-hour day. This is confirmed by Exodus 20:11:

> *For in six days the LORD made heaven and earth, the sea, and all that in them is, and rested the seventh day: wherefore the LORD blessed the Sabbath day, and hallowed it.*

The Lord refers directly to the days of creation as literal days, using the same word and literal meaning, even referring to the seventh literal

THE SUFFICIENCY OF SCRIPTURE

day in which He rested to define the Sabbath. There would have been absolutely no misunderstanding or conjecture that God meant for us to work for six-thousand years and then rest for a thousand years. The Bible distinctly says that just as God worked for six literal days and rested, so are we to do likewise. In the sentence, "In my day, we walked to the shop during the day, each day to buy milk," the meaning is clear from the context—the first day refers to a season, during my lifetime, the second refers to the daylight hours, and the third refers to a literal twenty-four-hour day. There is no ambiguity and no confusion. This is also true of every use of the word *yome* in the Bible.

When Christians allegorize away Genesis, they do away with the foundation of marriage (see Gen. 2:24). When they deny a global flood, they again shred the epistles (see 2 Peter 2:5-8). In fact, the first eleven chapters of Genesis declare man's dignity and superiority over animals (man being created in God's image, Gen. 1:27). They declare the first prophecy of the Savior (see Gen. 3:15), the origin of the many languages (see Gen. 11:1-9), much of the basis for our law, and much more. Almost every biblical doctrine has its origins in the first eleven chapters of Genesis. In fact, it is the denial of the sufficiency of Scripture that leads to racism, abortion and birth control, animal rights, euthanasia, promiscuity, homosexuality, the denigration of marriage, family disintegration, etc. Ideas have consequences.

Did you know that the ideas of Margaret Sanger, the founder of Planned Parenthood, have influenced our thinking to such an extent that more than fifty-million abortions have taken place since 1973 in the US alone? This is two-and-a-half times the population of Australia! Imagine that our entire nation has been murdered two and a half times over and this doesn't even include the abortions here in Australia, which are estimated at 100,000 per year, or the enumerable number in China or in other countries. We cringe at this but the birth control pill and other abortifacient methods (also her idea) have caused countless millions more to be aborted right at conception, and many Christians are ignorant of this fact.

THE SUFFICIENCY OF SCRIPTURE

A Third of South Australian Women Will Abort
The Advertiser
May 21, 2006

One in three South Australian women will have an abortion in their lifetime, according to predictions from latest figures.

The Pregnancy Outcome in South Australia report for 2004 also revealed the 17,522 SA women who gave birth in 2004 was the lowest since perinatal statistics were first collected in 1981.

Of the terminations, 1,879 or 38 percent of women, had previously had abortions, a slight increase from the past four years.

"The total first-time abortion rate for 2004 was 305.5 per 1,000 women aged 15-44 years," the report says. "This suggests that about one in three women would have had an abortion in their lifetime if they experienced the abortion rates of the different age groups for 2004."[2]

Shock Teen Abortion Rate
The Advertiser
January 4, 2008

More South Australian teenagers had abortions than gave birth in 2006, Health Department figures show.

The Pregnancy Outcomes report shows 982 women aged 15 to 19 had abortions, while 877 gave birth.

The 2006 statistics also show about one in three pregnancies in women aged between 20 and 24 was terminated.[3]

We are no longer taught what God thinks about children and how precious they really are to Him. Ideas have consequences. Based on his own evolutionary theory, Darwin theorized that indigenous Australians were pre-human, degrading God's special creation, made in His own image, to a mere "missing link" in the animal kingdom. Hitler built on this corrupt foundation by exterminating six-million Jews who, in like manner, he thought were inferior and unfit to live. Ideas have consequences and bad ideas have bad consequences. The animal rights movement asserts that the earthworm is more important than the human because we need worms but they don't need us. Consequently, millions of dollars are spent on saving the whales while children are murdered by the millions, and Christians leap on this bandwagon as zealously as humanists, not knowing the Scriptures. We have a magnet on our van showing a baby in the womb and a baby seal with the caption "Guess which one is not protected?" We need to return to the Scriptures to define and govern our personal lives, home lives, and church lives.

Time and again, God's wisdom has made man's wisdom total folly, as described in 1 Corinthians 1:19-21. We think it absurd that in the 1700s doctors used blood letting[4] as a method of treating certain diseases, killing such people as George Washington, the first president of the United States. Such an act today would no doubt be seen as murder, yet the Bible told us all along that "the life is in the blood" (see Gen. 9:4; Lev. 17:11-14; Deut. 12:23; Acts 15:20, 15:29, 21:25) and thus logically, spilling blood drains life. Up until the late 1800s, doctors thought it humiliating to have to wash their hands after touching a corpse and thought it ludicrous that germs could somehow be transferred through human contact, killing thousands of patients because of cross contamination[5], yet the Bible clearly teaches of a corpse's uncleanness and that hand-washing is important (see Num. 19:11-13; Hag. 2:13; Lev. 15:11). It was most likely the strict cleanliness of the Jewish people, who adhered to God's law, which saved them from the bubonic plague of the 1300-1400s, although, of course, they were erroneously blamed for its outbreak.

Today, birth is treated as an illness rather than a wonder of God's design. While things do go wrong because of sin, and we are grateful for medical intervention when it is necessary, birth is increasingly treated as an illness and aggressive obstetric intervention is too common. In the Scriptures, midwives attended births and women were free to give birth in the familiarity of their own home surrounded by their extended family. Evolutionary thinking has lead to a very detached, clinical, and often uncompassionate treatment of birth, illness and death. If a baby does die, rather than accepting that the Lord gives and takes, blame must be placed somewhere and is often laid at the feet of the mother for wanting a natural home birth. People have also been held in hospital against their will for resisting a particular treatment of an illness. Of course if a mother chooses to abort her baby, this is acceptable to the evolutionist. Unfortunately this whole inconsistent line of thinking is becoming common in Christian circles because of the humanistic education we have gullibly swallowed.

When we deny the sufficiency of Scripture, we begin to dress immodestly like the pagans, and with no distinction between that which is worn by a man and that which is worn by a woman, which God calls an abomination (see Deut. 22:5, 1 Tim. 2:9, Isa. 47:1-3). This was not a cultural custom, nor did God ever revoke His pronouncement of this as an abomination.

> *The woman shall not wear that which pertaineth unto a man, neither shall a man put on a woman's garment: for all that do so are abomination unto the LORD thy God.*
>
> *(Deut. 22:5)*

> *In like manner also, that women adorn themselves in modest apparel, with shamefacedness and sobriety; not with broided hair, or gold, or pearls, or costly array; But (which becometh women professing godliness) with good works.*
>
> *(1 Tim. 2:9-10)*

The attire of an harlot was distinguishable in biblical times from the dress of other women, but today there is little distinction (Prov. 7:10). Immodest dress is so common even amongst Christian women that

THE SUFFICIENCY OF SCRIPTURE

many don't even consider their attire as immodest. Yet, if they would consider their attire compared to even 50 years ago, what is commonly worn today used to be considered shameful. Tops with spaghetti straps or strapless tops, plunging neck lines, short or tight skirts or pants are just some of the styles which clearly violate scriptural modesty. God's standard of modesty has not changed. Immodesty is a direct rebellion against God's pronouncement of sin and His covering of Adam and Eve with coats (covering or robe) of skins (Gen 3:21). Today's attire tries to get as close to naked as possible without actual exposure of certain parts yet God's covering completely covered the flesh from the neck to below the knees. The very meaning of modest apparel meant appropriate or seemly long garment or dress. When Adam and his wife were convicted of the shame of their nakedness, their desire was to cover it, yet today, the desire is to expose it. We should obtain our dress code and distinction from the Word of God and not the fashion of the world (Rom. 12:2).

When we deny the sufficiency of Scripture, our Christian culture begins to borrow the language of the pagan culture surrounding us. How many Christians today have begun to speak like the pagans, changing the meaning of *wicked* to mean something good? Here is what the Bible has to say about this:

> *Woe unto them that call evil good, and good evil; that put darkness for light, and light for darkness; that put bitter for sweet, and sweet for bitter!*
> *(Isa. 5:20)*

Wicked will always be wicked in God's sight. Making it palatable by calling good things wicked will bring judgment.

When we deny the sufficiency of Scripture, our churches become filled with manmade traditions, pagan music and rituals, and an irrelevant and powerless gospel. The apostle Paul warns in Galatians 1:8 that he who preaches another gospel is cursed:

THE SUFFICIENCY OF SCRIPTURE

But though we, or an angel from heaven, preach any other Gospel unto you than that which we have preached unto you, let him be accursed.

When we deny the sufficiency of Scripture we risk losing our children to the world because we blindly send them to the humanists to be indoctrinated rather than discipling them ourselves. If they don't lose their faith altogether, many follow the godless and materialistic culture, resulting in delayed maturity, as they choose travel or career rather than starting a family to raise the next faithful generation.[6] When we deny the sufficiency of Scripture marriages and families may be compromised as wives become the helpmeet to other men, husbands spend long hours with women in the workforce who aren't their wives, and career rather than family consumes their focus.[7] When we deny the sufficiency of Scripture and do not distinguish the God-ordained roles for men and women, confusion reigns in society as women are ordained as church leaders to fight our spiritual battles, or are sent to the frontline of our physical wars. As women in the workforce increase[8] and men stay home and keep house, women then wonder why they need men at all. Homosexuality is then a natural consequence as women seek alternate ways of bearing children without a man.[9] Similarly, when marital intimacy is divorced from procreation, and loosed from its marital moorings as it now is in our culture, marriage loses its special and unique status and gives rise to same-sex marriage. This is not far-fetched. The Uniting Church of Australia already condones such actions and conclusions. The Uniting Church was not always this liberal. Seventy-five years ago, one would have thought anyone mad to predict that the then individual denominations, which later formed this denomination, would someday stray so far from orthodoxy. It happened slowly. Little by little the standard was lowered from one generation to the next. First truth is protected, then it is held but no-one remembers why, then it is questioned, then compromise begins, then truth gives way to pragmatism, and finally it is totally opposed. The Bible outlines principles for godly manhood and womanhood, how we should educate

THE SUFFICIENCY OF SCRIPTURE

our children, how they should find spouses, when they should find spouses, and the roles of men and women in the home, church, and community. The Bible speaks to dress, music, art, healthy eating, food production, work and business ethics, borrowing and lending money, property ownership, and literally everything we need to survive.

If only we would recognize that Christianity is indeed an entire worldview and not just a spiritual religion for Sunday. If enough Christians really applied the sufficiency of Scripture to all of life, our culture would be very different. Even the Muslims know the biblical principle of not charging interest on bank loans to their own (only to strangers, i.e., outside the household of faith—see Deut. 23:20, Luke 19:23). Imagine if enough Christians pooled their resources to do this instead of our having to cast our lot with unbelievers to secure finance (see Ex. 22:25, Lev. 25:36-37, Deut. 23:19-20, Neh. 5:7-10, Prov. 1:10-14, Acts 4:32-35).

Consider what could happen in the area of missionary outreach and evangelism if we simply applied the sufficiency of Scripture to our family planning, family worship, and discipleship. Amidst a culture of severely limited population growth, we might potentially fill this nation with godly men and women in just a few generations. We could outnumber the humanists just as the Muslims are doing right now in Europe and the U.K. The U.K. will be a Muslim nation by birthrate alone within twenty years—so too Germany.

'Muhammad boys' prove 'Islam will enter every house in Europe'
By Aaron Klein, www.worldnetdaily.com
December 19, 2007

JERUSALEM – Statistical information released yesterday showing Muhammad is the second most popular boys name in Britain "proves Islam is becoming the majority in the U.K. and will one day enter every house in Europe," a senior terror leader told WND in an interview.

THE SUFFICIENCY OF SCRIPTURE

> *According to statistics released yesterday by Britain's Office of National Statistics, Muhammad was the most popular boys' name in the U.K. when all of its spellings are accounted for. ... If trends continue, Muhammad could be the most popular boys' name in Britain next year.*
>
> *Abdel-Al is known for his fiery threats against Western targets, but he said statistical trends indicating Muslims are gaining a major foothold in the UK show there is no need for violence to spread Islam.*[10]

If we receive every blessing of God with joy, rather than controlling our birthrate like the pagans do, and if we raise our children in the nurture and admonition of the Lord according to the Scriptures, within just a few generations we could out-number the humanists without any trouble. This would be a far more effective means of evangelizing the world than the numerous non-multigenerational missionaries on the field today could achieve. I'm not saying we shouldn't send missionaries overseas—we should—but the emphasis is always *them* and *us*. Those of us who stay must recognize that we are also missionaries to our own children and their children and their children's children, as well as the communities in which we live. If each missionary had a multigenerational vision of faithfulness, how effective could we become? If each of my children has eight children and raises them to be godly, following their parents' example, they'll raise 64 Christians for the next generation. If they in turn each raise eight godly children, that's 512 in the third generation. If by God's grace this pattern continues, that's 4096 Christians in the fourth generation, 32768 Christians in the fifth generation, 262144 in the sixth generation and a staggering 2097152 Christians in the seventh generation. This is possible within 250 years if the Lord tarries. This is more than the population of Adelaide. If by God's grace we took this to the eighth generation, this is an incredible 16777216 Christians—that's three quarters of the population of Australia and it's possible within three hundred years. This is only the product of one faithful Christian family. I'm not saying for a moment

THE SUFFICIENCY OF SCRIPTURE

that we could achieve this perfect score, but by God's grace the impact Christians can have on a nation when they return to God's Word for all of life is truly phenomenal. Remember the children of Israel? The Egyptians were grieved because of the multitude of God's people as they multiplied dramatically and the Egyptians apparently didn't.

> *And the children of Israel were fruitful, and increased abundantly, and multiplied, and waxed exceeding mighty; and the land was filled with them. Now there arose up a new king over Egypt, which knew not Joseph. And he said unto his people, Behold, the people of the children of Israel are more and mightier than we: Come on, let us deal wisely with them; lest they multiply, and it come to pass, that, when there falleth out any war, they join also unto our enemies, and fight against us, and so get them up out of the land. Therefore they did set over them taskmasters to afflict them with their burdens. And they built for Pharaoh treasure cities, Pithom and Raamses. But the more they afflicted them, the more they multiplied and grew. And they were grieved because of the children of Israel.*
> *(Ex. 1:7-12)*

I'm not claiming that if we apply the sufficiency of Scripture we will have perfection in our lives, our family's lives, or in the church—no, until we put off this tabernacle we will have sin. But if we apply the sufficiency of Scripture we will be far more effective in our every endeavor.

> *Trust in the LORD with all thine heart; and lean not unto thine own understanding. In all thy ways acknowledge him, and he shall direct thy paths.*
> *(Prov. 3:5-6)*

> *This book of the law shall not depart out of thy mouth; but thou shalt meditate therein day and night, that thou mayest observe to do according to all that is written therein: for then thou shalt make thy way prosperous, and then thou shalt have good success.*
> *(Josh. 1:8)*

THE SUFFICIENCY OF SCRIPTURE

Before we can begin to apply the principle of the sufficiency of Scripture, however, there is one major thing we must do. Romans 12:2 plainly says that if we are to know God's perfect will, we must renew our minds. This means to take every thought captive to the Lord Jesus Christ and recognize and rid our thinking of man's philosophies.

Casting down imaginations, and every high thing that exalteth itself against the knowledge of God, and bringing into captivity every thought to the obedience of Christ.

(2 Cor. 10:5)

And be not conformed to this world: but be ye transformed by the renewing of your mind, that ye may prove what is that good, and acceptable, and perfect, will of God.

(Rom. 12:2)

1.5 Man Is Commanded to Live by Every Word That Proceedeth from the Mouth of God

God defines truth. No one else in the entire universe has that prerogative or ability. Not only is God the one who defines truth and the only wise God (see John 14:6, 17:3; 1 Tim. 1:17), but He has plainly commanded us that we are to live by every word that proceeds from His mouth:

And he humbled thee, and suffered thee to hunger, and fed thee with manna, which thou knewest not, neither did thy fathers know; that he might make thee know that man doth not live by bread only, but by every word that proceedeth out of the mouth of the LORD doth man live.

(Deut. 8:3)

And Jesus answered him, saying, It is written, That man shall not live by bread alone, but by every word of God.

(Luke 4:4)

THE SUFFICIENCY OF SCRIPTURE

Thy words were found, and I did eat them; and thy word was unto me the joy and rejoicing of mine heart: for I am called by thy name, O LORD God of hosts.

(Jeremiah 15:16)

Even if every man on the planet were to deny the truth of God's Word, long after the vain philosophies that govern their lives are gone "the Word of our God shall stand for ever" (Isa. 40:8). God's Word makes the bold statement, "Yea, let God be true and every man a liar" (Rom. 3:4). He Himself has declared that His Word is totally sufficient for all of life, if only we would study it and obey it:

Study to shew thyself approved unto God, a workman that needeth not to be ashamed, rightly dividing the word of truth.

(2 Tim. 2:15)

Thou hast commanded us to keep thy precepts diligently.

(Ps. 119:4)

Whoso despiseth the word shall be destroyed: but he that feareth the commandment shall be rewarded.

(Prov. 13:13)

The Scriptures are so bold as to plainly say that if we don't keep His Word we don't know Him:

And hereby we do know that we know him, if we keep his commandments. He that saith, I know him, and keepeth not his commandments, is a liar, and the truth is not in him. But whoso keepeth his word, in him verily is the love of God perfected: hereby know we that we are in him.

(1 John 2:3-5)

To the law and to the testimony: if they speak not according to this word, it is because there is no light in them.

(Isa. 8:20)

THE SUFFICIENCY OF SCRIPTURE

1.6 Summary of the Doctrine of the Sufficiency of Scripture

- The doctrine of the sufficiency of Scripture says God's Word is totally sufficient to instruct us either by direct commandment, principle, or pattern in every aspect of our lives.
- God has placed great emphasis on the importance of His Word, magnifying His Word even above His awesome name, which is a name above every name (see Eph. 1:21).
- He has warned of adding to or subtracting from His Word.
- He declared that His written Word is His revelation, word for word, to every jot and tittle, and that it is not open to private interpretation.
- He declares His Word to be powerful, piercing, and precise.
- He has declared it perfect and forever settled.
- He has declared it sufficient to fully equip the man of God for every good work.
- He has declared that His Word will not return to Him void but will accomplish that which He sends it forth to accomplish.
- He warns that in the latter days men will be burdened by their own word rather than God's Word (i.e., deny the sufficiency of Scripture in favor of their own wisdom).
- Denial of the sufficiency of Scripture not only is blasphemy against God's holy name, it destroys the effectiveness of Christianity in the world.
- Let's renew our minds that we may know God's perfect will in seeking to apply the Scriptures to all of faith and practice, a process we must start now but which may not be completed in our generation.
- He has declared that man must live by every Word that proceeds from His mouth. Let God be true and every man a liar.
- The doctrine of the sufficiency of Scripture is the key to revival of our own hearts, families, churches, and nation.

Chapter 2

PERSONAL REVIVAL

IT IS WITH great trepidation that I attempt to write on such a topic, as I am conscious of my own human frailty, and the perpetual need for revival in my own heart. There is no formula for revival—no, not personal, family, church, or national. There are, however, things that must happen for such revival to take place. In this chapter I would like to address the issue of personal revival and what must take place for it to occur.

It goes without saying that we must first be born again before any spiritual revival can occur. Let's first define what it means to be born again (see John 3:7-8, 1 Peter 1:23). What exactly is a Christian? No, it is not someone who simply believes in the one true God. The apostle James writes, "Thou believest that there is one God; thou doest well: the devils also believe, and tremble" (James 2:19). Yes, even the devils believe in God—and more than just believe, they tremble, something many of us who profess to be Christians do not even do.

The fear of the Lord is the beginning of wisdom (see Ps. 111:10), but a Christian is more than one who believes. A Christian is one who has the indwelling of the Holy Spirit (see Eph. 1:13-14). They are made alive spiritually. The spirit is that part of man that is God-conscious and communes with God. When Adam sinned, in that very day he died spiritually (see Gen. 2:17) and also began to die physically.

The apostle John writes, "But as many as received him, to them gave he power to become the sons of God, even to them that believe on his name: Which were born, not of blood, nor of the will of the flesh, nor of the will of man, but of God" (John 1:12-13). He also writes, "He that hath the Son hath life; and he that hath not the Son of God hath not life. These things have I written unto you that believe on the name of the Son of God; that ye may know that ye have eternal life, and that ye may believe on the name of the Son of God" (1 John 5:12-13).

The apostle Paul writes, "If thou shalt confess with thy mouth the Lord Jesus, and shalt believe in thine heart that God hath raised him from the dead, thou shalt be saved. For with the heart man believeth unto righteousness; and with the mouth confession is made unto salvation." (Rom. 10:9-10). A Christian is one who through the Holy Spirit's power openly confesses the Lord Jesus to the world through their life, both in words and deeds. A Christian is one who has confessed that they are a sinner, guilty before God and deserving of death (see Rom. 3:10, 3:23, 6:23). They understand that no good works can save them (see Gal. 2:6, Phil. 3:9) and that all their good works are as filthy rags (see Isa. 64:6). They have accepted the Lord's substitutionary death on their behalf (see Gal. 3:13). They understand that through the Lord Jesus Christ's atoning death on the cross and resurrection to prove God the Father's satisfaction with the propitiatory act of His only begotten Son, that God is just in forgiving their sin (see Rom. 3:25; 1 John 1:9, 2:2). This is not because of the person's own goodness but because of Christ's perfection.

A Christian then walks in newness of life, being a new creation (see 2 Cor. 5:17), putting to death the deeds of the flesh (see Rom. 8:13, Col. 3:5, Rom. 7:4) and instead feeds the spirit to walk in the law of Christ. This person recognizes that they are created in Christ Jesus unto good works (see Eph. 2:10), that they are no longer their own, but bought with a price, the precious blood of the Son of God (see 1 Peter 1:18-19) to glorify God in spirit and in body, which are God's (see 1 Cor. 6:19-20).

The apostle Paul reminds Timothy of what he has been teaching him through his discipleship as he outlines the healthy marks of a Christian. He writes, "But thou hast fully known my doctrine, manner of life, purpose, faith, longsuffering, charity, patience, persecutions, afflictions, ..." (2 Tim. 3:10-11). This truly is an excellent summary of a Christian affected by personal revival. Each of these marks is essential to a mature Christian life:

- doctrine - they know what they believe and how to communicate it,
- manner of life - they live what they believe, i.e. their application of the Scriptures,
- purpose - they know why they're alive, in order to glorify God (Rev. 4:11),
- faith - they demonstrate unquestioning and unwavering trust in God's Word,
- patience and long-suffering - they bear the fruit of the Spirit in adversity,
- charity - they love fervently with God's agape love,
- persecutions and afflictions - they are constantly being shaped by the fiery trials caused by living godly in an ungodly world.

When I speak of the Christian's spiritual revival, I do not mean regeneration—that is part of salvation. No, when I speak of revival I speak of calling the already saved to a closer walk with God. I speak of a Christian's heart burning with zeal, adoration of God, a recognition and hatred of their own wretched sin, desire for godliness, desire to serve others, desire to glorify God through good works, desire to constantly learn how to better apply the Scriptures, desire to hide God's Word in their heart that they might not sin against Him (see Ps. 119:11), and desire to see others saved and growing in their faith and knowledge of the

THE SUFFICIENCY OF SCRIPTURE

Lord Jesus Christ. In short, a returning to our first love (see Rev. 2:4). As I tell my children, it is not just knowing about God or His Word, though that is foundational and necessary, it is truly knowing the living God. It is knowing God as David knew God. Here are David's words—is it any wonder God called him a man after His own heart (see Acts 13:22)?

> *As the hart panteth after the water brooks, so panteth my soul after thee, O God. My soul thirsteth for God, for the living God: when shall I come and appear before God?*
>
> *(Ps. 42:1-2)*

> *O God, thou art my God; early will I seek thee: my soul thirsteth for thee, my flesh longeth for thee in a dry and thirsty land, where no water is; To see thy power and thy glory, so as I have seen thee in the sanctuary. Because thy lovingkindness is better than life, my lips shall praise thee. Thus will I bless thee while I live: I will lift up my hands in thy name. My soul shall be satisfied as with marrow and fatness; and my mouth shall praise thee with joyful lips: When I remember thee upon my bed, and meditate on thee in the night watches. Because thou hast been my help, therefore in the shadow of thy wings will I rejoice. My soul followeth hard after thee: thy right hand upholdeth me.*
>
> *(Ps. 63:1-8)*

> *My soul longeth, yea, even fainteth for the courts of the LORD: my heart and my flesh crieth out for the living God.*
>
> *(Ps. 84:2)*

> *In the multitude of my thoughts within me thy comforts delight my soul.*
> *(Ps. 94:19)*

> *My soul breaketh for the longing that it hath unto thy judgments at all times.*
>
> *(Ps. 119:20)*

PERSONAL REVIVAL

At midnight I will rise to give thanks unto thee because of thy righteous judgments.

(Ps. 119:62)

My soul hath kept thy testimonies; and I love them exceedingly.

(Ps. 119:167)

My soul waiteth for the Lord more than they that watch for the morning: I say, more than they that watch for the morning.

(Ps. 130:6)

I will praise thee; for I am fearfully and wonderfully made: marvellous are thy works; and that my soul knoweth right well.

(Ps. 139:14)

Oh, that David's words were our daily plea! What was the secret to David's hunger for the living God? Let's consider eight things necessary for personal revival:

- We must examine ourselves to see if we are in the faith.
- We must renew our minds and learn to take every thought captive to the obedience of the Lord Jesus Christ.
- We must understand God's character, titles, and attributes.
- We must understand what God means when He commands us to love Him with all of our heart, mind, soul, and strength.
- We must keep God in all our thoughts, with a constant prayerful attitude.
- We must remember God's works both in creation and history.
- We must understand our sinfulness and dependence on God, constantly humbling ourselves and submitting to His Lordship.
- We must present our body as a living sacrifice.

THE SUFFICIENCY OF SCRIPTURE

2.1 We Must Examine Ourselves to See If We Are in the Faith

If we are not saved, we are spiritually dead and need to repent of our sin and put our faith in the Lord Jesus Christ. We must understand that we rightly deserve death and hell and that there is nothing good in us. Even the wind and the waves obey the Lord Jesus Christ (see Mark 4:41), yet we have sinned not once or twice but continually, ever since our birth (see Ps. 51:5, 58:3)! We must understand that no good works can save us. All our good works are as filthy rags to God (see Isa. 64:6). We must cast ourselves in total dependence on the Lord Jesus Christ's shed blood for our sin. It is not a matter of simply accepting the Lord Jesus Christ and thinking we're basically good. We need a healthy recognition of our absolute abhorrence. Our sin separates us from God by an infinite chasm that can only be bridged by payment of the penalty of that filthy sin.

> *Examine yourselves, whether ye be in the faith; prove your own selves. Know ye not your own selves, how that Jesus Christ is in you, except ye be reprobates?*
>
> *(2 Cor. 13:5)*

How do we examine ourselves? We must consider our state in light of God's Word. Do we acknowledge and hate our sin, which separates us from peace with God? Do we believe in the Lord Jesus Christ's atoning work on our behalf? Are we willing to publicly confess the Lord Jesus to the point of martyrdom? Do we believe that God raised the Lord Jesus Christ from the dead? Do we love what God loves and hate what He hates? The Scripture is clear:

> *For God so loved the world, that he gave his only begotten Son, that whosoever believeth in him should not perish, but have everlasting life. For God sent not his Son into the world to condemn the world; but that the world through him might be saved. He that believeth on him is not*

condemned: but he that believeth not is condemned already, because he hath not believed in the name of the only begotten Son of God.
(John 3:16-18)

But what saith it? The word is nigh thee, even in thy mouth, and in thy heart: that is, the word of faith, which we preach; That if thou shalt confess with thy mouth the Lord Jesus, and shalt believe in thine heart that God hath raised him from the dead, thou shalt be saved.
(Rom. 10:8-9)

2.2 We Must Renew Our Mind

One of the most important prerequisites to personal revival is renewing our mind. It is something we often hear, but what does it mean, how do we do it, and why is it crucial?

First we must realize the ungodly philosophies with which our minds have been saturated since our birth. Humanism, socialism, feminism, hedonism, environmentalism, and every other "ism" of our upbringing and education mar our thinking and prevent us from knowing God's perfect will because we come to the Scriptures with worldly wisdom that opposes God's wisdom. Take careful note of the apostle Paul's inspired command, "And be not conformed to this world: but be ye transformed by the renewing of your mind, that ye may prove what is that good, and acceptable, and perfect, will of God" (Rom. 12:2). Note that the apostle Paul makes it clear that renewal of the mind must come in order that one may find God's perfect will.

The Apostle Paul teaches us that as part of the sanctification process of putting off the old and putting on the new, there must be a deliberate decision to renew the spirit of our mind, or, to renew that which influences and animates our rational thinking.

This I say therefore, and testify in the Lord, that ye henceforth walk not as other Gentiles walk, in the vanity of their mind, Having the understanding darkened, being alienated from the life of God through the ignorance that is in them, because of the blindness of their heart: Who being past feeling have given themselves over unto lasciviousness, to work all uncleanness with greediness. But ye have not so learned Christ; If so be that ye have heard him, and have been taught by him, as the truth is in Jesus: That ye put off concerning the former conversation the old man, which is corrupt according to the deceitful lusts; And be renewed in the spirit of your mind; And that ye put on the new man, which after God is created in righteousness and true holiness. (Eph. 4:17-24.)

Second we must recognize that God's ways are not our ways and that we must submit to His ways rather than our sinful human reasoning. We must take the desert island challenge. If we were on a desert island with only the Holy Bible, how would we live? What would we know about life, family, marriage, relationships, children, education, values, the church, etc.? God says through His prophet Isaiah, "For my thoughts are not your thoughts, neither are your ways my ways, saith the LORD. For as the heavens are higher than the earth, so are my ways higher than your ways, and my thoughts than your thoughts" (Isa. 55:8-9).

The apostle Paul also commands us that we should be constantly "Casting down imaginations, and every high thing that exalteth itself against the knowledge of God, and bringing into captivity every thought to the obedience of Christ" (2 Cor. 10:5).

It is almost impossible to renew our minds if they are constantly being filled with godless and worldly wisdom from television, movies, talk shows, radio, newspapers and other printed media, the Internet, humanistic education, the workplace, and even Christian bookshops, churches, and seminaries that do not teach the sufficiency of Scripture. Here we can make a very real application of the following verses:

> *Wherefore if thy hand or thy foot offend thee, cut them off, and cast them from thee: it is better for thee to enter into life halt or maimed, rather than having two hands or two feet to be cast into everlasting fire. And if thine eye offend thee, pluck it out, and cast it from thee: it is better for*

thee to enter into life with one eye, rather than having two eyes to be cast into hell fire.

(Matt. 18:8-9)

Whether it be television, ungodly books, magazines, music, or ungodly philosophy from Christians or non-Christians alike, if it doesn't lead to godly wisdom it should be discarded. Just because something has a "Christian" label on it, if it doesn't conform to the Scriptures it's not Christian.

2.3 We Must Study God's Character, Titles, and Attributes

One of the greatest hindrances to our relationship with God is a lack of a deep understanding of who God is. An interesting question was asked of a seminary student recently: "In all your studies, how much have you studied the character of God?"

The student was shocked. "Study the character of God?"

Yet knowing who God is is so foundational to our relationship with Him, just as knowing our spouse is foundational to a strong marriage.

Both Job and Isaiah really only had true revival in their hearts when they properly understood their wretchedness before the Holy God:

I have heard of thee by the hearing of the ear: but now mine eye seeth thee. Wherefore I abhor myself, and repent in dust and ashes.

(Job 42:5-6)

Then said I, Woe is me! for I am undone; because I am a man of unclean lips, and I dwell in the midst of a people of unclean lips: for mine eyes have seen the King, the LORD of hosts.

(Isa. 6:5)

It is essential to revival that we have a right understanding of who God is, not just in terms of his holiness but also in terms of His character and attributes. I remember the prayer of an elderly gentleman one time—for several minutes he simply recited off with fervor and affection God's titles. That was the extent of his prayer. It is paramount that we know who God is because it is only when we have a firm grasp of who He is that the constancy of His character will be able to comfort us during tribulation.

Consider with me for a minute that your wife has just gone missing. What are the options? Did she leave you? Did someone abduct her? What happened? Knowing her character at that point would be of great comfort to you. If you know she loved you and had proven herself trustworthy for many years, her leaving you would not even cross your mind. Instead you would be immediately seeking help to find her captors. If, however, your relationship with her was shaky at best and you had doubts about her character, you may well be filled with the heart-wrenching possibility that she left you. It is in our trials that a good understanding of God's character will really be able to comfort us. Let's consider for a moment some of His glorious titles and attributes:

- The only true God (John 17:3)
- Holy Father (John 17:11)
- Wonderful, Counselor, the mighty God, the everlasting Father, the Prince of Peace (Isa. 9:6)
- Excellent (Job 37:23; Ps. 148:13, 8:1, 36:7, 76:4, 150:2; Isa. 12:5; Heb. 8:6; 2 Peter 1:17)
- Love (1 John 4:8)
- The Good Shepherd (John 10:11, Ps. 23)
- The Chief Shepherd (1 Peter 5:4)
- The only wise God (1 Tim. 1:17, Rom. 16:27)
- The God of truth (Deut. 32:4, John 14:6)
- The Father of Mercies and the God of all comfort (2 Cor. 1:3-4)
- The God who provides (Gen. 22:14, Phil. 4:19)
- The Living Bread (John 6:51)

- The Door (John 10:9)
- The Light of the World (John 8:12)
- The True Vine (John 15:1-8)
- The Great I Am (Ex. 3:14)
- The Alpha and Omega (Rev. 1:8)
- The Chief Cornerstone (Eph. 2:20, 1 Peter 2:6)
- Righteous Judge (2 Tim. 4:8, 1 Peter 2:23)
- Father of Lights (James 1:17)
- The Amen (Rev. 3:14)

We haven't time nor space to study each of these few titles in great detail but summarizing just these few we can learn that the Almighty God is omnipotent, omnipresent, and omniscient. There is no one His equal in all of the universe. God defines wonderful. God defines wisdom. God defines truth. God defines love. God is a father—that is, He protects and provides for our soul. He is unchanging and therefore totally reliable and not subject to sudden changes in temperament or purpose as we are. As the Light of The World He shows us our true sinful nature. As the Vine, He gives us our identity and declares our utter dependence on Him. As the Door He provides the way of salvation. As the Bread He sustains us. As the Counselor and God of all comfort He gives us understanding, wisdom, and comfort through whatever trial He deems good for our character development. He is a "Man of His Word," so to speak—that which He promises will come to pass with utter certainty (see Rom. 11:29 and Isa. 55:10-11). As The Chief Cornerstone, He gives us a frame of reference and purpose. As the Father of Lights, He gives us every good and perfect gift and His will is that all things work together for the good of those who love Him and who are called according to His purpose (see Rom. 8:28). There is nothing that can separate us from the love of the Lord Jesus Christ (see Rom. 8:35, John 10:28-29). As Righteous Judge, every pronouncement of His mouth is totally right and just. His title as Amen speaks of His absolute and total trustworthiness in whatever trial we may face.

THE SUFFICIENCY OF SCRIPTURE

The following wonderful verses dispel the myth that we mere mortals cannot know God. The Lord goes as far as to say that if we are to glory, glory in this, that you understand and know Him and what He delights in:

> *Thus saith the LORD, Let not the wise man glory in his wisdom, neither let the mighty man glory in his might, let not the rich man glory in his riches: But let him that glorieth glory in this, that he understandeth and knoweth me, that I am the LORD which exercise lovingkindness, judgment, and righteousness, in the earth: for in these things I delight, saith the LORD.*
>
> (Jer. 9:23-24)

2.4 We Must Understand What It Means to Love God with All of Our Hearts, Minds, Souls, and Strength

> *And Jesus answered him, The first of all the commandments is, Hear, O Israel; The Lord our God is one Lord: And thou shalt love the Lord thy God with all thy heart, and with all thy soul, and with all thy mind, and with all thy strength: this is the first commandment.*
>
> (Mark 12:29)

If there is one thing that will contribute to personal revival and get a Christian through a life of trial and despair, it is his love for God, which is deeply rooted in God's love for him. Why did the Lord Jesus remind us of this fourfold love we should have for Him? As I look back over my experience in many churches and see the different ways in which Christians express their love for God, I see a pattern that often leaves one of these aspects of love for God out. It makes a Christian's love of God one-, two-, or three-dimensional instead of four-dimensional. Perhaps this is because the Christian's understanding of God's love is not four-dimensional. What do I mean? The Lord Jesus could have simply said, "Love God with your whole being." However, He spelled it out much more clearly than that and I believe this was for a good reason. Let's consider for a minute the four aspects of how we are to love God:

1. Heart (*kardia*): the center of all physical and spiritual life, will, vigor. The heart is the source of motive. If we do not love God with our hearts, there will be no desire to do His will, only a sense of duty and struggle. A horse is led by bit and bridle; a man is lead by his heartstrings. Whoever has your heart has your life.

> *My son, give me thine heart, and let thine eyes observe my ways.*
> *(Prov. 23:26)*

> *For where your treasure is, there will your heart be also.*
> *(Matt. 6:21)*

How do we love God with our hearts? We love God with our hearts when we are drawn to His character and love for us and this attraction creates in us that desire to please Him. We love God with our hearts when we from our very core desire to be like Him, to please Him, and to enjoy Him. We can love God with our hearts without knowing very much intellectually, similar to how a baby or child loves the affection of their parents. We love God with our hearts when what we find valuable and meaningful is in God's kingdom and not on the earth, as it is so aptly described in Matthew 6:21. Put very simply, if our affections and zeal are greater for earthly things than for what pleases God, we do not love God with our whole hearts.

2. Mind (*dianoia*): understanding, way of thinking, thoughts.

The mind is our understanding. We are commanded to love God with our minds. Without the mind, our knowledge of God would not grow. Without the mind, we would not be able to reason about the evidence that compels us to love God. Without the mind, any opposing "fine-sounding" folly could throw us off course—and in fact does to many Christians. Our minds, through investigation of the evidence, lead us to put faith in God. Our intellectual investigation is an anchor when emotions are flat, we are without strength, and even our hearts are broken. As we have already pointed out from Romans 12:2, it is impossible to know God's will for our lives unless we renew our minds. To renew our minds means to rid it of man's philosophies, which are rooted in man's ideas rather than God's Word. We thus can't love God with all of our minds if we do not renew our minds! We can't renew our minds if our main source of filling them are from the public education system, mass media, or unbelieving man's philosophies and –isms, which are opposed to God's Word and heart. Be not deceived: evil communications corrupt good manners (see 1 Cor. 15:33).

> *Come now, and let us reason together, saith the LORD: though your sins be as scarlet, they shall be as white as snow; though they be red like crimson, they shall be as wool.*
>
> *(Isa. 1:18)*

> *But grow in grace, and in the knowledge of our Lord and Saviour Jesus Christ.*
>
> *(2 Peter 3:18)*

> *Thou wilt keep him in perfect peace, whose mind is stayed on thee: because he trusteth in thee.*
>
> *(Isa 26:3)*

> *This I recall to my mind, therefore have I hope. It is of the LORD's mercies that we are not consumed, because his compassions fail not. They are new every morning: great is thy faithfulness.*
>
> *(Lam. 3:21-23)*

> *I thank God through Jesus Christ our Lord. So then with the mind I myself serve the law of God; but with the flesh the law of sin.*
>
> *(Rom. 7:25)*

And be not conformed to this world: but be ye transformed by the renewing of your mind, that ye may prove what is that good, and acceptable, and perfect, will of God.

(Rom. 12:2)

But his delight is in the law of the LORD; and in his law doth he meditate day and night.

(Ps. 1:2)

I remember the days of old; I meditate on all thy works; I muse on the work of thy hands.

(Ps. 143:5)

In the multitude of my thoughts within me thy comforts delight my soul.

(Ps. 94:19)

3. Soul (*psuche*): the seat of the feelings, desires, affections, life. Our souls are what make us different from dead people (see Gen. 2:7). It is our emotions, our attitudes, our feelings! We must love God with all of our souls. How do we do this? We do it by enjoying God through our senses. When we see a rainbow, a waterfall, a butterfly, or a flower; when we taste good food; when we hear a sweet melody; when we feel a loved one's embrace or hear their familiar and comforting voice; when we enjoy toddlers' antics or an infant's close contact; when we attribute all of these things to the God who created them, we taste and see that the Lord is good and we overflow in praise to Him. If a testimony of someone's conversion to Christ does not thrill us, if we do not attribute every pleasure enjoyed in godliness to Him, if we are not overwhelmed with awe when we perceive through our senses His marvelous works, we are not loving God with all of our souls.

Set your affection on things above, not on things on the earth

(see Col. 3:2)

THE SUFFICIENCY OF SCRIPTURE

O taste and see that the LORD is good: blessed is the man that trusteth in him.

(Ps. 34:8)

As the hart panteth after the water brooks, so panteth my soul after thee, O God. My soul thirsteth for God, for the living God: when shall I come and appear before God?

(Ps. 42:1-2)

O God, thou art my God; early will I seek thee: my soul thirsteth for thee, my flesh longeth for thee in a dry and thirsty land, where no water is.

(Ps. 63:1)

My soul longeth, yea, even fainteth for the courts of the LORD: my heart and my flesh crieth out for the living God.

(Ps. 84:2)

My soul breaketh for the longing that it hath unto thy judgments at all times.

(Ps. 119:20)

My soul waiteth for the Lord more than they that watch for the morning: I say, more than they that watch for the morning.

(Ps. 130:6)

4. Strength (*ischus*): ability, force, strength, might.

We love God through our strength when we serve Him with our hands and feet: This is the practical aspect of loving God. When we choose a life that is different from the world in order to fulfill His commandments or practice His clear precepts or patterns in our families, churches, workplace, etc., and when we give of our time and effort, we demonstrate loving God with our strength. "Be not deceived; God is not mocked: for whatsoever a man soweth, that shall he also reap" (Gal. 6:7). I think it is also clear from Scripture that it is not only what a man sows that is important but where a man sows—that is, where his energy is spent.

> *For God is not unrighteous to forget your work and labour of love, which ye have shewed toward his name, in that ye have ministered to the saints, and do minister. And we desire that every one of you do shew the same diligence to the full assurance of hope unto the end: That ye be not slothful, but followers of them who through faith and patience inherit the promises.*
> *(Heb. 6:10)*

> *For this is the love of God, that we keep his commandments: and his commandments are not grievous.*
> *(1 John 5:3)*

Matthew 25:14-30 describes the parable of the talents. The difference between the servant who was given five talents, which made another five, and the one who was given one and who buried it, was the amount they loved God with their strength. God gave them according to their ability and He was proven right in His judgment of their ability. Faith without works is dead, as we are told in James 2:17-26.

Now let's consider if any of these aspects of our love for God are absent, what happens.

If we do not love God with our hearts, everything is just duty. There is no motivation or desire to please God. Have you ever felt this way? If we do not love God with our minds, when our hearts are broken, our emotions and experience are bad, or we are faced with clever sounding opposition, without a love for God in this dimension, we will fall away. An intellectual love of God leads to reason, faith, and a desire to grow in knowledge. We can love God with our souls—that is, our emotions—and this is commanded. However, emotions come and go and so loving God with our souls alone lacks the motive when the emotions are flat.

We can love God with our strength, this too is commanded, but without the heart, this can become just duty and a Christian can feel burned out. We can love God with our minds—that is, an intellectual love of God, an understanding of what He has done, and a knowledge of doctrine and how we ought to live. But loving God with the mind without the heart and without strength lacks the motive and desire and, again, becomes a duty. It can also result in no practical application of His Word to our lives or obedience to what we intellectually know.

The Jews loved God with their strength. They religiously kept every feast but did not love God with their hearts and souls. This resulted in God uttering, "I hate, I despise your feast days, and I will not smell in your solemn assemblies" (Amos 5:21).

In Revelation 2:1-4, the Ephesian church loved God with their strength, they labored, they loved God with their minds, they didn't bear false doctrine, and they proved all things and teachers, but they did not love God with their hearts or souls, and they lost their first love (see Rev. 2:4). Thus, we can demonstrate our strength of love and intellectual love without our hearts and souls loving.

Josiah had this rare testimony: "And like unto him was there no king before him, that turned to the LORD with all his heart, and with all his soul, and with all his might, according to all the law of Moses; neither after him arose there any like him" (2 Kings 23:25).

We are also reminded of what God said to the children of Israel—that a failure to love Him would result in the following:

> *If thou wilt not observe to do all the words of this law that are written in this book, that thou mayest fear this glorious and fearful name, THE LORD THY GOD. ... And among these nations shalt thou find no ease, neither shall the sole of thy foot have rest: but the LORD shall give thee there a trembling heart, and failing of eyes, and sorrow of mind: And thy life shall hang in doubt.*
>
> (Deut. 28:58, 65-66)

While we are not the children of Israel, is it not true that without a deep love for God, we find no ease, no rest, a trembling heart, a failing of eyes, and sorrow of mind?

PERSONAL REVIVAL

We can only work toward the goal of loving God with all of our hearts, minds, souls, and strength if we realize there should be no separation of secular and sacred in our Christian lives. Loving God with all of our hearts, minds, souls, and strength requires that every aspect of our lives be subject to God's Word. While this sounds cliché, unless we understand the four dimensions of loving God, we won't submit each of these parts of our lives to His authority and will unknowingly compartmentalize those things to which we don't think the Scriptures speak and those we think it does. Remember the desert island challenge? If we did not have the influence of culture, media, philosophy, and trend, and only had God's Word on a desert island, how would we live? In truth, if we want to love the Lord our God with all our hearts, minds, souls, and strength, the Holy Bible should be all we treasure and consult for how we live.

How then do we get this love of God in these four dimensions? Paul wanted and prayed for the saints that they would be rooted and grounded in love, and that they would comprehend the breadth, length, depth, height of the love of Christ, which passes knowledge, and that they might be filled with all of God's fullness (see Eph. 3:16-19).

We love him, because he first loved us.

(1 John 4:19)

It is our love for God, deeply rooted and grounded in His love for us, that gives us stability, rest, clear vision, and a sound heart and mind, which results in fruitfulness. I believe we must be rooted and grounded in God's love for us in these four areas of our life. This is why the Lord Jesus explained the first commandment as He did.

And the Lord direct your hearts into the love of God, and into the patient waiting for Christ.

(2 Thess. 3:5)

THE SUFFICIENCY OF SCRIPTURE

Keep yourselves in the love of God, looking for the mercy of our Lord Jesus Christ unto eternal life.

(Jude 1:21)

And hope maketh not ashamed; because the love of God is shed abroad in our hearts by the Holy Ghost which is given unto us.

(Rom. 5:5)

What do you see when you look at a photo close up? What do you miss at a distance? I know in my life when my love for God in any of these areas is lacking, it is because my perception of God has diminished and my senses have been dulled to His love surrounding me, like taking a beautiful picture and removing it far from our view until the detail becomes blurred and indistinguishable. Our hearts must commune with God's heart in meaningful prayer, our minds must be filled with the wonder of everything we can know about God. We must apply our mind to attempt to comprehend the incredible immensity of the atoning work of the Lord Jesus Christ for our deprave and abhorrant sinful state! Our senses must be filled with the wonder of His creation around us. Our strength must be directed to every work that both achieves these goals and also glorifies Him.

So when they had dined, Jesus saith to Simon Peter, Simon, son of Jonas, lovest thou me more than these? He saith unto him, Yea, Lord; thou knowest that I love thee. He saith unto him, Feed my lambs. He saith to him again the second time, Simon, son of Jonas, lovest thou me? He saith unto him, Yea, Lord; thou knowest that I love thee. He saith unto him, Feed my sheep. He saith unto him the third time, Simon, son of Jonas, lovest thou me? Peter was grieved because he said unto him the third time, Lovest thou me? And he said unto him, Lord, thou knowest all things; thou knowest that I love thee. Jesus saith unto him, Feed my sheep.

(John 21:15-17)

While we read this as a reversal to the denial of his Lord three times (see Mark 14:72), it also shows the extent of Peter's love for his Lord. The Lord Jesus asked Peter twice if he loved Him with agape love, the deep and comprehensive love with which God loves us and with which we should love Him. Agape is based on worth or esteem rather than emotion—our love for God should be based on His character rather than on our frail feelings. Twice Peter answered that he loved Jesus with phileo love—that is, he was fond of him. This is more a fondness based on emotion rather than a love for Him based on the intrinsic value of His character.

The third time, after Peter's less than convincing answer, the Lord Jesus asked him if he loved Him with a phileo love. This brought Peter to grief. We see in this example that Peter only loved the Lord with his emotions or soul, not his heart (will), mind (comprehension of God's character), or strength (willingness to feed His flock). We also learn of the futility of deceiving ourselves about the lack of depth of love for God—as the Lord Jesus demonstrated to Peter, He knew Peter's heart better than Peter did.

Some Christians love God with their hearts but think it wrong to bring the intellect into their faith and think faith is opposed to reason rather than firmly founded on reason. Others have an intellectual but emotionless love. Others still worship God emotionally but lack practical obedience, not loving with their strength (or works). Still others love God with their works but not their minds. It is interesting to observe the different kinds of Christians and how we easily point a finger at the other kind to find fault with the expression of their love for God. Which kind of Christian are you? If you lack one aspect of love for God, you fail to obey this very first commandment.

While we know we cannot keep the law in our flesh, it should be every born-again Christian's earnest desire to love the Lord our God with all of our hearts, minds, souls, and strength!

2.5 We Must Keep God in All Our Thoughts with a Constant Prayerful Attitude

We often are exhorted to have a quiet time when we first awake. While this is beneficial, even more beneficial is a constant attitude of contemplation of God's Word and a constant attitude of prayer in our hearts throughout the day, regardless of what we're doing. Limiting our prayer life to a few minutes in the morning only adds to that wrong practice of the separation of secular and sacred. We are God's children full-time, not only for a few minutes when we awake, a few seconds when we give thanks for food, and an hour or two on the Lord's Day.

> *The wicked, through the pride of his countenance, will not seek after God: God is not in all his thoughts.*
>
> (Ps. 10:4)

Notice that the wicked do not have God in all their thoughts, conversely, the child of God should have God in all his thoughts.

> *This book of the law shall not depart out of thy mouth; but thou shalt meditate therein day and night, that thou mayest observe to do according to all that is written therein: for then thou shalt make thy way prosperous, and then thou shalt have good success.*
>
> (Josh. 1:8)

> *Blessed is the man that walketh not in the counsel of the ungodly, nor standeth in the way of sinners, nor sitteth in the seat of the scornful. But his delight is in the law of the LORD; and in his law doth he meditate day and night.*
>
> (Ps. 1:1-2)

> *When I remember thee upon my bed, and meditate on thee in the night watches.*
>
> (Ps. 63:6)

I will meditate in thy precepts, and have respect unto thy ways.
(Ps. 119:15)

At midnight I will rise to give thanks unto thee because of thy righteous judgments.
(Ps. 119:62)

Mine eyes prevent the night watches, that I might meditate in thy word.
(Ps. 119:148)

Let the word of Christ dwell in you richly in all wisdom; teaching and admonishing one another in psalms and hymns and spiritual songs, singing with grace in your hearts to the Lord.
(Col. 3:16)

Pray without ceasing.
(1 Thess. 5:17)

2.6 We Must Constantly Consider the Works of God Both in Creation and History

David had many hours to contemplate God's glory in creation as he sat under many a starry night keeping his father's sheep. Today we are bombarded with information, much of little importance, from radio, TV, Internet, e-mail, billboards, printed media, and books. We would do well to, "Be still, and know that I am God: I will be exalted among the heathen, I will be exalted in the earth" (Ps. 46:10).

Consider the number of times David spoke of God's works throughout the Psalms and how he made it his mission to make them known to all.

I will meditate also of all thy work, and talk of thy doings.
(Ps. 77:12)

THE SUFFICIENCY OF SCRIPTURE

I remember the days of old; I meditate on all thy works; I muse on the work of thy hands.

(Ps. 143:5)

I will praise thee, O LORD, with my whole heart; I will shew forth all thy marvellous works.

(Ps. 9:1)

The works of the LORD are great, sought out of all them that have pleasure therein.

(Ps. 111:2)

He hath made his wonderful works to be remembered: the LORD is gracious and full of compassion.

(Ps. 111:4)

The Lord's works in the earth:

Come, behold the works of the LORD, what desolations he hath made in the earth.

(Ps. 46:8)

O LORD, how manifold are thy works! in wisdom hast thou made them all: the earth is full of thy riches.

(Ps. 104:24)

God's works in the ocean's depths:

They that go down to the sea in ships, that do business in great waters; These see the works of the LORD, and his wonders in the deep.

(Ps. 107:23-24)

PERSONAL REVIVAL

The Lord's works in the heavens:

The heavens declare the glory of God; and the firmament sheweth his handywork. Day unto day uttereth speech, and night unto night sheweth knowledge. There is no speech nor language, where their voice is not heard.
(Ps. 19:1-3)

Whether in the earth, the ocean's depths, or the far reaches of the universe, God has displayed His handiwork and we should both contemplate it and glorify Him for it. We should also diligently teach our children history, that is, His story, so they also set their hope in God, as Psalm 78 so clearly teaches:

I will open my mouth in a parable: I will utter dark sayings of old: Which we have heard and known, and our fathers have told us. We will not hide them from their children, shewing to the generation to come the praises of the LORD, and his strength, and his wonderful works that he hath done. For he established a testimony in Jacob, and appointed a law in Israel, which he commanded our fathers, that they should make them known to their children: That the generation to come might know them, even the children which should be born; who should arise and declare them to their children: That they might set their hope in God, and not forget the works of God, but keep his commandments: And might not be as their fathers, a stubborn and rebellious generation; a generation that set not their heart aright, and whose spirit was not stedfast with God.
(Ps. 78:2-8)

Remember the days of old, consider the years of many generations: ask thy father, and he will shew thee; thy elders, and they will tell thee.
(Deut. 32:7)

Remember the former things of old: for I am God, and there is none else; I am God, and there is none like me, Declaring the end from the beginning,

THE SUFFICIENCY OF SCRIPTURE

and from ancient times the things that are not yet done, saying, My counsel shall stand, and I will do all my pleasure.

(Isa. 46:9-10)

Of course the central event of history is the event which should captivate the focus of every believer, that of the coming to earth of God Himself, in the person of the Lord Jesus Christ. Who, at the cruel hands of sinful men, his very pinnacle of creation, was beaten and scourged,[11] had His beard ripped from His face, was spat upon,[12] and had thrust upon His head a crown of the sharpest thorns.[13] We then nailed Him to a rugged wooden cross, naked and humiliated.[14] This exemplifies the true nature of man against His Creator. How do we comprehend though that this was allowed by God the father in order to pay the penalty for all sin including that very act of the highest treason? Yet it did not end there, for the Lord of Glory rose again, death unable to hold Him. He was seen of more than 500 before His bodily ascension and promise of His certain return. Yes we must teach history. For the Lord's incarnation is not some mythical event divorced from our experience of time on earth but was the most incredible act man has ever participated in. To have those loving and purposeful hands touch the eyes of the blind, raise the dead, unstop the ears of the deaf and hold little children. To have those eyes of omniscience probe the hearts of his disciples and look upon a poor widow who gave her last mite. To hear that voice of comfort speak words of solace to Mary as she wept outside His tomb on that resurrection day, or to hear that voice of thunderous authority command the wind and waves to be still in that tumultuous storm as they were tossed violently in a small fishing boat! To consider how the two disciples felt their hearts burn within them as they walked with that "mysterious" person on the road to Amaus. To see the Son of God ascend to the heavens and hear the voices of the angels proclaim His coming again! Yes, we must teach history in its entirety from God's perspective as it is His story.

We will look more at God's hand in history in the chapter on education. Even now, what we do as Christians in our lifetimes will one day be part of history. Will we impact the world for good or ill? Will we make a name for ourselves or glorify God?

2.7 We Must Humbly Submit to His Lordship

Know ye that the LORD he is God: it is he that hath made us, and not we ourselves; we are his people, and the sheep of his pasture.
(Ps. 100:3)

Humble yourselves therefore under the mighty hand of God, that he may exalt you in due time.
(1 Peter 5:6)

Humble yourselves in the sight of the Lord, and he shall lift you up.
(James 4:10)

The LORD is nigh unto them that are of a broken heart; and saveth such as be of a contrite spirit.
(Ps. 34:18)

Submit yourselves therefore to God. Resist the devil, and he will flee from you. Draw nigh to God, and he will draw nigh to you. Cleanse your hands, ye sinners; and purify your hearts, ye double minded.
(James 4:7-8)

For thus saith the high and lofty One that inhabiteth eternity, whose name is Holy; I dwell in the high and holy place, with him also that is of a contrite and humble spirit, to revive the spirit of the humble, and to revive the heart of the contrite ones.
(Isa. 57:15)

2.8 We Must Present Our Bodies as Living Sacrifices

I beseech you therefore, brethren, by the mercies of God, that ye present your bodies a living sacrifice, holy, acceptable unto God, which is your reasonable service.

(Rom. 12:1)

What? know ye not that your body is the temple of the Holy Ghost which is in you, which ye have of God, and ye are not your own? For ye are bought with a price: therefore glorify God in your body, and in your spirit, which are God's.

(1 Cor. 6:19-20)

Presenting our bodies as living sacrifices means that we make ourselves and all we have available to the Lord's service. There is nothing we have that the Lord didn't first give us (see 1 Chron. 29:16). It is even He who gives us the power to get wealth (see Deut. 8:18) but even this is for His own purpose, not for the gratification of our flesh.

2.9 Summary of Eight Necessary Prerequisites to Personal Revival

There is no shortcut to personal revival. We may at times experience a spiritual high such as after attending a camp, but the mundane will quickly bring us back to earth. The mountaintop thrills are good for us to help us cast vision for the future and get our thoughts and lives in perspective, but we do come down from the mountain and sometimes with a thud. As we seek personal revival, let's remember the eight necessary prerequisites:

- Let's examine ourselves to see if we are in the faith.
- Let's renew our minds and seek to take every thought captive to the obedience of the Lord Jesus Christ.
- Let's study God's character, titles, and attributes.

PERSONAL REVIVAL

- Let's understand what it means to love God with all of our hearts, minds, souls, and strength.
- Let's keep God in all our thoughts with a constant prayerful attitude.
- Let's constantly consider God's works both in creation and history.
- Let's understand our sinfulness and dependence on God, constantly humbling ourselves and submitting to His lordship.
- Let's present our bodies as living sacrifices.

Chapter 3

REVIVAL IN THE HOME

3.1 Marriage (Poem)
(From *More than Meets the Eye*, Copyright ©2009, Joseph Stephen)

> A house divided against itself,
> Will certainly come to ruin.[15]
> God hath made the man and wife,
> A single blessed union.[16]
> Let not man tear what God hath joined,
> No let there not be schism.[17]
> Infighting and disunity,
> Will only yield confusion.
>
> The husband cries, "Wife submit!"[18]
> The wife asks "Where's the love?"[19]
> The fingers point, the blame is cast,
> A solution seems far off.
> Each one of us must guard our hearts[20]
> Against pride and selfishness;
> For these things often rob the home
> Of God's most perfect rest.

REVIVAL IN THE HOME

Know that when one member hurts,
The whole body feels the pain;
And when one member celebrates,
All the members gain.[21]
Marriage is the union,
Of two members tightly joined;
So when one causes anguish,
He will not escape, be warned.

Remember, oh dear husband,
How your Master loves the church.
He gave His very life for her
And bestows the highest worth.[22]
The church is never perfect and
His love does not depend
On her actions good or lacking,
He is faithful to the end.

Dwell with your wife in knowledge.
You are joint heirs together.
Your prayers will be hindered,
If you fail to remember.[23]
Give honor to the weaker
And never become bitter.[24]
Shepherd her and show her,
That you'll cherish her forever.

Oh wife, you are his help meet;[25]
He is your head and your protection.[26]
Bear with him in patience,
In spite of his imperfection.

THE SUFFICIENCY OF SCRIPTURE

Encourage him and love him,
Your impact is profound.
A wise woman builds her house,
But the foolish plucks it down.[27]

May your husband safely trust in you,
Look well to all your ways.
Obey the law of kindness and
Do him goodness all his days.[28]
Favor is deceitful
And beauty is truly vain,
But a woman who fears the Lord,
She surely will be praised.[29]

It is better to dwell in the wilderness,
Than with a contentious wife;[30]
And as wood is to a fire,
A contentious man will kindle strife.[31]
So stop that drip drip dripping.
O woman, please take heed[32]
And man, do not be wrathful,
It worketh not the will of God.[33]

Marriage in all is honourable,[34]
It's God's perfect will.
He gave the woman to the man,
This plan is perfect still.
The purpose is to procreate,
A line of godly seed,[35]
Of women meek and virtuous[36]
And visionary men who lead.[37]

REVIVAL IN THE HOME

In this chapter I'd like to discuss family revival. It is very important to say from the outset that I did not grow up knowing about the biblical pattern for the home. I came from a tumultuous family background of several dysfunctional generations. I never knew my biological father and my mother married multiple times. Though we attended church and a Christian school for a few years, there was a typical disconnect between professed religion and reality. My family grew to reflect the moral abomination of the culture surrounding us. I grew up in an area where promiscuity, substance abuse and violence were common. My sister was murdered in 2013, never escaping the snare of this culture. I lay this foundation so you don't think I came from a perfect Christian home and thus don't know what it is like to know a dysfunctional family. I was saved out of this mess by God's glorious grace, but not without scars and much baggage.

I also need to say that even now we are not a perfect family. I am simply God's messenger, one who by God's grace seeks revival in my own home. Family revival requires effort. There are no shortcuts. It is not a matter of simply praying and sitting back waiting for God to do what He has commanded you to do. A Scripture verse that has been a challenge to me and that puts things simply is:

Through wisdom is an house builded; and by understanding it is established: And by knowledge shall the chambers be filled with all precious and pleasant riches.
(Prov. 24:3-4)

Revival in the home begins with a deliberate choice to break the cycle of the sins of our fathers, the traditions of men, and the humanistic baggage inherited from our own education. By wisdom is it built. Not by accident.

God has defined three basic institutions in His great design: the family, the church, and the state. The family is His basic atom, so it is no wonder that today Satan is trying to destroy it with all his vehement hatred. Christians have largely not been taught God's pattern for the family, which is why Christian families often look no different to unbelieving families except perhaps for their weekly church attendance.

The purpose of the family is to exemplify and transmit God's character, works, Word, providences, and glorious gospel from one generation to the next. Similar to how the Jew was to be a light to the nations, so too the family as a unit is to be a living epistle. Mark 3:25 says a house divided against itself will fall. We often only think of division as the separation of parents. Division, however, can cause ruin simply when a family is individualistic rather than unified in its goal and mission. If children do not catch the biblical convictions their parents hold, communication of God's providence, works, and character will not reach the next generation and that Christian household will end at that generation, as will the local church of that generation. When children and parents are united in vision, purpose, and action, it is only then that multigenerational faithfulness can occur and that the Christian household will stand.

The apostle Paul exhorts us to, "Rebuke not an elder, but intreat him as a father; and the younger men as brethren; The elder women as mothers; the younger as sisters, with all purity" (1 Tim. 5:1-2). Where do we learn how to treat a brother or a sister, to respect a father or a mother? In the family. Of course, today in many families, brothers and sisters are treated identically and there is no respect of the father above anyone else. We've lost this important picture because our families do not follow the biblical pattern. This is, of course, one of the major reasons for weak churches today. It is thus vitally important that we understand what a family is in God's economy and do our best by His grace to conform our family to His design. If we don't, we will continue to reap the rapid destruction of society that we observe every day. God's absolutes are not determined by social norms—rather, social norms should be conformed to God's absolutes. God's absolutes do not change with the passing of time. What God once thought was an abomination is still an abomination today, but sadly many Christians have given up God's absolutes in favor of the social norms that the humanists have defined.

What I mean by revival in the home is a home in which God's Word, love, and order is foundational. It is a home in which the father knows and demonstrates he is under the headship of the Lord Jesus Christ. His attitude is of a servant willing to lay down his life for those under his care. His role is shepherd, teacher, protector, and provider. The mother's role is as helper to her own husband—a homemaker, teacher, and coworker with her husband. Their mission and marriage is to raise godly children (see Mal. 2:15) who will in turn raise godly children, etc., until the Lord Jesus Christ returns. That is a deliberate vision for instilling multigenerational faithfulness. Their children are raised in the nurture and admonition of the Lord and educated according to the scriptural pattern of family-based discipleship. They are prepared for a purpose, sharpened and straightened as arrows in the hand of a mighty man (see Ps. 127:4) to be used in spiritual warfare. They are to be those who endure hardness as soldiers of the Lord Jesus Christ (see 2 Tim. 2:3), not entangling themselves with the affairs of this life such as the latest fashion, sports, or pop idol; movie or video game; or subculture slang or fad (see 2 Tim. 2:4). They have a mission to take dominion of the world for the glory of the Lord Jesus Christ, making disciples of all nations and teaching them all He has commanded (see Gen 1:28 and Matt. 28:19-20).

This may sound radical and in today's largely humanistic, feministic, materialistic, and socialist culture, it is. However, it wasn't always radical. Up until only about two-hundred years ago, this was by far the norm in Christian homes.

I'd like to briefly touch on several of these points, which are foundational if we want to see revival in the home. They are foundational because they are God's design and anything that is not God's design will ultimately fail. Make no mistake, I'm not talking about manufacturing a perfect family—that won't happen. What I am talking about is a family governed by God's design, Word, and purpose.

3.2 The Father's Role

The father is defined and patterned in Scripture as the:

3.2.1 HEAD OF THE FAMILY

But I would have you know, that the head of every man is Christ; and the head of the woman is the man; and the head of Christ is God.

(1 Cor. 11:3)

Headship does not imply tyranny. Headship rightly understood means servanthood. A husband is entrusted with loving, cherishing, and leading a daughter of the King of kings to the point of laying down his life for her just as Christ demonstrated to the church, over which He is head. This is no light matter of throwing our weight around to accomplish our selfish desires. It is critical that as husbands and fathers we remember that although we are the heads of our homes, we must rule with a servant's heart and not a dictatorial manner. King Solomon warns us, "Envy thou not the oppressor, and choose none of his ways. For the froward is abomination to the LORD: but his secret is with the righteous" (Prov. 3:31-32). Solomon continues, "He that is slow to wrath is of great understanding: but he that is hasty of spirit exalteth folly" (Prov. 14:29). He also says, "Be not hasty in thy spirit to be angry: for anger resteth in the bosom of fools" (Eccl. 7:9).

The most serious of warnings, however, is that of anger resulting in failure to obtain the very results our chastisement is supposed to achieve: "He that soweth iniquity shall reap vanity: and the rod of his anger shall fail" (Prov. 22:8). While firmness is necessary to keep the home in godly order, anger and despotic force are not God's way. The father is commanded to use the rod in the training of his children, as we shall see later, but even this is to be done in patience and love rather than anger and frustration. The apostle James tells us plainly, "For the wrath of man worketh not the righteousness of God" (James 1:20).

The words of the apostle Paul to Timothy about a servant of the Lord's character and attitude hold true as we deal with our wives and children, who may at times oppose us when we are convinced of God's will by His Word on a particular matter:

> *And the servant of the Lord must not strive; but be gentle unto all men, apt to teach, patient, In meekness instructing those that oppose themselves; if God peradventure will give them repentance to the acknowledging of the truth; And that they may recover themselves out of the snare of the devil, who are taken captive by him at his will.*
>
> *(2 Tim. 2:24-26)*

Headship does not imply inequality. Just as God the Son is not inferior to God the Father, the wife is not inferior to the husband. Yet God the Son willingly submits to God the Father just as the wife is to submit to the husband, and, the husband must submit to God. Headship simply put means that we as husbands are totally accountable to God for everything that happens in our families under our jurisdictions. God is a God of order (see 1 Cor. 14:33), and as we'll see, defying this creation order is very serious.

3.2.2 Physical and Spiritual Protector of the Family

Read Genesis 14:12-16 (Abraham rescues his nephew, Lot, who he cared for as a son); Numbers 32:6, 32:17-26 (the children of Gad and Reuben fight but leave their children and wives in the protection of fenced cities); 1 Samuel 30:5-18 (David rescues his wife, Abigail); Nehemiah 4:14 (Nehemiah tells the men to fight for their children, wives, and property); and Mark 3:27 and Luke 11:21 (describe the strong man protecting his house).

God Himself is referred to as a strong tower (see Ps. 144:2); shelter (see Ps. 61:3); a refuge (see Ps. 9:9, 14:6, 46:1); protecting wings (see Ps.

17:8, 36:7, 57:1); rock, fortress, deliverer (see Ps. 18:2); hiding place and shield (see Gen. 15:1 and Ps. 3:3, 28:7, 32:7, 91:4, 115:11, 119:114), etc.

It is important to note that women were never left without protection in the Scriptures. A woman was either in her father's house, with a brother or relative, married, or looked after by the local church (see Est. 2:7, 2 Sam. 13:20, Gen. 2:24, Gen. 38:11, Num. 30:3, 30:16, etc.). Even the Lord Jesus did not leave Mary without protection. From His very cross He committed Mary into the care of the disciple whom He loved and trusted—Mary presumably was widowed at that time (see John 19:25-27).

Protection also includes protecting against anything that might defile your family spiritually, whether it be acquaintances, predatory young men after your daughters, or Proverbs 7 women after your sons. Whether it be printed or electronic media, godless philosophies, or false doctrine. Perhaps it is the idolatry of sports, music, TV, or video games, or simply laziness. In fact, we are to do more than protect—we are to equip our families to handle such warfare. Do you know why you believe what you believe? Do your wife and children know why you believe what you believe? Can your family defend your beliefs from the Scriptures? Fathers, this is part of our job.

There is a very practical lesson we must learn from the children of Israel. When they did not evict the nations whom God told them to drive out from among them, those very people became a snare and thorn in their flesh even to this very day (see Deut. 7:16, Josh. 23:13, Judg. 2:1-3, Num. 33:55). So too, if we do not protect our families from the idolatrous and worldly influences God tells us to hate, these very things will be a vexation and thorn in our side for multiple generations. It has rightly been said that what we allow in moderation, our children allow in excess. This is why it is critical to protect our families from such influences before they take hold. Television and music are particularly insidious, as is wrong use of the Internet. What starts out as watching the nightly news and an occasional documentary soon becomes an all-night addiction, replacing family discussion, devotions, Scripture memorization, and the nurturing of relationships. It is the quality of these very relationships that keeps a family together when the devil's wiles and fiery darts seek to divide the family asunder.

3.2.3 Provider for the Family

But if any provide not for his own, and specially for those of his own house, he hath denied the faith, and is worse than an infidel.
(1 Tim. 5:8)

For even when we were with you, this we commanded you, that if any would not work, neither should he eat.
(2 Thess. 3:10)

Again, God the Father models this, as the Lord Jesus reminds us, "Be not ye therefore like unto them: for your Father knoweth what things ye have need of, before ye ask him" (Matt. 6:8). Also see Matthew 6:11 and 6:32 about providing us our daily bread; and Matthew 7:11 and James 1:17 about giving good things to our children when they ask.

3.2.4 Shepherd and Teacher of the Family

Consider Abraham's testimony, which caused the Lord to utter, "For I know him, that he will command his children and his household after him, and they shall keep the way of the LORD, to do justice and judgment; that the LORD may bring upon Abraham that which he hath spoken of him" (Gen. 18:19).

Abraham successfully passed on God's Word to Isaac, Jacob, and Joseph. This was four generations of faithfulness to God, not four generations of perfection, but four generations of faithfulness. It was Joseph's godly character that enabled him to survive mistreatment from his brothers and continuous temptation from Potiphar's wife, to endure the injustice of wrongful detention, to nourish and provide for his family who had previously despised and abused him, and thus to save the entire household of Israel. Multigenerational faithfulness

THE SUFFICIENCY OF SCRIPTURE

was very real. Consider how Joseph commanded his family to carry his bones to the Promised Land before he died in Egypt in Genesis 50:25 and how Moses remembered this and took them with him from Egypt (see Ex. 13:19). His descendents eventually buried them after Joshua's death (see Josh. 24:32), more than two-hundred years from the time of Joseph's death. Will our descendents remember what we commanded two-hundred years from now if the Lord tarries?

Another incredible story of multigenerational faithfulness is found in a seldom-taught passage in Jeremiah 35. Rechab, by no means a perfect father as none of us are or ever will be, through vision and training, raised several generations of children who kept his sayings. At the time of this writing in Jeremiah, his commandments and traditions had been kept for hundreds of years. God was so impressed with the children of Rechab that He used them as a national example. According to Jeremiah 35:18-19, his line of faithfulness still continues even to this day:

> *The word which came unto Jeremiah from the LORD in the days of Jehoiakim the son of Josiah king of Judah, saying, Go unto the house of the Rechabites, and speak unto them, and bring them into the house of the LORD, into one of the chambers, and give them wine to drink. ... And I set before the sons of the house of the Rechabites pots full of wine, and cups, and I said unto them, Drink ye wine. But they said, We will drink no wine: for Jonadab the son of Rechab our father commanded us, saying, Ye shall drink no wine, neither ye, nor your sons for ever: Neither shall ye build house, nor sow seed, nor plant vineyard, nor have any: but all your days ye shall dwell in tents; that ye may live many days in the land where ye be strangers. Thus have we obeyed the voice of Jonadab the son of Rechab our father in all that he hath charged us, to drink no wine all our days, we, our wives, our sons, nor our daughters; Nor to build houses for us to dwell in: neither have we vineyard, nor field, nor seed: But we have dwelt in tents, and have obeyed, and done according to all that Jonadab our father commanded us. ... Then came the word of the LORD unto Jeremiah, saying, Thus saith the LORD of hosts, the God of Israel; Go and tell the men of Judah and the inhabitants of Jerusalem,*

REVIVAL IN THE HOME

Will ye not receive instruction to hearken to my words? saith the LORD. The words of Jonadab the son of Rechab, that he commanded his sons not to drink wine, are performed; for unto this day they drink none, but obey their father's commandment: notwithstanding I have spoken unto you, rising early and speaking; but ye hearkened not unto me. I have sent also unto you all my servants the prophets, rising up early and sending them, saying, Return ye now every man from his evil way, and amend your doings, and go not after other gods to serve them, and ye shall dwell in the land which I have given to you and to your fathers: but ye have not inclined your ear, nor hearkened unto me. Because the sons of Jonadab the son of Rechab have performed the commandment of their father, which he commanded them; but this people hath not hearkened unto me: Therefore thus saith the LORD God of hosts, the God of Israel; Behold, I will bring upon Judah and upon all the inhabitants of Jerusalem all the evil that I have pronounced against them: because I have spoken unto them, but they have not heard; and I have called unto them, but they have not answered. And Jeremiah said unto the house of the Rechabites, Thus saith the LORD of hosts, the God of Israel; Because ye have obeyed the commandment of Jonadab your father, and kept all his precepts, and done according unto all that he hath commanded you: Therefore thus saith the LORD of hosts, the God of Israel; Jonadab the son of Rechab shall not want a man to stand before me for ever.

(Jer. 35:1-19)

Psalm 23 is the most quoted psalm, but have you ever considered it as the pattern for us fathers as shepherds of our families? Does the sheep ever ask for green pastures? Still waters? To dwell in the safety of the shepherd's house forever? No, the sheep never ask—the shepherd knows his role and does it without grudging. The good shepherd anticipates the needs of his sheep and fulfills their needs even before they have them. The shepherd is proactive, not reactive. We already saw this as the pattern of our heavenly Father in Matthew 6:8.

Man's original sin was abdication of his role to the woman. The education system has reinforced this abdication. Today, some men still believe they are the provider, others may agree that they are the protectors, and some even think that they are the head. Few, however, realize they are accountable to God for the provision, protection, and shepherding of the family. Some give lip service to this but in practice delegate almost every one of these roles to either the State or to another organization. Christian shepherding has been delegated to the Sunday school, teaching of life skills has been delegated to the state, and the provider role has been delegated in part or in whole to the wife. Even the protector role is slowly disappearing as we send women to the battlefield, forgetting that men are to give their life for women and children (see Neh. 4:14).

Here is what Isaiah said of the corruption of the roles of men, women and children: "As for my people, children are their oppressors, and women rule over them. O my people, they which lead thee cause thee to err, and destroy the way of thy paths" (Isa. 3:12).

We are also warned, "Where there is no vision, the people perish: but he that keepeth the law, happy is he" (Prov. 29:18).

Fathers, if we have no vision for our families' futures, now is the time to find that vision. There is a lot of wonderful material to help undo the programming of our humanistic education. Even if we had fathers who lacked vision or never shepherded our hearts, we can break the cycle of our fathers' sin and begin as Rechab (see Jeremiah 35) and other notable godly fathers did who started a long line of godly faithfulness through prayer, training, example, and, of course, God's wisdom and grace. We are not left alone to fend for ourselves.

How can you start this in your own home? Reformation must always begin somewhere. Start by confessing your failure to God, your wife, and your children, and then begin. One simple way is to read the Bible at meal times. Pray with your children or grandchildren. Memorize Scripture with them. Remember, you are always discipling, for good or for bad. Everything we do as fathers is watched by others. Others are discipling you too, consciously or subconsciously. We must be deliberate in our efforts to positively disciple those in our care. Even if you are a grandfather or simply have children or young men in your life, you can make a conscious effort to disciple them through your example, words, choices, attitudes, and care. This goes beyond your own biological children to all children and young men in your life. When we're tired and irritable, impatient and angry, we are still discipling and sons are watching. We do not stop discipling.

It is also worth noting that our training as fathers makes us eligible to be elders in the local church. The strains and lessons we learn as fathers in dealing with conflict, discipling, teaching, and protecting are directly applicable to an elder's role. Note that the apostle Paul made it clear that "if a man know not how to rule his own house, how shall he take care of the church of God?" (1 Tim. 3:5).

3.3 The Mother's Role

The mother is patterned in Scripture as:

3.3.1 Helpmeet to Her Own Husband

The heart of her husband doth safely trust in her, so that he shall have no need of spoil. She will do him good and not evil all the days of her life.
(Prov. 31:11-12)

Also see Genesis 2:18.

3.3.2 Home Keeper

Manager of the home under her husband's direction (see Prov. 31:13-22 and 31:27-28).

To be discreet, chaste, keepers at home, good, obedient to their own husbands, that God's Word be not blasphemed.
(Titus 2:5)

The women of my people have ye cast out from their pleasant houses; from their children have ye taken away my glory for ever.
(Micah 2:9)

THE SUFFICIENCY OF SCRIPTURE

It is interesting to note that Micah 2:9 records the casting out of women from their homes and from their children as a sign of a rebellious nation, not a progressive and enlightened one. It is also interesting that a mother's nurture of children in the home is described here as the glory of God which is taken away. Indeed a home in which God's creation order is harmoniously reflected and humbly obeyed is glorious.

Some have argued that the Proverbs 31 woman had her own independent career (Prov 31:24). While it is not wrong for a wife to contribute financially to the family economy, this verse must be taken in the context of the other principles discussed in this chapter:

- She is to be her husband's help-meet, not another man's (Gen. 2:18-24; Prov. 31:11-12, 31:28);
- She is to be the keeper of the home, implying that her primary responsibilities are in the home (Tit. 2:5; 1 Tim. 5:14; Ps. 68:12b; Prov. 7:11, 5:8, 9:14,14:1; 2 Ki. 4:8-10);
- She is to train and nurture children (Tit. 2:4-5; Sol. 8:2; Ps. 113:9; 1 Sam. 2:19; Prov. 31:13, 31:15, 31:19-22, 31:27-28, 31:1-9);
- It is her husband who has the primary task of providing financially, not her (Gen. 3:17-19; 1 Tim. 5:8; 2 Thess. 3:10-15);

This is borne out by other verses in Proverbs 31 such as verses 15, 18 and 27, which demonstrate that her business was conducted within the context of her home. Throughout the Scriptures, men are described as being in the gate and the women in the home. Even Deborah worked from her own dwelling, see Judg. 4:5.

While we obviously need women to provide services such as midwifery, we should not just blindly accept the cultural expectation that all women must seek a career outside the home and put off having children, then delegate their nurture to day-care if they do have any. Rather, we should train both our daughters and sons for their normative role, considering carefully the best way of imparting necessary skills without unnecessarily drowning them in a culture which is at war with God.

3.3.3 Instructor and Bearer/Main Nurturer of Children

He maketh the barren woman to keep house, and to be a joyful mother of children. Praise ye the LORD.

(Ps. 113:9)

Also see Solomon 8:2; Proverbs 1:8b, 4:3, 6:20b; Psalms 128:3, 131:2; Isaiah 49:15, 66:13; 1 Samuel 2:19; Proverbs 31:1; 2 Timothy 1:5; and Titus 2:4.

3.3.4 Minister of Practical Help

She stretcheth out her hand to the poor; yea, she reacheth forth her hands to the needy.

(Prov. 31:20)

See also Luke 8:1-3 (describes women providing for the Lord and His disciples), Matthew 8:14-15 (Peter's mother-in-law serving), and Acts 9:36-39 (account of Tabitha, full of good works).

This is an extremely practical role that a woman can often exercise with her children (when they are older and able) as part of the local church's role (1 Tim. 2:10). Her ability to fulfill this role has a direct bearing on her eligibility to be counted in the number of widows after the age of sixty, according to 1 Timothy 5:10.

3.3.5 Who Bears a Double Curse Today?

What was the curse given to men? "Cursed is the ground for thy sake ... In the sweat of thy face shalt thou eat bread" (Gen. 3:17-19)—providing for his family through hard work. What was the curse given to women? "In sorrow thou shalt bring forth children" (Gen. 3:16)—pain in childbirth. How many men today bear their own curse plus the women's curse? I know of none! How many women today are bearing a double curse? Too many!

THE SUFFICIENCY OF SCRIPTURE

It is not a question of whether a woman can do a job better than a man but whether God ordained her to do that job. We must not confuse the roles God has ordained for the sexes lest we blur that distinction and defy God's creation order. If men do not provide for their own, God says they are worse than an infidel (see 1 Tim. 5:8). If women are not keepers of the home, God says they blaspheme God's Word (see Titus 2:5). These are strong words—they indicate the importance God places on preserving His creation order. We must keep this distinction in mind and purposefully prepare our sons and daughters for the roles God has ordained for them rather than their stumbling into their roles when they marry, or worse still, never knowing their roles.

Mothers, like fathers, have also been educated out of their God-given roles. They have been taught that the critically important role of raising godly children is unfulfilling. They have been taught that raising virtuous and responsible sons who will be the next judges, police officers, prime ministers, scientists, doctors, builders, husbands, and fathers is worthless. They have been taught to raise daughters to seek careers rather than the most noble and God honoring role of a virtuous and content wife and mother. Mothers have been taught that they can't teach their children and that teaching must be left to "professionals." They are taught that their role as helper to their own husbands is demeaning, inferior, and somehow incomplete. This change in attitude from the joyful mothers who keep house—described in Psalms 113:9—to today's career-seeking, miserable, discontent, frustrated, and ill-prepared mothers is a direct result of the departure from the scriptural pattern for the family due to the feministic agenda.

Even older women or grandmothers should disciple young women in their lives. Remember, older women, that you are to teach younger women how to love their children and husbands (Tit. 2:5). You know from experience that this often doesn't come naturally. You, too, are discipling when you usurp your husband's authority or are irritable with your children. You are always discipling, and daughters are watching.

REVIVAL IN THE HOME

3.3.6 A Word to Single Mothers

My heart goes out to single mothers who are forced to bear the responsibility of their children alone. We live in a society where boys often do not grow up, but remain irresponsible and immature. Let's break this cycle by teaching our sons to be godly men. Single mothers, I encourage you to seek refuge and help from your churches. Older women in the church, please take care of these sisters. Men, remember single sisters in their need for home maintenance and discipling of their sons.

Although you are a single parent, you can still see revival in your home. Be encouraged by these verses:

A father of the fatherless, and a judge of the widows, is God in his holy habitation.

(Ps. 68:5)

The LORD preserveth the strangers; he relieveth the fatherless and widow: but the way of the wicked he turneth upside down.

(Ps. 146:9)

3.4 What the Bible Says About Children

In this section we will consider the devastating impact of modern anti-scriptural attitudes toward children upon the family and church. This is not the first time in history that children have been so wrongly viewed. Satan has always realized the power of training godly children on a nation and thus has tried to destroy the potential for godly seed several times throughout history (see Ex. 1:22, 2 Kings 23:10, Jer. 32:35, Matt. 2:16). Today, millions upon millions of babies are aborted or prevented from being born for many and varied excuses, and Christians are largely no different from pagans. Even if these children are allowed to be born, they are often sent to pagans for indoctrination in their humanistic education, or the state tells parents how to raise them using anti-scriptural methods. True revival can only come when we recognize

THE SUFFICIENCY OF SCRIPTURE

and reverse this terrible trend. Godly children are the hope for any local church's future, and Satan knows it.

When I got married, I said I'd never have children. I did not want to bring children into this evil world. I had no idea at all what the Bible said about children or what God thought about them. Its not that I did not want to know, I just was never taught. My wife was brought up to go to university and have a career, not to be a wife and mother. The negativity toward children was part of the baggage we had both inherited from our parents and culture.

Three years after we were married, we found out Florence was pregnant with our first son, Caleb. Then eighteen months later Gideon was born. When Micah came along, we thought he'd be the last. What a handful—three boys under three! I was ready to be sterilized and even had a doctor's referral, but by God's providence I did not make the appointment. That year, through reading and research, Florence began to see that not all Protestant parents thought like we did. This began a journey that caused me to search the Scriptures from cover to cover to see what God thought about children. It was life changing! It was also a challenge to us, my being blind and coming from a dysfunctional family, and Florence not having any relatives in Australia. Also, neither of us was particularly fond of the challenges children brought!

After giving this to the Lord, the next test of our faith came when we discovered that Florence was pregnant with twins! We surrendered our wills to God and accepted the challenge and purposed to live by faith, trusting that God would provide in our lack of ability and experience. Hannah was born naturally at home and Esther by emergency cesarean at the hospital. Florence almost died from excessive blood loss during surgery, requiring blood transfusions. The Lord, in His wisdom, chose to take Esther home when she was just two days old. Amos and Moses followed via caesareans two and three, and Noah and Abigail were both delivered naturally at home, three years apart, after three prior caesareans.

REVIVAL IN THE HOME

While this section might contain some new truths for you, I encourage you that we did not always see things as we do today and remind you of God's grace, which covers us in our journey from obscurity to understanding on all matters of life we entrust to God.

It is not easy to have a large family. My wife has had three caesareans—each time God brings us a blessing, there is much trepidation as we deal with the hospital system and all it entails, such as the rapid downward spiral of intervention, the disapproval toward large families and the constant encouragement to use birth control. Raising children is not easy, as any parent will tell you, however God has not left us alone but has provided us a lot of wisdom and guidance through precept, pattern, and principle in His infallible Word. It does, however, take diligence and grace to apply these principles in a consistent manner.

Can you guess who made the following rather strong remarks about the lack of love for children?

> *The purpose of marriage is not to have pleasure and to be idle but to procreate and bring up children, to support a household. This, of course, is a huge burden full of great cares and toils. But you have been created by God to be a husband or a wife and that you may learn to bear these troubles. Those who have no love for children are swine, stocks, and logs unworthy of being called men or women; for they despise the blessing of God, the Creator and Author of marriage.*

Those were Martin Luther's words.

While our standard is God's Word and not our fathers in the faith, it is encouraging to know that Christians' prevailing understanding for nineteen centuries was what I am about to share with you, and, that our modern attitudes are at odds with the history of God's people right from creation.

Charles D. Provan, in his helpful book, *The Bible and Birth Control*, said, "We have found not one orthodox theologian to defend birth control before the 1900s. Not one! On the other hand, we have found that many highly regarded Protestant theologians were enthusiastically opposed to it, all the way back to the very beginning of the Reformation. ... Those in favor of birth control will find no one in the orthodox Protestant camp for the first four centuries to ally themselves with."[38]

Man's opinions aside, let's see what the Bible says about children.

> *So God created man in his own image, in the image of God created he him; male and female created he them. And God blessed them, and God said unto them, be fruitful, and multiply, and replenish the earth, and subdue it: and have dominion over the fish of the sea, and over the fowl of the air, and over every living thing that moveth upon the earth.*
>
> *(Gen. 1:27-28)*

The very first commandment given to both animals and man was to multiply and replenish the earth, to take dominion of it and subdue it. For nineteen centuries of church history this was well accepted and rarely an issue. This century, with the prominence of feminism, the power of the media, and the carnality and worldliness of the church, the majority of Christians have embraced without question the ways of the surrounding culture. Even animals, who only received one command (see Gen. 1:22), still multiply in abundance. This command was repeated to Noah in Genesis 9:1 and again to Jacob in Genesis 35:11. It was never revoked.

Modern experts teach us that the world is overpopulated but this is a myth. If this were a danger, God would have told us—after all, He has revealed a lot about this time period but the overpopulation danger is not part of that revelation. His command was to be fruitful, multiply, and replenish the earth. Since we have only populated less than 1 percent of the earth's useable surface, we've got a long way to go. In countries where starvation is occurring, it is due to political corruption, mismanagement of resources, and man worshiping animals rather than having dominion over them, worshiping the created rather than the Creator (see Prov. 13:23; Genesis 1:26, 28; Romans 1:22-25). Besides, in the West we are literally dying of obesity!

REVIVAL IN THE HOME

Much food is in the tillage of the poor: but there is that is destroyed for want of judgment.

(Prov. 13:23)

3.4.1 What About Large Families Contributing to Global Warming?

From *Global Warming, Global Governance*, a film produced by Sovereignty International:

> *If you were to ask ten people on the street if mankind was causing global warming, at least eight out of ten would say yes. After all, Al Gore's Inconvenient Truth provides incontrovertible evidence that this is the case. Yet contrary to what is heard in the media, there is overwhelming evidence that the warming we are experiencing is natural, part of natural cycles caused by the sun and solar activity, with maybe a small amount contributed by man's activities and emissions of carbon dioxide. Nor is there any scientific consensus. The debate is still raging within the scientific community. Sovereignty International has put together interviews of climate scientists and biologists from numerous sources who explain, step by step, why Al Gore and the global warming alarmists are incorrect—in some cases blatantly so. It also provides evidence that the global warming agenda is being funded with tens of billions of dollars as a mechanism to create global governance with treaties and laws like the Kyoto Protocol. Hear from congressmen, experts, and even well-known news broadcasters how global governance puts global institutions, especially the United Nations, that are not accountable to the American people in control of every aspect of our economy. The US government is very close to making this a reality. Very close. Every American, every citizen of the world, needs to hear the other side of the global warming story.*[39]

In this film, proponents of global warming use two separate graphs to show how CO_2 influences global warming. The scientist explains the fallacy of this graph this way: We all die, and we all breathe oxygen, therefore breathing oxygen causes death. We all know this to be a crazy conclusion for what is actually the opposite, i.e., oxygen is necessary for life. He points out that if you superimpose the graphs on each other, CO_2 rises as temperature rises, not the other way around. CO_2 emissions, for which mankind is responsible, make up about 3 percent to 4 percent of all CO_2 emissions, which is negligible. We also know that CO_2 is good for plants and that increasing CO_2 causes plants to thrive, which in turn produces more oxygen.

So, large families, fear not—you will not be contributing to the planet's destruction.

3.4.2 The Foundation and Purpose of Marriage

And the LORD God said, It is not good that the man should be alone; I will make him an help meet for him. And out of the ground the LORD God formed every beast of the field, and every fowl of the air; and brought them unto Adam to see what he would call them: and whatsoever Adam called every living creature, that was the name thereof. And Adam gave names to all cattle, and to the fowl of the air, and to every beast of the field; but for Adam there was not found an help meet for him. And the LORD God caused a deep sleep to fall upon Adam, and he slept: and he took one of his ribs, and closed up the flesh instead thereof; And the rib, which the LORD God had taken from man, made he a woman, and brought her unto the man. And Adam said, This is now bone of my bones, and flesh of my flesh: she shall be called Woman, because she was taken out of Man. Therefore shall a man leave his father and his mother, and shall cleave unto his wife: and they shall be one flesh.

(Gen. 2:18-24)

Marriage was established and the woman created for the man as his help meet because no animal was suitable. (The saying that a dog is a man's "best friend" is humanistic and not God's design).

Note in verse 24 that the leaving of father and mother does not necessarily mean physical leaving but the leaving of one's jurisdiction to establish one's own. Abraham dwelt with Isaac and Jacob (see Heb. 11:9).

REVIVAL IN THE HOME

When parents are elderly, it is also fitting that they should live with their children in order for their children to take care of them, (see 1 Tim. 5:3-8).

Verse 24 also indicates the intimacy of the marriage covenant—since they were now one flesh, one flesh shouldn't be divided.

Malachi reinforces not only the importance and sanctity of the marriage covenant but the purpose of it: "And did not he make one? Yet had he the residue of the spirit. And wherefore one? That he might seek a godly seed. Therefore take heed to your spirit, and let none deal treacherously against the wife of his youth" (Mal. 2:15).

We will return to the purpose of raising godly seed later.

And Adam knew Eve his wife; and she conceived, and bare Cain, and said, I have gotten a man from the LORD.

(Gen. 4:1)

Eve acknowledged that her child was from God. These are not the words of a simplistic "cave woman" as some would have us believe, but the words of the most intelligent woman who ever lived. Adam and Eve had perfect knowledge of the body's biological functions but Eve still acknowledged God's provision of her son. Jacob also acknowledged that his children were gracious gifts from God (see Gen. 33:5) as did Joseph in Genesis 48:9.

Lo, children are an heritage of the LORD: and the fruit of the womb is his reward. As arrows are in the hand of a mighty man; so are children of the youth. Happy is the man that hath his quiver full of them: they shall not be ashamed, but they shall speak with the enemies in the gate.

(Ps. 127:3-5)

How many is a "quiver full"? The quiver here is a warrior's quiver and it probably held twelve to fifteen arrows. The point is not so much how many but that God is the one who fills it until He deems it full.

THE SUFFICIENCY OF SCRIPTURE

Blessed is every one that feareth the LORD; that walketh in his ways. For thou shalt eat the labour of thine hands: happy shalt thou be, and it shall be well with thee. Thy wife shall be as a fruitful vine by the sides of thine house: thy children like olive plants round about thy table. Behold, that thus shall the man be blessed that feareth the LORD.

(Ps. 128:1-4)

Children are likened to olive plants and arrows (see Ps. 127:3-5, 128:1-4). Olive plants, if not pruned and controlled, become a wild nuisance. On the other hand, small olive plants that are nurtured and trained in the way they should grow do not grow wild and have no scars from pruning since the pruning is done while they are young and tender. The later you do the training, the more scars and the less likely there will be success in directing their growth. Olive oil in the Scriptures is a symbol of the Holy Spirit. "Olive plants" nurtured by godly parents are more likely to yield Holy Spirit-filled and directed children of God as the children embrace their parents' God as their own.

Arrows in the wrong hands can cause a lot of destruction. Well-trained arrows, however, can save a nation. No arrow will change course mid-flight. I am not saying that a right environment guarantees our children's salvation. It most certainly does not. Children are born sinners (see Ps. 51:5, 58:3, and Rom. 5:12). We do, however, give them a great head start by helping them to curb passions and learn self-control and other godly character traits. They must ultimately repent and believe in the Lord Jesus Christ for personal salvation, and they will still deal with sin as we all must. We do, however, prepare the soil for receiving the seed of God's Word. Seed sowed in good soil will bear much fruit (see Mat 13:4, 13:8).

Note carefully: "Behold, that thus shall the man be blessed that feareth the LORD." Are these just the psalmist's words?

REVIVAL IN THE HOME

Take heed that ye despise not one of these little ones; for I say unto you, That in heaven their angels do always behold the face of my Father which is in heaven.
(Matt. 18:10)

And they brought young children to him, that he should touch them: and his disciples rebuked those that brought them. But when Jesus saw it, he was much displeased, and said unto them, Suffer the little children to come unto me, and forbid them not: for of such is the kingdom of God.
(Mark 10:13-14)

There are only three incidents recorded in the Gospels where the Lord Jesus was provoked to sore displeasure or anger—this incident, the incident where the people had turned the temple into a house of merchandise, and the time when the Lord Jesus healed a man with a withered hand on the Sabbath (see John 2:13-17 and Mark 3:5). I believe this says something very powerful about what God thinks of children, as does the following:

And he took a child, and set him in the midst of them: and when he had taken him in his arms, he said unto them, Whosoever shall receive one of such children in my name, receiveth me: and whosoever shall receive me, receiveth not me, but him that sent me. And whosoever shall offend one of these little ones that believe in me, it is better for him that a millstone were hanged about his neck, and he were cast into the sea.
(Mark 9:36, 37, 42)

Do we recognize children—as Jacob describes in Genesis 33:5—as gracious gifts from God? The word *receive* in Mark 9:37 is *decomai*. Strong's definition 1209 gives as some of the senses of this word which seem to fit this context, i.e. to receive into one's family; to bring up or educate; and to receive favorably, give ear to, embrace, make one's own, approve, and not to reject. This is very significant and means so much more than a mental ascent to liking children.

Read what the Lord said as the women bewailed him on the way to Golgotha. While this might have direct application to Jerusalem's destruction in 70 AD and to the Great Tribulation, it certainly reflects the sentiments of many today and indicates the rapid social decline leading up to the end.

> *But Jesus turning unto them said, Daughters of Jerusalem, weep not for me, but weep for yourselves, and for your children. For, behold, the days are coming, in the which they shall say, Blessed are the barren, and the wombs that never bare, and the paps which never gave suck.*
> (Luke 23:28-29)

Note it says "they shall say," not that God says. In 70 AD people might have thought it better not to have to bring children through such a terrible time but their motive was to save the children. These days it is often selfishness that creates that sentiment. Today, children are portrayed as a nuisance, a burden, and something that stands in the way of a career or leisure. The majority of Western society limits its number by birth control.

I know of a godly woman who was branded filthy by a church elder when he learned she was expecting her sixth child. The parents of any large family, especially a home-schooling one that perhaps also run a family business, will tell you they are extremely busy people. Marital intimacy is not at the top of the list of the ways they spend their time! I don't know how many comments I've had over the past few years implying "this is what happens when you don't have a television." I mention this to dispel that myth. Even if it were true, Hebrews 13:4 says, "Marriage is honourable in all, and the bed undefiled," and Isaiah 5:20 says, "Woe to them that call evil good and good evil." The filthiness was in that elder's mind, not in this dear sister's heart. For if believers search the Scriptures they will see God never calls children a nuisance or something to be avoided or limited. God never called a woman filthy for having a lot of children. Rebekah's family sent her off with the following blessing, written for our learning, "And they blessed Rebekah, and said unto her, Thou art our sister, be thou the mother of thousands of millions, and let thy seed possess the gate of those which hate them" (Gen. 24:60). On the contrary, children are a blessing, and those who had none were the cursed ones in Scripture, not those who had children. Besides, God commanded us to be fruitful, and throughout the Scriptures it is assumed that marriage would result in children (except where the woman was barren). Even in barrenness there are examples of where prayer turned this barrenness into fruitfulness (see Gen. 25:21 and 1 Sam. 1:11-17).

Certainly no offense is intended to those sisters in the Lord who through no fault of their own remain childless even after prayer. For the unmarried, the childless, or elderly, the encouragement is to love what God loves and hate what God hates and to recognize that the modern attitudes toward children are anti-scriptural. Even if you are without children, knowing what the Scriptures teach should dictate your attitude toward children or young families around you. Give practical help to meet the needs of a growing young family, a pregnant mother, or a mother with a newborn, or help care for children whose parents are ill. At the very least you can show encouragement rather than disdain for what God loves.

Genesis 38:8-10 offers the only case of the use of birth control, when Onan spills his seed on the ground. God showed His displeasure at Onan's selfish attitude about raising up seed to his dead brother by destroying Onan. His motive was selfishness, not just that he didn't want to raise up seed. This had a punishment far less severe, which amounted to humiliation (see Deut. 25:7-9) where the wife was to take off his shoe and spit in his face.

THE SUFFICIENCY OF SCRIPTURE

Some may disagree with this interpretation of Onan's account and yet the absolute majority of commentators agree with this interpretation, which I believe is borne out by other Scriptures. In 1 Corinthians 12:23, God bestows honor on the members of our body whom we think are less honorable. This is, of course, analogous to our physical bodies, where God bestows very high honor to the man's procreative member—this is clear from Deuteronomy 25:11-12, where a woman's hand was to be cut off if she damaged a man's secret part while rescuing her husband from a fight. Just as life is in the blood and God tells us to respect blood (see Lev. 17:14), He also makes it clear that we are to respect the procreative seed. It is God who has the prerogative to open or close the womb in Scripture, not man's will (see Gen. 4:25, 20:18, 29:31, 30:22; Ex. 23:26; Deut. 7:14; Ps. 113:9; John 1:13).

The question could be asked: What about finances? Isn't it bad stewardship not to use birth control? But if God gives the increase (which He does) and no child is an accident but a gift from God, won't He supply for the need provided we are obedient?

> *Neither did we eat any man's bread for nought; but wrought with labour and travail night and day, that we might not be chargeable to any of you: Not because we have not power, but to make ourselves an ensample unto you to follow us. For even when we were with you, this we commanded you, that if any would not work, neither should he eat. For we hear that there are some which walk among you disorderly, working not at all, but are busybodies. Now them that are such we command and exhort by our Lord Jesus Christ, that with quietness they work, and eat their own bread.*
>
> *(2 Thess. 3:8-12)*

Also see Proverbs 6:6-8, 13:4, 10:4, 12:24, 12:27, 20:4, 22:29, and 27:23.

David said, "I have been young, and now am old; yet have I not seen the righteous forsaken, nor his seed begging bread" (Ps. 37:25). The apostle

Paul said, "But my God shall supply all your need according to his riches in glory by Christ Jesus" (Phil. 4:19). The Lord Himself said, "Therefore take no thought, saying, What shall we eat? or, What shall we drink? or, Wherewithal shall we be clothed? (For after all these things do the Gentiles seek): for your heavenly Father knoweth that ye have need of all these things. But seek ye first the kingdom of God, and his righteousness; and all these things shall be added unto you" (Matt. 6:31-33).

It has been said, if the Lord is not Lord *of* all, He is not Lord *at* all. If children are a gift from the Lord, which the Scriptures say they are, then He will provide for His gifts provided we as fathers are willing to work, and that as parents we are obedient and choose wisely when it comes to how we use our time, money, and other resources.

In considering what God thinks of children, let's return to the primary reason why God loves children and commanded us to be fruitful and multiply. The key to the entire subject of why children are a blessing and why as parents we are to treat our task of training, protecting, and eventually releasing these precious gifts with the utmost diligence was described by the prophet Malachi, who wrote, "And did not he make one? Yet had he the residue of the spirit. And wherefore one? That he might seek a godly seed. Therefore take heed to your spirit, and let none deal treacherously against the wife of his youth" (Mal. 2:15). The purpose of marriage has always been to raise godly children.

3.4.3 CHILDREN (POEM)

Here is a poem I wrote a few years ago as I pondered this whole subject:

(From *More than Meets the Eye*, Copyright ©2009, Joseph Stephen)

> Children are blessings from the Lord
> According to His holy Word.
> As arrows in the warrior's hands
> Sharpened by training in God's commands.[40]

THE SUFFICIENCY OF SCRIPTURE

Just as they sacrificed their sons of old,
Career and lifestyle are the gods of gold.[41]
Abortion and the use of birth control,
Are the modern fires that take their toll.

If we love God our hearts should grieve.
We should love what He loves, if we believe.
God loves children, He hath said,[42]
Yet even Christians want dogs instead.

Some may ask who will provide?
Faith and wisdom will decide.
One who works, who chooses well,
To them the floodgates are opened wide.[43]

Take note of the psalms
As David said,
"The righteous not forsaken,
Nor his seed begging bread."[44]

Today it seems the tables are turned:
The barren are blessed and the fruitful are scorned;[45]
But whatever our worldview, God's Word hasn't changed.
Humanism and feminism are now what is learned.

How far we've strayed from God's holy plan
And forgotten the first task given to man.[46]
Did you know, overpopulation is just a lie,[47]
Our selfish lifestyles to justify.

If we would raise up godly seed,
And train up warriors who can lead,
Revival would spread across the land,
The difference made would be profound.

Even Muslims know this rule[48]
Yet Christians have learned from the wrong school.
It's time to stop believing the lie
And be fruitful and multiply.

3.5 The Biblical Pattern for the Education and Training of Our Children

We know, at least in theory, that we are to train up our children in the nurture and admonition of the Lord, but have you ever considered what this actually means? The Bible has a lot to say about child training and education, and I can't hope to cover everything in this short section. I would like to outline the biblical pattern and precepts for training and educating our children.

I need not elaborate on what happens when the biblical methods of child training and education are abandoned. What many don't realize, however, is just how bad things really are. It is no exaggeration to say that the moral decline due to abandoning God's methods for this important task has reached a slope that is almost straight downward.

What I submit to you is that biblical training and discipline goes far beyond giving your child academic know-how and punishment when disobedient. Biblical training has the future in mind—not just the grown child, but the grown child's grandchildren. Training and discipline is far more than surviving today's tantrums and hoping to keep your child off the streets and out of bad company tomorrow. I hope after reading this that you'll go away with a multigenerational vision for passing on biblical conviction and context to your children so they know where

THE SUFFICIENCY OF SCRIPTURE

they fit in God's providence and in shaping history as your progeny. After all, revival could take several generations.

By the way, who was the most influential home-educated person in history? You'll find out at the end of this chapter.

Due to our own baggage, we have a concept of education that has no doubt been formed by the modern school or university system. This system is based largely on humanistic rather than biblical philosophies, a system that in many points is vastly opposed to scriptural patterns and precepts, a system that separates faith from facts. Let's strip away the baggage of our own education and look solely at what God's Holy Word says about this most important subject. Indeed, Romans 12:2 clearly says that if we want to know God's perfect will, we must renew our minds, as we already discussed.

We can easily examine our own mindsets to see the humanistic influence of our own education by considering the following statements. Which of the following cause us to wow with admiration?

Carnal	Spiritual
I have a Ph.D. in rocket science.	Enoch "had this testimony, that he pleased God." (Heb. 11:5)
I am a CEO of a multinational conglomerate.	"I have found David the son of Jesse, a man after mine own heart, which shall fulfil all my will." (Acts 13:22)
I have a Bible college degree.	"When I call to remembrance the unfeigned faith that is in thee." (2 Tim. 1:5) "And that from a child thou hast known the holy Scriptures." (2 Tim. 3:15)

Carnal	Spiritual
My daughter is a successful business woman.	"She openeth her mouth with wisdom; and in her tongue is the law of kindness. She looketh well to the ways of her household, and eateth not the bread of idleness. Her children arise up, and call her blessed; her husband also, and he praiseth her. Many daughters have done virtuously, but thou excellest them all." (Prov. 31:26-29) "Well reported of for good works; if she have brought up children, if she have lodged strangers, if she have washed the saints' feet, if she have relieved the afflicted, if she have diligently followed every good work" (1 Tim. 5:10). "Sober, to love their husbands, to love their children, to be discreet, chaste, keepers at home, good, obedient to their own husbands." (Titus 2:4-5)

I am not saying that studying rocket science is wrong, but our emphasis on education without regard to the fulfillment of God's purposes, God's distinct roles for men and women, or godly character, is wrong. Daniel and Joseph are just two examples—both wise and skilful in all they did, yet it was their fear of God and good character that highlighted their skills and abilities, not their skills on their own. We must be careful that what we are remembered for is godliness and not the name we have made for ourselves, as was the case at the Tower of Babel (see Gen. 11:4).

3.5.1 What Is Education?

R. J. Rushdoony wrote, "The dictionary definition of education describes it as 'the impartation or acquisition of knowledge, skill, or discipline of character.' The function of education is thus to school persons in the ultimate values of a culture. This is inescapably a religious task. Education has always been a religious function of society and closely linked to its religion. When a state takes over the responsibilities for education from the church or from Christian parents, the state has not thereby disowned all religions but simply disestablished Christianity in favour of its own statist religion, usually a form of humanism. To see education as an expression of religion is not an approach limited to orthodox Christians. Liberals, anthropologists, and statist educators have so viewed it."[49]

John Dewey, humanist and co-author and signer of *Humanist Manifesto 1*, is considered by many to be the father of "modern" education. His goals for public education were no secret to those in his circle, although most students today are oblivious to this agenda. Two of his main goals were to remove the God of the Bible from education and to make a society of servants to the Socialist State. He said, "There is no God, and there is no soul. Hence, there are no needs for the props of traditional religion. With dogma and creed excluded then immutable truth is also dead and buried. There is no room for fixed, natural law or permanent moral absolutes."[50]

In a public address to educators in 1899, he also said (emphasis mine), "You can't make Socialists out of individualists—*children who know how to think for themselves spoil the harmony of the collective society* which is coming, where everyone is interdependent."

Jean-Jacques Rousseau, another very influential voice in modern education theory who abandoned his own children, had a similar philosophy. He said, "Submit yourself to the State, and my philosophy will liberate you from submission to intermediate authorities like the Church and the family."

Charles F. Potter and John J. Dunphy were two other prominent secular humanists who unashamedly revealed the agenda of the modern education system. Potter wrote, "Education is thus a most powerful ally of humanism, and every American public school is a school of humanism. What can a theistic Sunday school's meeting for an hour once a week and teaching only a fraction of the children do to stem the tide of the five-day program of humanistic teaching?" ("Humanism: A New Religion," 1930)

Dunphy said, "The battle for humankind's future must be waged and won in the public school classroom by teachers who correctly perceive their role as the proselytizers of a new faith: A religion of humanity—utilizing a classroom instead of a pulpit to carry humanist values into wherever they teach. The classroom must and will become an arena of conflict between the old and the new—the rotting corpse of Christianity, together with its adjacent evils and misery, and the new faith of humanism." ("The Humanist (1983").

The Christian apologist Henry Van Til describes culture as "religion externalized."[51] Education's function, then, is to teach the ultimate values of externalized religion. Our culture of promiscuity, sports idols, peer acceptance, fantasy, and rebellion reflects our society's religion and education's priorities.

The great reformer Martin Luther wrote, "I am much afraid that schools will prove to be great gates of hell, unless they diligently labour in explaining the Holy Scriptures, engraving them in the hearts of youth. I advise no one to place his child where the Scriptures do not reign paramount. Every institution in which men are not increasingly occupied with God's Word must become corrupt."

THE SUFFICIENCY OF SCRIPTURE

3.5.2 THE REWRITING OF HISTORY

History is His story.

R.J. Rushdoony later wrote, "But, some might object, can we not agree that Columbus 'discovered' America in 1492? As a matter of fact, we must dissent with the whole interpretation of that event. For us as Christians the facts are very different. Humanistic historians give us an economic motive, but Columbus had a very different goal. ... The Gospel had to be carried to the far corners of the earth. He also believed that some 'lost' tribes of Jews might dwell in the unknown lands, and he therefore took along an interpreter of Hebrew on his first voyage. A Christian motive was present in virtually all the explorers. ... The near coincidence of exploration and the Reformation is not an accident: both have a common theological source."[52]

Humanists have rewritten history to remove God. They will not tell you that the first message Samuel Morse transmitted was, "What hath God wrought!" Many of the greatest scientists of all time unequivocally attributed their discoveries to the God of the Bible. Indeed, the Bible gave them the very motivation, foundation, and framework in which to inquire. We will briefly look at just four to demonstrate how many educators, both Christian and humanist, suppress the truth. While the theology of some of these scientists may at times be questionable, nevertheless, they demonstrated a fear and awe of God, and recognition of His Word as the all-important foundation to their work.

Johannes Kepler (1571-1630), a German Lutheran, developed three famous laws of planetary motion after many years of arduous experimentation and observation in which he compared facts with theory.

Kepler did not hide the motivations for his work under a bushel. He understood his discoveries and writings as hymns to his Creator and Redeemer, and he often punctuated his writings with prayers and psalms of praise to God, as illustrated in *The Harmonice Mundi* ("The Harmonies of the World"), published in 1619.[53]

REVIVAL IN THE HOME

Kepler wrote:

Accordingly let this do for our envoi concerning the work of God the Creator. It now remains that at last, with my eyes and hands removed from the tablet of demonstrations and lifted up towards the heavens, I should pray, devout and supplicating, to the Father of lights: O Thou who dost by the light of nature promote in us the desire for the light of grace, that by its means. Thou mayest transport us into the light of glory, I give thanks to Thee, O Lord Creator, who hast delighted me with Thy makings and in the works of my profession, having employed as much power of mind as Thou didst give to me; to the men who are going to read those demonstrations I have made manifest the glory of Thy works, as much of its infinity as the narrows of my intellect could apprehend. Great is our Lord and great His virtue and of His wisdom there is no number praise Him, ye heavens, praise Him, ye sun, moon, and planets. Use every sense for perceiving, every tongue for declaring your Creator. Praise him, ye celestial harmonies, praise Him, ye judges of the harmonies uncovered ... and thou my soul, praise the Lord thy Creator, as long as I shall be: for out of Him and through Him and in Him are all things.[54]

Galileo Galilei (1564-1642) was responsible for discovering the laws of falling bodies and of the parabolic path of projectiles. He studied the motions of pendulums, and he investigated mechanics and the strength of materials.

In a letter to a friend on January 30, 1610, Galileo wrote, "I give thanks to God, who has been pleased to make me the first observer of marvelous things unrevealed to bygone ages."[55] In another letter in 1615, he wrote, "God is known ... by nature in His works, and by doctrine in His revealed word."[56]

He understood "the phenomena of nature ... as the observant executrix of God's commands."[57] Continuing his letter, he wrote, "To prohibit the whole science would be but to censure a hundred passages of holy Scripture which teach us that the glory and greatness of almighty God are marvelously discerned in all His works and divinely read in the open book of heaven. For let no one believe that reading the lofty concepts written in that book leads to nothing further than the mere seeing of the splendor of the sun and the stars and their rising and setting, which is as far as the eyes of brutes and of the vulgar can penetrate. Within its pages are couched mysteries so profound and concepts so sublime that the vigils, labors, and studies of hundreds upon hundreds of the most acute minds have still not pierced them, even after continual investigations for thousands of years."[58]

Galileo's creative science was anchored in his belief in the full rationality of the universe as the product of a fully rational Creator, whose finest product was the human mind, which shared in the rationality of its Creator.[59]

Sir Isaac Newton (1642-1727) was born in the year Galileo died. Newton was going to be a farmer but became the greatest mathematician of all time. He not only did work in mathematics and science, he also wrote volumes of material expositing Scripture passages that cost him a comparable effort as *The Principia*. To Newton, the Scriptures provided the basic foundation and motivation for all his scientific works.

In the third edition of *The Principia*, Newton wrote, "The most beautiful system of sun, planets, and comets could only proceed from the counsel and dominion of an intelligent and powerful Being. And if the fixed stars are the centers of other like systems, these, being formed by the like wise counsel, must be all subject to the dominion of One; ... This Being governs all things, not as the Soul of the world, but as Lord over all; and on account of his dominion He is wont to be called Lord God."[60] He continues, "The Supreme God is a Being eternal, infinite, absolutely perfect; but a being, however perfect, without dominion, cannot be said to be Lord God. ... And from His true dominion it follows that the true God is a living, intelligent, and powerful Being: and, from His other perfections, that He is supreme, or most perfect. He is eternal and infinite, omnipotent and omniscient; that is, His duration reaches from eternity to eternity; His presence from infinity to infinity; He governs all things, and knows all things that are or can be done. ... We know Him only by His most wise and excellent contrivances of things, and final causes; we admire Him for his perfections; but we reverence and adore Him on account of His dominion: for we adore Him as his servants; and a God without dominion, providence, and final causes, is nothing else but Fate and Nature."[61]

Blaise Pascal (1623-1662) was another great scientist and mathematician. He wrote of the heart of man's emptiness without God. He said, "What else does this craving, and this helplessness, proclaim but that there was once in man a true happiness, of which all that now remains is the empty print and trace? This he tries in vain to fill with everything around him, seeking in things that are not there the help he cannot find in those that are, though none can help, since this infinite abyss can be filled only with an infinite and immutable object; in other words by God Himself."[62]

From the above quotes, it is obvious that many of the greatest scientists who ever lived did not separate secular and sacred, as we are told science and faith must be today. Science indeed does not and cannot make sense without the foundation of the God of absolutes. Science, like the rest of education, is built on faith assumptions, whether those faith assumptions are Christian, humanist, or something else. History without God is similarly absurd, as God gives history meaning and relevance.

3.5.3 True Discipleship

If all we had was the Bible, we would find a pattern of education very different from what we see in the modern world. The pattern for our children's education has always been (that is, up until the past few hundred years) discipleship from their own parents, not the church or the State. Even the Lord Jesus demonstrated this principle of discipleship by calling twelve men and living with them for three years, teaching and showing by example the way He wanted them to live. He never started a seminary or school. He didn't live separately and just meet up with them to teach them. He walked with them and talked with them throughout the day, every day, for the duration of His ministry. He even went as far as calling them little children (see John 13:33, 21:5). He gave them a vision that carried them forward even after His ascension. He gave them more than facts—He gave them context in which to interpret those facts, conviction, and purpose!

Consider the very example revealed to us in the Father/Son relationship within the Godhead: "Then answered Jesus and said unto them, Verily, verily, I say unto you, The Son can do nothing of himself, but what he seeth the Father do: for what things soever he doeth, these also doeth the Son likewise. For the Father loveth the Son, and sheweth him all things that himself doeth: and he will shew him greater works than these, that ye may marvel" (John 5:19-20).

The apostle Paul also understood the father's important educational role, as opposed to just an instructor, as he said in 1 Corinthians 4:15-16, "For though ye have ten thousand instructors in Christ, yet have ye not many fathers: for in Christ Jesus I have begotten you through the Gospel. Wherefore I beseech you, be ye followers of me."

Consider also these beautiful words the apostle Paul said of Timothy, "But ye know the proof of him, that, as a son with the father, he hath served with me in the Gospel" (Phil. 2:22).

Fathers, do we have a desire for and vision of our sons serving alongside us in the gospel or in whatever work in which we are skilled?

The job of the discipler is to prepare his disciple to be like his master. That pattern of discipleship was not new to the New Testament. The very writing of the Old Testament was a demonstration of discipleship in action as father passed God's Word to son, generation after generation (see Ex. 13:14, Ps. 44:1, Deut. 6:20, Prov. 1:8, 4:1, 13:1, 15:5, 23:26). The commandment was formally decreed in Deuteronomy 6 and repeated in Psalm 78.

What about the Christian school? If indeed a school teaches all subjects from a distinctly Christian worldview, it still misses the point that in Scripture it is the parents who are given the task of training their children (see Prov. 1:8, 4:1, 13:1, 15:5, 23:26; Song 8:2; Eph. 6:4). In truth, however, most Christian schools still teach their curricula from a humanistic standpoint. They teach Math, English, History, and then the Holy Bible. You can't just add a smattering of verses to a humanistic view of the world. In fact, Christian schools in South Australia are not even allowed to teach that the biblical account of creation is literal truth.[63] Biblical education starts with the Holy Bible as the indisputable foundation and builds math, language, history, etc., on it. Faith is not separate to reason but built on reason, either God's reason or man's reason.

Most modern schools also segregate pupils by age according to the fraudulent humanistic philosophy Ernst Haeckel invented and G. Stanley Hall made popular, which claims that each stage of a child's development mirrors a stage of evolution (ontogeny recapitulates phylogeny) and thus mixing the different age groups is detrimental. In Scripture, children were not age segregated or separated from their parents during times of public teaching, worship, or meeting (see Deut. 29:10-12, 31:12; Josh. 8:35; 2 Chron. 20:13; Ezra 10:1; Neh. 8:1-3; Matt. 14:21, 15:38).

There are two recorded cases of peer grouping that come to mind from Scripture: The first ended in the death of forty-two young people who banded together to mock Elisha (see 2 Kings 2:23-24), and the second, Solomon's son Reheboam listened to his peers rather than his elders' wisdom and lost the kingdom (see 1 Kings 12:6-16). Both incidents reinforce God's wisdom revealed through Solomon, who said, "He that walketh with wise men shall be wise: but a companion of fools shall be destroyed" (Prov. 13:20).

Does this mean that parents can never delegate the teaching of certain subjects to others or even to a Christian school? Not at all. The problem comes when we presume it is someone else's responsibility to educate our children and delegate all teaching to others, without serious consideration of what is being taught through textbooks, teachers' personal examples, and peers. We must also remember that schools tend to be egalitarian in their objectives, educating children to satisfy a centralised bureaucratic notion of a common curriculum, not to fulfil their unique role and function in God's eternal purpose. If we do delegate to a Christian school, we must also be certain of the level to which Biblical authority is upheld by the school in practice. As school principals and teachers change, so may the doctrines being taught. Ultimately, as parents, we own the responsibility and are accountable for the consequences. Therefore we should be cautious when delegating.

3.5.4 THE FOUNDATION OF BIBLICAL EDUCATION

Let's consider the biblical model of Hebrew discipleship formally commanded in Deuteronomy 6 and demonstrated throughout Scripture, including by the Lord Jesus Christ Himself:

Hear, O Israel: The LORD our God is one LORD: And thou shalt love the LORD thy God with all thine heart, and with all thy soul, and with all thy might. And these words, which I command thee this day, shall be in thine heart: And thou shalt teach them diligently unto thy children, and shalt talk of them when thou sittest in thine house, and when thou walkest by the way, and when thou liest down, and when thou risest up. And thou shalt bind them for a sign upon thine hand, and they shall be as frontlets between thine eyes. And thou shalt write them upon the posts of thy house, and on thy gates.

(Deut. 6:4-9)

1. First, we as parents must worship the one true God and love Him with all our hearts, all our souls, and all our might. Without the deepest love for God all we will communicate through our teaching are rules and facts. Both loving God and understanding God's love for us in all His commandments is vitally important.

2. As parents, we must diligently seek to hide His Word in our own hearts. Hiding God's Word in our hearts has a most important purpose, that we might not sin against God (see Ps. 119:11).

REVIVAL IN THE HOME

You say, "I thought you were going to talk about training our children." I am, but the truth is, the best teaching is caught and not taught—if we love God it will be infectious! If we have hidden His word in our own hearts, it can't help but come out. You can't give what you don't have. The Lord Jesus said, "A good man out of the good treasure of his heart bringeth forth that which is good; and an evil man out of the evil treasure of his heart bringeth forth that which is evil: for of the abundance of the heart his mouth speaketh" (Luke 6:45).

We can't fill our hearts with sci-fi or who knows what and then expect to exude God's Word. The Personal Revival chapter will equip us well in this area. Let's take our example from Ezra, to prepare, seek, do and teach, "For Ezra had prepared his heart to seek the law of the LORD, and to do it, and to teach in Israel statutes and judgments" (Ezra 7:10).

3. We must diligently train our children in God's whole counsel throughout the day through the living of life, teaching them all the practicality of God's Word: from language (to read and study God's law) to history (His Story, the dealings of God with man since the beginning) to science (God's unchanging principles on which the universe was founded) to math (to understand the chronological events that unfolded in the Scriptures and the practical application men of God used to build, trade, etc.) to cleanliness and food preparation to business skills to common law and the respecting of authority and jurisdictional power (i.e., laws governing human relationships) to any other skill necessary to take dominion of the earth (see Gen. 1:28 and Matt. 28:18-20)—all in the framework and from the foundation of God's complete and infallible Word. Yes, God's law is far more than the Ten Commandments. God's Word contains principles and patterns as well as commandments for dealing with every aspect of life including mathematics, language, science, law, politics, finance, geography, history, music, homemaking, nutrition, etc.

The quality and quantity of time spent training is clear from Deuteronomy 6:7: "And thou shalt teach them diligently unto thy children, and shalt talk of them when thou sittest in thine house, and when thou walkest by the way, and when thou liest down, and when thou risest up." In short, all day every day, not just from nine to three.

4. Fill their environment with the knowledge of God (on the doorposts, gates, etc.) that they might remember God's providences, set their hope in Him, remember His works, and not be like their fathers, a stiff-necked and rebellious generation (see Ps. 78:7-8). In short, this is a walking, talking, spending time, living education to prepare our children for life.

God gave the responsibility and privilege of training, education, and discipline of children to their parents, particularly fathers. The goal of this training and education was not to raise brilliant but morally destitute citizens. The goal was first to train the character, which would then create the right foundation for developing life skills in anything necessary for doing God's work and will, whether that is studying science built on His laws or raising a godly family. It was also to ensure that God's glorious Word, work, and providential intervention in history was faithfully communicated from one generation to the next.

Today we are told that education must be left to the experts, that we are all born basically good (without a sin nature), that physical discipline psychologically damages our children, that parents are incapable of raising their children without the state's intervention, that boys and girls are a product of environment rather than different by design, that children need the socialization of peers, and that our parenting really has no impact on the way children turn out anyway. God's Word, however, teaches the opposite to all of these things. God commands and empowers parents to raise and educate their children for life and gives us the assurance of success.

Be not deceived; God is not mocked: for whatsoever a man soweth, that shall he also reap.

(Gal. 6:7)

REVIVAL IN THE HOME

Train up a child in the way he should go: and when he is old, he will not depart from it.

(Prov. 22:6)

The rationale for family-based discipleship is multigenerational faithfulness to God. We must learn the lessons of history lest we repeat the mistakes of the past. As soon as the Jews stopped teaching their children, they fell into moral and spiritual decline. Take careful note of the reason the children of Israel in Joshua's day went astray after the elders' death:

> *And Israel served the LORD all the days of Joshua, and all the days of the elders that overlived Joshua, and which had known all the works of the LORD, that he had done for Israel.*
>
> *(Joshua 24:31)*

> *And Joshua the son of Nun, the servant of the LORD, died, being an hundred and ten years old. ... And also all that generation were gathered unto their fathers: and there arose another generation after them, which knew not the LORD, nor yet the works which he had done for Israel.*
>
> *(Judg. 2:8, 10)*

Why? It was because fathers forsook their duty and did not pass on God's providences and praises to the next generation. Oh, yes, the next generation enjoyed the fruits of the prior generation's labors, but they did not embrace their values or their God. It is no different today. This generation enjoys the prosperity and freedoms secured by prior God-fearing generations, but has largely abandoned the prior generation's values. God will not tolerate this for much longer and is already beginning to pour out judgment on this generation, just as He did on the children of Israel.

This lack of biblical home discipleship education is one of the greatest contributors to why even the most fundamental of Bible-believing churches today has trouble keeping young people from apostasy. When

THE SUFFICIENCY OF SCRIPTURE

we allow the Philistines to educate our children or their peers to dictate wisdom, we are almost guaranteed to fail, no matter how godly the parents and biblical the church.

Let's turn our attention to the New Testament:

Children, obey your parents in the Lord: for this is right. Honor thy father and mother; which is the first commandment with promise; That it may be well with thee, and thou mayest live long on the earth. And, ye fathers, provoke not your children to wrath: but bring them up in the nurture and admonition of the Lord.

(Eph. 6:1-4)

Let us consider the meaning of this word nurture which is translated from the greek word Paideia:

Strong's Definition 3809 παιδεια Paideia:
1. The whole training and education of children (which relates to the cultivation of mind and morals, and employs for this purpose now commands and admonitions, now reproof and punishment). It also includes the training and care of the body.
2. Whatever in adults also cultivates the soul, esp. by correcting mistakes and curbing passions.
2a. Instruction that aims at increasing virtue.
2b. Chastisement, chastening (of the evils with which God visits men for their amendment).

The word *nurture* is very rich in meaning. Readers of that time readily understood it to mean the all-encompassing "whole" aspect of training and education, of mind and morals, to fully equip the child for life. In 2 Timothy 3:16-17, the same word is used: "All Scripture is given by inspiration of God, and is profitable for doctrine, for reproof, for correction, for instruction (paidea) in righteousness: That the man of God may be perfect, thoroughly furnished unto all good works." In other words, the Word of God is sufficient to fully equip and mature the man of God for any and every work that God may call him to. In the same way, as fathers, we are to fully train, equip and mature our children for life.

The problem today is we separate spiritual training from academic training, and while some may concede that parents are responsible for their children's spiritual learning, most still think it is the school that is responsible for the rest. But in the Bible there is actually no distinction at all between spiritual and academic instruction. It is the humanists who have dishonestly convinced many that one can teach mathematics, science, language, and history without God. But in truth, none of these make any sense without the God who created the laws on which all disciplines rest. As we have seen from Rushdoony and Van Til, education is inescapably religious and thus never neutral.

There is also a very overbalanced emphasis given to the acquisition of knowledge without character. In fact, this is the hallmark of the "modern education system," Christian or humanistic. This is hugely detrimental, and we know from Scripture that a man is brutish who acquires knowledge without wisdom. Read the confession of Agur the son of Jakeh, "Surely I am more brutish than any man, and have not the understanding of a man. I neither learned wisdom, nor have the knowledge of the holy" (Prov. 30:2-3). Jeremiah observed, "Every man is brutish in his knowledge: every founder is confounded by the graven image: for his molten image is falsehood, and there is no breath in them" (Jer. 10:14).

Every man of God chosen for the Lord's service first had to learn the character qualities necessary for the job and be proven in them. The earthly knowledge necessary for doing the job, while important, was secondary to character training and was learned as character was being molded. It was also critical that the knowledge was acquired in God's framework as Creator, as Agur reminds us: "Who hath ascended up into heaven, or descended? who hath gathered the wind in his fists? who hath bound the waters in a garment? who hath established all the ends of the earth? what is his name, and what is his son's name, if thou canst tell? Every word of God is pure: he is a shield unto them that put their trust in him. Add thou not unto his words, lest he reprove thee, and thou be found a liar" (Prov. 30:4-6). In 2 Timothy 3:7 people are described as "Ever learning, and never able to come to the knowledge of the truth." This so aptly describes the world's education system!

We also see a tragedy even in our home-schooling circles as the homemakers of one generation do not realize their own daughters will not have the same vision they did. In the words of my wife who was brought up a feminist before God's providence enabled her to discover His will for her, "We cannot expect our daughters to love being homemakers if we start them on a path that teaches them their entire self-worth is attained by a piece of paper. We cannot send our daughters out to work and then expect them to dutifully come home and love being a keeper at home." Unless we train them from the start that their fulfillment and self-worth are based solely on God's Word and pattern for them, they will only see and experience contradiction. We need to have a vision for our daughters if we want them to carry on the godly legacy of the faithful, capable, happy homemaker.

As a father, I say this also applies to sons. If all they are taught is that the highest paying job is the goal they should be attaining, or that ministry or some profession is always more important than raising a godly family, the Christian legacy we have begun will last but one generation. We must be so careful as parents to ensure that the worldview we present to our children is consistent with our own convictions and that we don't allow a subconscious overemphasis on the worth of a man-made qualification, which has no value in the courts of heaven.

If you already home-educate your children, it is vitally important to realize the scriptural foundation for doing it. Many get caught up in the curriculum, social activities, academia, and other reasons people decide to home-educate, but we must realize that home education is the pattern laid down in Scripture and its purpose is multigenerational faithfulness to God. As home educators we must return to the foundation lest we lose the multigenerational vision and just bring the humanistic school system into our homes.

3.5.5 Teach Your Children the Sufficiency of Scripture

Teaching the sufficiency of Scripture must begin as soon as our children can understand language. We often immunize our children against the Word of God by raising them on a diet of cartoons and perversions of biblical history presented as fables. They become so accustomed to such presentations that they find it a chore to sit through a simple Bible reading, let alone an in-depth exegetical sermon. A simple test is to sit your children down and watch their reaction as you read them the Scriptures. Do they become bored easily or do they listen with interest? As adults who ourselves were raised on Hollywood, we think it almost cruel to simply read our children the Scriptures, and yet for thousands of years, this is all they got taught, as fathers passed to their children the Word of God by mouth through family-based discipleship. Even with food, the diet we raise our children with will inevitably impact their taste, they will either enjoy junk food or relish fresh fruit and vegetables. It is all in the standard that we as parents set in our homes. The more we pander to the lust of the eyes, the more "eye candy" we need in order to hold our attention. King Solomon reminds us of the futility and vanity of trying to satisfy our senses when he says, "… the eye is not satisfied with seeing, nor the ear filled with hearing." (Eccl 1:8). We need more action, more special effects, more entertainment, more jokes, more, more, more of everything but the truth itself. This simply breeds lust, greed, and a desire for instant gratification. It ultimately leads to dissatisfaction with what God says as the most important thing in all of life, His very Word. If a picture paints a thousand words, and the picture distorts, detracts from, or otherwise adds to or takes away from God's Word, this is a most grievous sin (Prov 30:5-6, Rev 22:18-19). I discuss the dangers of children's books and media presentations in my book, *If a Picture Paints a Thousand Words*. Following is a short extract from this book on the purpose of reading:

THE SUFFICIENCY OF SCRIPTURE

"The purpose of reading is to equip the reader to fear God and keep His commandments. That is, to draw his attention back to his awe inspiring and worship desiring Creator. It is to cause him to be silent before the true God whose character and works should fill every sense given him by God, to bring him into the place of total and utter dependence upon and submission to Him. Reading should not be time filler, entertainment, lust gratification or a stumbling block to idolatry. Knowledge for knowledge's sake puffeth up (1 Cor. 8:1), yet knowledge mixed with wisdom is a gem worthy of our diligent and deliberate desire and search (2 Chron. 1:10-12; Prov. 1:7, 2:6, 2:10, 8:12, 9:10, 24:13-14; Eccles. 2:26, 7:12; Isa. 33:6; Dan. 1:4, 2:21; Eph. 1:17; Col 1:9; and, James 3:13). If knowledge mixed with wisdom is the goal for believers, it should also be the goal of believers for their children. Thus, any book we lay before the eyes of our precious blessings should result in bringing that young soul into a love relationship of total dependence and faith in our Creator and Saviour."

3.5.6 DISCIPLINE

The Bible clearly discusses not only the method and purpose of training and educating our children through family discipleship, but it also clearly outlines the respect and honor children should give their Parents, and which parents should instill in their children. It clearly outlines the method of that taboo word *discipline*.

> *If his children forsake my law, and walk not in my judgments; If they break my statutes, and keep not my commandments; Then will I visit their transgression with the rod, and their iniquity with stripes. Nevertheless my loving-kindness will I not utterly take from him, nor suffer my faithfulness to fail.*
>
> *(Ps. 89:30-33)*

> *If ye endure chastening, God dealeth with you as with sons; for what son is he whom the father chasteneth not? Furthermore we have had fathers*

of our flesh which corrected us, and we gave them reverence: shall we not much rather be in subjection unto the Father of spirits, and live? For they verily for a few days chastened us after their own pleasure; but he for our profit, that we might be partakers of his holiness. Now no chastening for the present seemeth to be joyous, but grievous: nevertheless afterward it yieldeth the peaceable fruit of righteousness unto them which are exercised thereby.
(Heb. 12:7, 8-11)

This is almost lost on us today as *chastening* in today's language rarely means the severe and unpleasant correction described in these verses.

Foolishness is bound in the heart of a child; but the rod of correction shall drive it far from him.
(Prov. 22:15)

The rod and reproof give wisdom: but a child left to himself bringeth his mother to shame.
(Prov. 29:15)

Chasten thy son while there is hope, and let not thy soul spare for his crying.
(Prov. 19:18)

The blueness of a wound cleanseth away evil: so do stripes the inward parts of the belly.
(Prov. 20:30)

Let's be clear. We are not talking about uncontrolled beating in anger, but controlled, calm administering of a rod after the child has first been trained to know what is expected of him or her. Remember, "He that soweth iniquity shall reap vanity: and the rod of his anger shall fail." (Prov. 22:8)

Do we expect obedience at our first command or do we wait for five or ten times before we lose the plot in anger? If children can obey after five commands, they can obey after one. We just need to get them used to obeying on our first gentle command. This takes a great deal of effort and consistency but it can be done.

God has given us a tool to correct our children: the rod. It is not the only tool in our biblical toolbox but it is the tool largely abandoned in today's politically correct humanistic society. It is described as the only tool to correct issues of the heart, whether foolishness or disobedience. There is no alternative to the use of this tool for these heart issues.

No one would argue that the pain of having a rotten tooth pulled out is unpleasant, but nor would they argue that pulling it out is a bad thing. Nor too is discipline given correctly, especially when God is the one who commanded this method of chastisement. Who are we to stand in judgment of God's methods?

> *He that spareth his rod hateth his son: but he that loveth him chasteneth him betimes.*
>
> *(Prov. 13:24)*

> *There is a generation that curseth their father, and doth not bless their mother. There is a generation that are pure in their own eyes, and yet is not washed from their filthiness. There is a generation, O how lofty are their eyes! and their eyelids are lifted up.*
>
> *(Proverbs 30:11-13)*

When God held Eli accountable for the sin of his sons, it was when his sons were mature men (see 1 Sam. 2:12, 2:22-25, 27-36, 3:13-14, 4:11). Even as adults, corporal punishment was a scriptural discipline for certain crimes that was never revoked (see Deut. 25:3; 2 Sam. 7:14; Ps. 89:32; Prov. 17:10, 19:29, 20:30; Isa. 53:5; 1 Peter 2:24; Luke 12:47-48; Acts 16:23; 2 Cor. 6:5, 11:23-24). The point is that even as adults, children were expected to still honor and take guidance from their parents. Do you remember the account of Bathsheba coming to Solomon as king and asking him for a favor? Solomon, even as king, bowed in reverence to his mother (see 1 Kings 2:19). There is no such thing as a child automatically being free from honoring their parents at the age of eighteen.

3.5.7 Requiting Parents

It is worth noting here that it is the children's responsibility to look after aged or widowed parents, not the state. A widow is only supposed to be taken into the number of the church under certain conditions, one being that she has no children or nephews to take care of her. This is so strongly put that the apostle Paul wrote that one who doesn't take care of those of his own household is worse than an infidel. He also made it clear that children should first show piety at home by requiting their parents (see 1 Tim. 5:3-8). The Lord Jesus addresses this issue in Mark 7:10-13, where He chides the Jews for nullifying the commandment of God by the Jewish tradition of corban. Children could shirk their responsibility to honor their parents by claiming that the money which should have been used to support them was a gift to God. It is a disgrace that today's children are so quick to place their elderly parents in nursing homes when the children are able to take care of them. Surely honoring our parents doesn't stop when they can no longer look after themselves (see Lev. 19:32, Prov. 16:31, Eph. 6:2-3). Having elderly parents stay with the next generation when they are still able is also an added blessing as they can help with the grandchildren and add that extra dimension of wisdom and family cohesion (see Heb. 11:9). Having multiple generations live together also helps solve that generation gap, which has become so difficult to bridge in the modern nuclear family. This alone can do wonders for revival in the home.

3.5.8 Summary of Education and Discipline

In conclusion, God gave parents the responsibility to educate their children. This education was not the school-like system of today but discipleship as described in Deuteronomy and exemplified by the Lord

Jesus Christ Himself. We call it "home education" rather than "home schooling" because the goal is not simply to bring school into the home but to bring godly wisdom into the heart.

The foundation of this education is God's Word, which gives every subject context. The Bible commands fathers to take charge of their children's entire training of mind and morals and to, when necessary, use the rod for correction. The mother, the keeper of the home and the husband's helper, does much of the practical work in this area while the father provides, but this does not mean fathers should just sit back and watch. We should oversee the education and give our wife vision and direction in it. We must also take the lead in family worship and discipline. The goal of such education must recognize God's creation order and the distinction of men's and women's roles. The goal is not to make brilliant but morally destitute individuals, but to pass on to the next generation the providences, works, and Word of God—that is, multigenerational faithfulness. If we want to see enduring fruit from our evangelistic endeavours, we need to seriously consider the quality of our discipleship. Enduring fruit will be dramatically helped if Christian families return to God's methods of training, discipline, and multigenerational vision.

Who was the smartest and most influential home-educated person in history? Was it Alexander Graham Bell, Thomas Edison, Orville and Wilbur Wright, Albert Einstein, or Blaise Pascal? Yes, all of these great men were home educated. No, it was none other than the Lord Jesus Christ Himself. He was educated in the Deuteronomy 6 Hebrew tradition, taught by Joseph, and trained in the skill of carpentry, yet He was so knowledgeable that He astonished the doctors and teachers of the law in the temple at just twelve years old (see Luke 2:42-52).

During this period of Jewish history, boys typically spent several hours a day learning the law at the synagogue and several hours learning a trade under their father. Girls learned to be home makers from their mothers. The majority of their learning was still discipleship by their own parents according to Deut 6:6-9.[64]

3.6 The Family Economy

Throughout the Scriptures, the basic economic unit is not the individual but the family. Indeed the very word economy comes from the Greek word oikonomia, which means household management. While children were under their father's roof, the family's collective productivity was used to build the family economy, not the prosperity of each individual (Gen. 29:9, 37:2, 37:12, Exod. 2:16; 1 Sam. 17:15; Luke 15:25-31; Php 2:22; Luke 2:49-by inference). The wife did not pursue her own career, but as keeper of the home, oikouros, her economic productivity was under the jurisdiction of her husband as part of the family economy (Prov. 31:11-27; Num. 30:6-8, 30:10-16). It was not until a son left his father and mother and cleaved to his wife that a new household was formed (Gen. 2:24). It was not until a daughter was given in marriage that her provision ceased to be the responsibility of her father or brothers (Lev. 22:13; Num. 30:3, 30:16; 2 Sam. 13:20). The family economy demonstrated the cohesive unit of its members. They didn't just stay together under the same roof, but learned life skills and wisdom together, and worked daily together. It was indeed an environment which nurtured strong relationships.

Though some would argue that this economic model was because their culture was mostly agrarian, there is no doubt that this economic family unit was God's pattern and reflects God's wisdom. Where there is a pattern but no command, it is often the principles which we must learn wisdom from, rather than trying to duplicate a pattern which may not fit precisely in our context. If you are able to get back to a simple farming model, well and good, there are obvious benefits in doing this. If not, consider the ultimate goals which such a family economy produces in terms of family cohesion, God-reliance (rather than self-reliance), and multigenerational faithfulness. After all, family wealth, which is what we will be discussing in this section, is not necessarily financial but may in fact be a myriad of physical resources including a very fruitful farm.

THE SUFFICIENCY OF SCRIPTURE

God almost always deals with entire households throughout Scripture. There are about 845 occurrences of the phrase "house of" in the KJV Bible. We begin with this fact to lay the foundation for this section in which we will explore what the Bible says about wealth. We will demonstrate from Scripture that wealth should be used for the building of a godly dynasty, rather than fuel for individual consumption. A right understanding of the family economy and wealth, in conjunction with the doctrine previously outlined in this chapter, will thus provide a tool for sustaining revival in the home for future generations if the Lord so chooses to tarry.

> *Through wisdom is an house builded; and by understanding it is established: And by knowledge shall the chambers be filled with all precious and pleasant riches.*
>
> *(Proverbs 24:3-4)*

3.6.1 THE TWO EXTREME VIEWS OF WEALTH

Wealth is like a rope. To some it is a vital tool for saving life, and for others it is a noose of death. On the one hand we have Christians teaching that unless you live like a pauper you are carnal, and on the other hand, you have Christians teaching that unless God is blessing you financially, you aren't living in the fullness of Christ. We have those who insist that we must live by the principals of Luke 10:1-7 where the Lord Jesus told 70 disciples to take nothing for their journey but live "by faith," who often condemn those who live as commanded in Luke 22:35-38 where the Lord Jesus instructed His disciples to do the exact opposite and provide for their own needs as the Apostle Paul did (1 Thes. 2:9; 2 Thes. 3:8, Acts 18:1-3).

> *And he said unto them, When I sent you without purse, and scrip, and shoes, lacked ye any thing? And they said, Nothing. Then said he unto them, But now, he that hath a purse, let him take it, and likewise his scrip: and he that hath no sword, let him sell his garment, and buy one.*

REVIVAL IN THE HOME

For I say unto you, that this that is written must yet be accomplished in me, And he was reckoned among the transgressors:
(Luke 22:35-37)

It appears that this second passage supersedes the passage in Luke 10:1-7 and describes the situation when The Lord Jesus would no longer be physically present with His disciples. He was about to go to Calvary and then shortly thereafter to His Father. The comforter would then be sent who would lead them into all truth.
(John 14:26, 16:13)

God has obviously honoured the faith of many believers who have gone out on missionary journeys without anything as described in Luke 10:1-7, but equally others have found themselves having to return because they lacked the support necessary to continue. Supporting oneself does not negate living by faith. One must still rely upon God to direct his steps, provide the opportunities to cross paths with those whom God wills, give wisdom to know what to say when, etc. The Apostle Paul chose to support himself so as not to be a burden to the church. (1 Thes. 2:9; 2 Thes. 3:8; Acts 18:1-3), yet his life was a life of faith and obedience.

We must not despise the poor nor treat the rich preferentially, because wealth is no indication of God's favour of one person over another.

The rich and poor meet together: the LORD is the maker of them all.
(Proverbs 22:2)

For ye have the poor with you always, and whensoever ye will ye may do them good: …. (Mark 14:7a i.e. there will always be poor amongst us.

Then Peter opened his mouth, and said, Of a truth I perceive that God is no respecter of persons: (Acts 10:34, also see James 2:1-9 for a strong warning about despising the poor.)

THE SUFFICIENCY OF SCRIPTURE

3.6.2 THE ABILITY TO GET WEALTH IS FROM GOD

It is God who gives us the ability to get wealth. This is for a reason, to establish His purposes.

> *But thou shalt remember the LORD thy God: for it is he that giveth thee power to get wealth, that he may establish his covenant which he sware unto thy fathers, as it is this day.*
>
> *(Deuteronomy 8:18)*

> *Both riches and honour come of thee, and thou reignest over all; and in thine hand is power and might; and in thine hand it is to make great, and to give strength unto all.*
>
> *(1 Chronicles 29:12)*

> *Praise ye the LORD. Blessed is the man that feareth the LORD, that delighteth greatly in his commandments. His seed shall be mighty upon earth: the generation of the upright shall be blessed. Wealth and riches shall be in his house: and his righteousness endureth for ever.*
>
> *(Psalms 112:1-3)*

> *By humility and the fear of the LORD are riches, and honour, and life.*
>
> *(Proverbs 22:4)*

> *There is nothing better for a man, than that he should eat and drink, and that he should make his soul enjoy good in his labour. This also I saw, that it was from the hand of God.*
>
> *(Ecclesiastes 2:24)*

> *Behold that which I have seen: it is good and comely for one to eat and to drink, and to enjoy the good of all his labour that he taketh under the sun all the days of his life, which God giveth him: for it is his portion. Every man also to whom God hath given riches and wealth, and hath*

given him power to eat thereof, and to take his portion, and to rejoice in his labour; this is the gift of God.

(Ecclesiastes 5:18-19)

I know both how to be abased, and I know how to abound: every where and in all things I am instructed both to be full and to be hungry, both to abound and to suffer need.

(Philippians 4:12)

For the scripture saith, Thou shalt not muzzle the ox that treadeth out the corn. And, The labourer is worthy of his reward.

(1 Timothy 5:18)

And in the same house remain, eating and drinking such things as they give: for the labourer is worthy of his hire.

(Luke 10:7)

Woe unto him that buildeth his house by unrighteousness, and his chambers by wrong; that useth his neighbour's service without wages, and giveth him not for his work;

(Jeremiah 22:13)

I have rejoiced in the way of thy testimonies, as much as in all riches.

(Psalms 119:14)

How could David speak of rejoicing in riches if it were sin like adultery? Could you imagine David saying that he rejoiced in the way of God's testimony as much as in all adultery?

And God said unto him, Because thou hast asked this thing, and hast not asked for thyself long life; neither hast asked riches for thyself, nor hast asked the life of thine enemies; but hast asked for thyself understanding to discern judgment; Behold, I have done according to thy words: lo, I have given thee a wise and an understanding heart; so that there was none like

thee before thee, neither after thee shall any arise like unto thee. And I have also given thee that which thou hast not asked, both riches, and honour: so that there shall not be any among the kings like unto thee all thy days.
(1 Kings 3:11-13)

God gave Solomon riches. Would God give something evil to Solomon, especially when he didn't ask for them (Mat. 7:11)? Riches are not evil in and of themselves if one is able to be a good steward of them without being ensnared. Solomon was eventually ensnared by women, not his riches.

Abraham was also rich yet he was called the friend of God: And Abram was very rich in cattle, in silver, and in gold.
(Genesis 13:2)

And the scripture was fulfilled which saith, Abraham believed God, and it was imputed unto him for righteousness: and he was called the Friend of God.
(James 2:23)

All of the above verses clearly demonstrate that God gives us the power or ability to get wealth primarily for His purposes but also for godly enjoyment. I say godly enjoyment because just heaping up goods to satisfy our own lusts is clearly not what is meant by the enjoyment of the fruit of our labor. Godly enjoyment of the fruit of our labour is giving God the glory and praise for whatever we enjoy in moderation.
(Php. 4:5; 1 Pet. 4:3-4)

3.6.3 THE IDOLATRY AND SNARES OF RICHES

Money is not evil. What is evil is the idolatry of money. As riches increase, so do the deceitful snares associated with them. God's wisdom says that such snares lead to hurtful lusts, and ultimately destruction and perdition. Clearly if one has a weakness toward the love of money, they are more likely to be ensnared. In such a case, Mark 9:43-47 would be wise advice, i.e. remove the opportunity to be snared. Let the numerous Scriptures speak for themselves.

> *For the love of money is the root of all evil: which while some coveted after, they have erred from the faith, and pierced themselves through with many sorrows.*
>
> *(1 Timothy 6:10)*

> *No man can serve two masters: for either he will hate the one, and love the other; or else he will hold to the one, and despise the other. Ye cannot serve God and mammon.*
>
> *(Matthew 6:24)*

> *He also that received seed among the thorns is he that heareth the word; and the care of this world, and the deceitfulness of riches, choke the word, and he becometh unfruitful.*
>
> *(Matthew 13:22)*

> *And Jesus looked round about, and saith unto his disciples, How hardly shall they that have riches enter into the kingdom of God!*
>
> *(Mark 10:23)*

> *Trust not in oppression, and become not vain in robbery: if riches increase, set not your heart upon them.*
>
> *(Psalms 62:10)*

> *For where your treasure is, there will your heart be also.*
>
> *(Luke 12:34)*

> *Love not the world, neither the things that are in the world. If any man love the world, the love of the Father is not in him. For all that is in the world, the lust of the flesh, and the lust of the eyes, and the pride of life,*

THE SUFFICIENCY OF SCRIPTURE

is not of the Father, but is of the world. And the world passeth away, and the lust thereof: but he that doeth the will of God abideth for ever.
(1 John 2:15-17)

A little that a righteous man hath is better than the riches of many wicked.
(Psalms 37:16)

Labour not to be rich: cease from thine own wisdom.
(Proverbs 23:4)

Remove far from me vanity and lies: give me neither poverty nor riches; feed me with food convenient for me: Lest I be full, and deny thee, and say, Who is the LORD? or lest I be poor, and steal, and take the name of my God in vain.
(Prov. 30:8-9)

He that oppresseth the poor to increase his riches, and he that giveth to the rich, shall surely come to want.
(Proverbs 22:16)

Wealth gotten by vanity shall be diminished: but he that gathereth by labour shall increase.
(Proverbs 13:11)

He that is faithful in that which is least is faithful also in much: and he that is unjust in the least is unjust also in much.
(Luke 16:10)

As the partridge sitteth on eggs, and hatcheth them not; so he that getteth riches, and not by right, shall leave them in the midst of his days, and at his end shall be a fool.
(Jeremiah 17:11)

Wilt thou set thine eyes upon that which is not? for riches certainly make themselves wings; they fly away as an eagle toward heaven.
(Proverbs 23:5)

REVIVAL IN THE HOME

But godliness with contentment is great gain. For we brought nothing into this world, and it is certain we can carry nothing out. And having food and raiment let us be therewith content. But they that will be rich fall into temptation and a snare, and into many foolish and hurtful lusts, which drown men in destruction and perdition.
(1 Timothy 6:6-9)

There is a sore evil which I have seen under the sun, namely, riches kept for the owners thereof to their hurt.
(Ecclesiastes 5:13)

And he spake a parable unto them, saying, The ground of a certain rich man brought forth plentifully: And he thought within himself, saying, What shall I do, because I have no room where to bestow my fruits? And he said, This will I do: I will pull down my barns, and build greater; and there will I bestow all my fruits and my goods. And I will say to my soul, Soul, thou hast much goods laid up for many years; take thine ease, eat, drink, and be merry. But God said unto him, Thou fool, this night thy soul shall be required of thee: then whose shall those things be, which thou hast provided? So is he that layeth up treasure for himself, and is not rich toward God.
(Luke 12:16-21)

For what is a man profited, if he shall gain the whole world, and lose his own soul? or what shall a man give in exchange for his soul?
(Matthew 16:26; Psalm 49:6-7)

Go to now, ye rich men, weep and howl for your miseries that shall come upon you. Your riches are corrupted, and your garments are moth-eaten. Your gold and silver is cankered; and the rust of them shall be a witness against you, and shall eat your flesh as it were fire. Ye have heaped treasure together for the last days. Behold, the hire of the labourers who have reaped down your fields, which is of you kept back by fraud, crieth: and the cries of them which have reaped are entered into the ears of the Lord of sabaoth. Ye have lived in pleasure on the earth, and been wanton; ye

THE SUFFICIENCY OF SCRIPTURE

have nourished your hearts, as in a day of slaughter. Ye have condemned and killed the just; and he doth not resist you.

(James 5:1-6)

I can't write a section about riches without considering the words of the richest man that ever lived, King Solomon. We'd be very foolish not to learn from God's wisdom revealed through this great king.

I said in mine heart, Go to now, I will prove thee with mirth, therefore enjoy pleasure: and, behold, this also is vanity. I said of laughter, It is mad: and of mirth, What doeth it? I sought in mine heart to give myself unto wine, yet acquainting mine heart with wisdom; and to lay hold on folly, till I might see what was that good for the sons of men, which they should do under the heaven all the days of their life. I made me great works; I builded me houses; I planted me vineyards: I made me gardens and orchards, and I planted trees in them of all kind of fruits: I made me pools of water, to water therewith the wood that bringeth forth trees: I got me servants and maidens, and had servants born in my house; also I had great possessions of great and small cattle above all that were in Jerusalem before me: I gathered me also silver and gold, and the peculiar treasure of kings and of the provinces: I gat me men singers and women singers, and the delights of the sons of men, as musical instruments, and that of all sorts. So I was great, and increased more than all that were before me in Jerusalem: also my wisdom remained with me. And whatsoever mine eyes desired I kept not from them, I withheld not my heart from any joy; for my heart rejoiced in all my labour: and this was my portion of all my labour. Then I looked on all the works that my hands had wrought, and on the labour that I had laboured to do: and, behold, all was vanity and vexation of spirit, and there was no profit under the sun.

(Eccl 2:1-11)

And Jesus looked round about, and saith unto his disciples, How hardly shall they that have riches enter into the kingdom of God! And the disciples were astonished at his words. But Jesus answereth again, and saith unto them, Children, how hard is it for them that trust in riches to enter into the kingdom of God! It is easier for a camel to go through the eye of a

> *needle, than for a rich man to enter into the kingdom of God. And they were astonished out of measure, saying among themselves, Who then can be saved? And Jesus looking upon them saith, With men it is impossible, but not with God: for with God all things are possible. Then Peter began to say unto him, Lo, we have left all, and have followed thee. And Jesus answered and said, Verily I say unto you, There is no man that hath left house, or brethren, or sisters, or father, or mother, or wife, or children, or lands, for my sake, and the gospel's, But he shall receive an hundredfold now in this time, houses, and brethren, and sisters, and mothers, and children, and lands, with persecutions; and in the world to come eternal life. But many that are first shall be last; and the last first.*
>
> (Mark 10:23-31)

Note verses 23 and 24. Often verse 23 is quoted alone but verse 24 clarifies that it is not merely riches but the trust put in riches which is wrong. The Lord Jesus also makes it clear that God is no man's debtor, as He tells Peter in response to his query about those who have given up all to follow him, "…But he shall receive an hundredfold now in this time, houses, and brethren, and sisters, and mothers, and children, and lands, with persecutions; and in the world to come eternal life…" (Mark 10:29-30; Prov. 19:17; Eph. 6:8.) Thus the Lord makes it clear that God will abundantly supply our needs so long as our affection is toward Him, and our faith and trust is in Him and not in our material possessions. (Also see Php. 4:19; Heb. 13:5-6.) This provision however is not without persecutions. We are never promised that this life will be a bed of roses even though all our needs are met.

The following verses from Jeremiah 9 really summarize this section well.

> *Thus saith the LORD, Let not the wise man glory in his wisdom, neither let the mighty man glory in his might, let not the rich man glory in his riches: But let him that glorieth glory in this, that he understandeth and knoweth me, that I am the LORD which exercise lovingkindness,*

judgment, and righteousness, in the earth: for in these things I delight, saith the LORD.

(Jeremiah 9:23-24)

3.6.4 God Commands Us To Live By Faith

God commands us to live by faith, not self-reliance (which is what we tend to do if we have an abundance).

(Rom. 1:17; Gal. 3:11; Heb. 10:38)

They that trust in their wealth, and boast themselves in the multitude of their riches; None of them can by any means redeem his brother, nor give to God a ransom for him:

(Psalms 49:6-7)

He that trusteth in his riches shall fall; but the righteous shall flourish as a branch.

(Proverbs 11:28)

Charge them that are rich in this world, that they be not highminded, nor trust in uncertain riches, but in the living God, who giveth us richly all things to enjoy;

(1 Timothy 6:17)

Therefore I say unto you, Take no thought for your life, what ye shall eat, or what ye shall drink; nor yet for your body, what ye shall put on. Is not the life more than meat, and the body than raiment? Behold the fowls of the air: for they sow not, neither do they reap, nor gather into barns; yet your heavenly Father feedeth them. Are ye not much better than they? Which of you by taking thought can add one cubit unto his stature? And why take ye thought for raiment? Consider the lilies of the field, how they grow; they toil not, neither do they spin: And yet I say unto you, That even Solomon in all his glory was not arrayed like one of these. Wherefore, if God so clothe the grass of the field, which to day is, and to morrow is cast into the oven, shall he not much more clothe you, O ye of little faith?

Therefore take no thought, saying, What shall we eat? or, What shall we drink? or, Wherewithal shall we be clothed? (For after all these things do the Gentiles seek:) for your heavenly Father knoweth that ye have need of all these things. But seek ye first the kingdom of God, and his righteousness; and all these things shall be added unto you.
(Matthew 6:25-33)

Some take this passage from Matthew to mean that we should solely rely on God to provide without the need to work. This is taking the verses out of context and ignoring the clear teaching of other Scriptures. Our goal must be to seek first His kingdom, but in doing so we will learn that God expects us to labour rather than expect food for naught. The fowls of the air need to collect the seeds they eat, God doesn't just drop them into their mouth. The lillies of the field must dig their roots into the soil and draw up the nourishment. What these verses teach us is that if we are willing to seek work and do it, we can trust that God will provide the employment opportunity. This is living by faith. It doesn't mean that we don't need to actively gain useful skills, seek the employment or diligently work at a job. Our priority should thus be to obey God, not worry about what we will wear or eat. God will do the impossible while we must do what He has commanded.

3.6.5 THE PURSUIT OF WISDOM AHEAD OF RICHES

The pursuit of Wisdom is more important than riches

Happy is the man that findeth wisdom, and the man that getteth understanding. For the merchandise of it is better than the merchandise of silver, and the gain thereof than fine gold. She is more precious than rubies: and all the things thou canst desire are not to be compared unto her.
(Proverbs 3:13-15)

Yea, if thou criest after knowledge, and liftest up thy voice for understanding; If thou seekest her as silver, and searchest for her as for hid treasures; Then shalt thou understand the fear of the LORD, and find the knowledge of God. (Prov. 2:3-5.) Note that the above verse doesn't say we shouldn't search for silver or hidden treasure, it says that we should search for wisdom more than them.

> *The law of the LORD is perfect, converting the soul: the testimony of the LORD is sure, making wise the simple. The statutes of the LORD are right, rejoicing the heart: the commandment of the LORD is pure, enlightening the eyes. The fear of the LORD is clean, enduring for ever: the judgments of the LORD are true and righteous altogether. More to be desired are they than gold, yea, than much fine gold: sweeter also than honey and the honeycomb.*
>
> (Psalm 19:7-9)

> *Riches profit not in the day of wrath: but righteousness delivereth from death.*
>
> (Proverbs 11:4)

> *A GOOD name is rather to be chosen than great riches, and loving favour rather than silver and gold.*
>
> (Proverbs 22:1)

> *There is that maketh himself rich, yet hath nothing: there is that maketh himself poor, yet hath great riches.*
>
> (Proverbs 13:7)

> *The law of thy mouth is better unto me than thousands of gold and silver.*
>
> (Psalm 119:72)

> *These were not the empty words of someone who didn't know what it was like to be rich, but rather the utterance of someone who experientially knew great wealth as the King of Israel, yet knew also the unfathomable riches of God's truth and the blessedness of a close relationship with his Creator. David was called a man after God's own heart.*
>
> (Acts 13:22)

3.6.6 COMMUNISM OR "COMMONISM?"

Neither was there any among them that lacked: for as many as were possessors of lands or houses sold them, and brought the prices of the things that were sold, And laid them down at the apostles' feet: and distribution was made unto every man according as he had need.

(Acts 4:34-35)

Now concerning the collection for the saints, as I have given order to the churches of Galatia, even so do ye. Upon the first day of the week let every one of you lay by him in store, as God hath prospered him, that there be no gatherings when I come. And when I come, whomsoever ye shall approve by your letters, them will I send to bring your liberality unto Jerusalem.

(1 Cor. 16:1-3, also see Gal. 2:10)

... let him labour, working with his hands the thing which is good, that he may have to give to him that needeth.

(Ephesians 4:28b)

Only they would that we should remember the poor; the same which I also was forward to do.

(Gal 2:10)

It is important to clarify the point that the Bible does not teach socialism or Communism but social cohesion which we may call, "commonism." What is the difference? Communism says, "what is yours is mine by force and right." "Commonism" says, "What is mine is yours by my free-will and compassion if you are in need." For more on Socialism and Communism, see Chapter 5. For a discussion of tithing vs freewill offering, see section 4.5.

The Bible clearly teaches that private ownership of property, and wealth gained by honest labour are acceptable to God and the normative pattern for life. (Exod. 20:15, 20:17; Exod. 2:9; Gen. 30:28; Lev 19:13;

> *Jer 22:13.) God teaches us that we are to help the genuinely poor, not the lazy. It teaches that women should be provided for by their father, husband, or even older brother (2 Sam. 13:20), and that children should be provided for by parents as already discussed (1 Tim. 5:8; 2 Thes. 3:10; 2 Cor. 12:14b.) It also teaches that the elderly widows should be taken care of by the church if they have no living family and have a testimony of godliness and good works.*
>
> (1 Tim. 5:3-10)

When helping the poor, the distinction needs to be made between providing for one's needs versus their wants, between the genuinely poor and those who won't work because they are lazy. This often requires a delicate balance between mercy and truth. (Prov. 12:24, 12:27, 18:9, 21:13, 21:25-26, 22:9, 22:13, 24:30-34.) Ultimately one who is not willing to work will remain poor regardless of how many handouts they are given. Others however when given a hand-up, will be able to get their life in order and sustain themselves from the help they were given.

3.6.7 THE PARABLE OF THE NOBLEMAN
Luke 19:12-26:

> He said therefore, A certain nobleman went into a far country to receive for himself a kingdom, and to return. And he called his ten servants, and delivered them ten pounds, and said unto them, Occupy till I come. But his citizens hated him, and sent a message after him, saying, We will not have this man to reign over us. And it came to pass, that when he was returned, having received the kingdom, then he commanded these servants to be called unto him, to whom he had given the money, that he might know how much every man had gained by trading. Then came the first, saying, Lord, thy pound hath gained ten pounds. And he said unto him, Well, thou good servant: because thou hast been faithful in a very little, have thou authority over ten cities. And the second came, saying, Lord, thy pound hath gained

five pounds. And he said likewise to him, Be thou also over five cities. And another came, saying, Lord, behold, here is thy pound, which I have kept laid up in a napkin: For I feared thee, because thou art an austere man: thou takest up that thou layedst not down, and reapest that thou didst not sow. And he saith unto him, Out of thine own mouth will I judge thee, thou wicked servant. Thou knewest that I was an austere man, taking up that I laid not down, and reaping that I did not sow: Wherefore then gavest not thou my money into the bank, that at my coming I might have required mine own with usury? And he said unto them that stood by, Take from him the pound, and give it to him that hath ten pounds. (And they said unto him, Lord, he hath ten pounds.) For I say unto you, That unto every one which hath shall be given; and from him that hath not, even that he hath shall be taken away from him.

This parable and its parallel passage in Matthew 25:14-29 clearly teach that God expects us to be fruitful with what He entrusts to our care. It has been argued that this parable solely deals with talents but the passage in Luke uses money as its example. The Lord surely would not use money as an example if strategically and deliberately increasing money was sinful. Whether talents or finances, God expects good stewardship. Good stewardship means multiplying, honing, improving, and generally using whatever it is for the glory of God. The conclusion of this passage is that those who prove good stewards are entrusted with more, while those who are bad stewards are dispossessed of the little they have.

Moreover it is required in stewards, that a man be found faithful.
(1 Cor. 4:2)

There is that scattereth, and yet increaseth; and there is that withholdeth more than is meet, but it tendeth to poverty.
(Prov. 11:24)

THE SUFFICIENCY OF SCRIPTURE

> *There is a difference between contentment and complacency. Contentment as described in 1 Tim. 6:8 means that we do not covet. Complacency however is what leads us to bury the treasure entrusted to us rather than seeking to increase it. The increase of wealth is not sinful, it is the love of that increase which maybe a snare. ... if riches increase, set not your heart upon them.*
>
> (Psalms 62:10b)

It is interesting that those who go out as missionaries preaching that we should all live as paupers are often the very ones who expect those with riches to support them. Indeed they should be supported if they are doing an honest day's work labouring in the gospel but they should not expect everyone to live as they do. The body is made up of many members (1 Cor. 12-31; Rom. 12:4-13). Some go down the well, others hold the rope for them. If there is no-one to hold the rope, no-one can go down the well. If all are on the mission field looking to others to support them, there wouldn't be anyone to support them. The problem comes when Christians do not support the work of others financially when they themselves have the ability to do so and are not labouring in any other part of the vineyard.

> *Some Christians think that selling resources is wrong. They say that physical resources should be free, citing verses like Matthew 10:8, freely ye have received, freely give. These verses in context prohibit charging for the resultant transformation of lives through the working of the power of the gospel. If one is able to provide physical resources freely, that is great, but someone somewhere must pay for the publishing and other costs of those making the resources available. The apostle Paul, though he himself chose not to do so, made it clear that it was indeed acceptable to receive support for doing the Lord's work (1 Cor. 9:13-14.) The motive of our heart, whether it be to cover costs and provide for one's family, or to make a greedy profit will however not go unnoticed by the righteous judge!*
>
> (Php. 4:19; Mark 10:29-30; Jude 11; 1 Pet. 5:2; Tit. 1:11)

3.6.8 Debt

The Bible tells us to owe no man anything but love. It does not outright forbid debt. It does however warn that we should do our utmost to avoid it. It outlines the very important fact that debt changes the nature of an otherwise equal relationship. Debt brings the borrower under servitude. We live in a culture where debt is accepted as normal and necessary. Keynesian Economics is taught in almost every school and university. One of its most famous theories which has created the sixteen trillion plus dollar debt of the US, and which is accepted practice by most western nations, is wealth creation through government borrowing. Unfortunately this theory is also accepted at a personal level so that many gullibly think that debt is okay. This goes against God's revealed wisdom. The Bible treats debt as a state of judgment from which we should strive to be free. The Apostle Peter notes "... for of whom a man is overcome, of the same is he brought in bondage."

(2 Peter 2:19b., 1 Cor. 7:21-23)

The rich ruleth over the poor, and the borrower is servant to the lender.

(Proverbs 22:7)

Owe no man any thing, but to love one another: for he that loveth another hath fulfilled the law.

(Romans 13:8)

Under the Mosaic law, we learn that this servant-master relationship was often entered into when a man couldn't pay a debt and thus became a bond-servant. After six years, however, his master was to let him go free with pay and provision unless he chose to remain with his master forever. (Exod. 21:2-6; Deut 15:12-18.) It thus seems reasonable to consider entering into such an agreement whereby you lend money in return for an agreed amount of labour if such an agreement is possible and practical for both parties.

If we do lend money, we should not lend with interest to fellow believers, only unbelievers. This principle was expected of the Jews and it seems reasonable to take this as a general principle for the household of faith when lending for personal use, that is to help them out of financial difficulty rather than for them to make profit from your loan.

> *If thou lend money to any of my people that is poor by thee, thou shalt not be to him as an usurer, neither shalt thou lay upon him usury.*
> *(Exodus 22:25)*

> *Thou shalt not give him thy money upon usury, nor lend him thy victuals for increase.*
> *(Leviticus 25:37)*

> *Thou shalt not lend upon usury to thy brother; usury of money, usury of victuals, usury of any thing that is lent upon usury: Unto a stranger thou mayest lend upon usury; but unto thy brother thou shalt not lend upon usury: that the LORD thy God may bless thee in all that thou settest thine hand to in the land whither thou goest to possess it.*
> *(Deuteronomy 23:19-20)*

> *He that hath pity upon the poor lendeth unto the LORD; and that which he hath given will he pay him again.*
> *(Proverbs 19:17)*

Rather than lending to one in need, we should consider giving them a gift. This avoids that servant-master relationship. (For an example, see 2 Kings 4:1-7; Philemon 1:18.)

> *And if ye lend to them of whom ye hope to receive, what thank have ye? for sinners also lend to sinners, to receive as much again. But love ye your enemies, and do good, and lend, hoping for nothing again; and your reward shall be great, and ye shall be the children of the Highest: for he is kind unto the unthankful and to the evil.*
> *(Luke 6:34-35)*

In terms of borrowing money, we should avoid it wherever possible because of the status of servitude it brings us under. In our current climate, it is difficult to avoid debt when purchasing a family home. If we however are able to acquire the resources, we can certainly aim at helping our children to avoid or at least reduce debt when it is their turn to purchase a home, and then encourage them to do the same for the next generation. Under the Mosaic law, no debt took longer than six years to repay as we have seen. In our context, we should attempt to repay debt as quickly as possible rather than taking as long as allowable. For example, if one can pay back a house loan within six years rather than extending it to thirty years, one should do so.

It is also worth noting that the Scriptures explicitly warn against being a guarantor for someone else's debt.

> *Be not thou one of them that strike hands, or of them that are sureties for debts. If thou hast nothing to pay, why should he take away thy bed from under thee?*
>
> *(Proverbs 22:26-27)*

> *My son, if thou be surety for thy friend, if thou hast stricken thy hand with a stranger, Thou art snared with the words of thy mouth, thou art taken with the words of thy mouth. Do this now, my son, and deliver thyself, when thou art come into the hand of thy friend; go, humble thyself, and make sure thy friend. Give not sleep to thine eyes, nor slumber to thine eyelids. Deliver thyself as a roe from the hand of the hunter, and as a bird from the hand of the fowler.*
>
> *(Proverbs 6:1-5)*

> *He that is surety for a stranger shall smart for it: and he that hateth suretiship is sure.*
>
> *(Proverbs 11:15)*

> *A man void of understanding striketh hands, and becometh surety in the presence of his friend.*
>
> *(Proverbs 17:18)*

3.6.9 INHERITANCE

A good man leaveth an inheritance to his children's children: and the wealth of the sinner is laid up for the just.
(Proverbs 13:22)

House and riches are the inheritance of fathers: and a prudent wife is from the LORD.
(Proverbs 19:14)

...for the children ought not to lay up for the parents, but the parents for the children. (2Corinthians 12:14b, note this is a statement made in the NT by the Apostle Paul who inferred that this case would still stand, even under the new covenant. He couldn't tell us that parents were to "lay up" or save for our children if we were to live as paupers.)

Wisdom is good with an inheritance: and by it there is profit to them that see the sun.
(Ecclesiastes 7:11)

The Lord expects us to not only provide for our children, but if resources enable, our children's children also. This is in direct opposition to those who think it wrong to own their own home or accumulate wealth for the next generation. Interestingly, those who choose to rent because of this often don't consider that renting from someone causes them to be a debtor to their landlord, which is not a wise state to be in (see previous section on Debt). Also, we should carefully consider the strong words of the Apostle Paul when he said,

"But if any provide not for his own, and specially for those of his own house, he hath denied the faith, and is worse than an infidel."
(1 Tim 5:8)

When considering Acts 4:34-35 as a justification for not owning one's own house, many overlook the fact that those who sold their lands and houses firstly owned them and secondly owned multiple of them, i.e. they sold their excess, not their primary residence. Take careful note:

> *Neither was there any among them that lacked: for as many as were possessors of lands or houses sold them, and brought the prices of the things that were sold, And laid them down at the apostles' feet: and distribution was made unto every man according as he had need.*
>
> *(Acts 4:34-35)*

Others point to the example of the Lord Jesus himself when He said,

> *"The foxes have holes, and the birds of the air have nests; but the Son of man hath not where to lay his head."*
>
> *(Mat. 8:20b)*

Indeed, we are also told that we are to live as strangers or pilgrims:

> *Dearly beloved, I beseech you as strangers and pilgrims, abstain from fleshly lusts, which war against the soul;*
>
> *(1Peter 2:11)*

> *But pilgrims and strangers still need to live somewhere and participate in society as Christ's ambassadors.*
>
> *(2 Cor. 5:20)*

The Lord's example highlights the rejection of His people, and the temporal nature of His earthly ministry. His statement must be taken in its context and not as a normative example for the mere mortal who is encouraged to procreate and provide for his household to the second generation, be salt and light in the world but not of it, and to occupy until He comes.

THE SUFFICIENCY OF SCRIPTURE

What we can take from this statement is that as strangers and pilgrims, we must not set our affections on things below but upon things above (Col. 3:1-5, especially v2). This does not mean we should be bad stewards of earthly things, on the contrary, in order to glorify God and fulfil His will for our family, we should make every effort to increase whatever He entrusts to us without falling into the snare of idolatry. Managing wealth is thus an exercise of stewardship, not accumulating fuel for the fulfilment of our lusts. Its purpose is to provide for the needs of our family and for the needs of the saints, not to attempt to satisfy a bottomless carnal desire for things which can never satisfy.

(Eccl 1:8)

The common view that all Christians should live as paupers, not increasing wealth or owning assets, is a subtle Satanic snare because the Christian is made dependent upon the unbeliever and is at his mercy for everything. This leads to the situation described in 1 Sam. 13:19-20 where the children of Israel were trodden underfoot by the Philistines and couldn't even sharpen their own tools without relying on the enemy to do so.

Now there was no smith found throughout all the land of Israel: for the Philistines said, Lest the Hebrews make them swords or spears: But all the Israelites went down to the Philistines, to sharpen every man his share, and his coulter, and his axe, and his mattock.

(1 Samuel 13:19-20)

Hear what the Lord said, "Behold, I send you forth as sheep in the midst of wolves: be ye therefore wise as serpents, and harmless as doves."

(Matthew 10:16)

And the lord commended the unjust steward, because he had done wisely: for the children of this world are in their generation wiser than the children of light. And I say unto you, Make to yourselves friends of the mammon of

REVIVAL IN THE HOME

unrighteousness; that, when ye fail, they may receive you into everlasting habitations.

(Luke 16:8-9)

Why should the children of this world be wiser than the children of light? This should not be. We have the truth. It is Christianity which has brought civilization to the world. We must consider the whole counsel of God, not make the mistake of many in the church today who think that the red letters of the Bible are all that should be considered. All of the Scriptures taken in context are God's revealed Word and profitable for our learning (2 Tim. 3:16-17; 1 Cor 10:11.). Christians should be the best stewards of all resources including wealth, not for selfish gain but for the support and ministry of future generations. Everything on earth costs, from the printing of literature to the cost of travel and upkeep of mission workers. Even the good Samaritan did not expect the inn keeper to look after the beaten man for naught, (Luke 10:30-35, especially v35. Also see Exod. 2:9; Gen. 30:28.) God has given us a tool to support this work, namely the generosity of believers who manage their wealth in order to increase it without being ensnared by it. Let us not be short sighted. The temple of the Lord's day took forty-six years to build (John 2:20). King David accumulated wealth for his son Solomon to build God's temple (1 Chron. 28:3-20). What we accumulate today helps the generation of tomorrow and inheritance is one of the means by which this is accomplished. (See Num. 27:8-11 for guidance.) Note too that disinheritance is also Scriptural under certain extreme situations, if adult children forsake the Lord and commit certain abominations. (See Lev 18, especially v29; Num. 15:31; Exod. 20:12.)

Finally, we must not think that inheritance is solely material. The legacy of wisdom and godly input which we inculcate in the next generation is far more important than the material inheritance we might leave behind (Eccl 7:11; Ps. 78:4-8.)

THE SUFFICIENCY OF SCRIPTURE

3.6.10 Summary

- The basic economic unit is the family, not the individual.
- Wealth is from God to accomplish His purposes. It does not however indicate God's favor or ill favor of a person though it may indicate that they are a good steward of His provisions.
- Private ownership of property, and wealth gained by honest labour are acceptable to God and are the normative pattern in Scripture.
- Wealth maybe enjoyed but not idolized.
- Wealth can easily become a destructive snare to many.
- The Bible does not teach communism but "commonism", Communism says that what is yours is mine by force or right. "Commonism" says that what is mine is yours by my free will if you are in need.
- God commands us to live by faith which is harder to do when we are self-reliant because of abundance.
- Living by faith requires action on our part. God will not do for us what He has commanded us to do.
- The pursuit of wisdom is more important than the pursuit of riches.
- Debt is discouraged as it indicates servitude. Lend without expectation of repayment. Interest should not be charged to help those of the household of faith out of financial difficulty. A loan in return for agreed labour is acceptable but a gift is even better.
- Inheritance is a means by which we can help equip the next generation for their service of the Lord. Disinheritance is Biblical for rebellious children who dishonor their parents and forsake the Lord. Inheritance includes godly wisdom and instruction, not just material provision.

3.7 Final Thoughts on the Biblical Pattern for the Family

What we haven't dealt with in this chapter is how to practically implement this biblical pattern. While home education might seem way off and too daunting, reformation must begin somewhere.

Fathers, do you have dinnertime devotions around your table to teach your children the Scriptures? Do you even eat together at meal times? Remember, Psalm 128:3 describes children "round about thy table." Do you pray for and with your children? Do you teach them why you as a family believe what you believe? Do you yourself know why you believe what you do? Have you made job choices that have taken you away from your home for long periods? Do you have a life outside your family that is more important than your children? Do you realize that the most important ministry of all is first to your own children? (Sol. 1:6b.)

Mothers, do you understand that God has made you the keeper of the home and your husband's dedicated helper? Do you train your daughters to be homemakers or do you encourage them to be career-seeking?

Parents, do you encourage deep and meaningful relationships between your children? Do you acknowledge and distinguish the differences between brothers and sisters in their roles toward each other? Do you teach your sons that they must be protectors, providers, and shepherds; and your daughters to be quiet, gentle, and virtuous helpers?

Family cohesion is a Scriptural principle we hear very little about today. Psalm 133:1 describes the pleasantness of brethren dwelling together in unity. We almost take it for granted that sibling rivalry should be the family norm. Proverbs 7:4 personifies wisdom as one's sister. Do you teach your sons to cherish their sisters as they should cherish and jealously guard wisdom? Psalm 50:20 equates those who slander their own brother as one who condones the actions of a thief or adulterer. Do you teach your daughters to respect their brothers? This Psalm goes on to imply that slandering of one's brother is in effect dishonoring one's own mother. The Apostle Paul writing to Timothy in 1 Tim. 5:1-2 teaches that appropriate relationships in the church are first learned through right relationships in the family. Perhaps this is why our churches are often so individualistic and dysfunctional.

Parents, do you have a Biblical understanding of the family economy? Do you understand wealth and inheritance as a tool to equip your children and grand-children for the service of the Lord? Are you training your children to comprehend that all we have and are is from the Lord and to be used for His glory?

Don't be deceived, the people with whom your children spend the majority of their time will be their role models and exert the greatest influence whether they are teachers, peers, sports idols, youth groups, pop stars and actors, or Mum and Dad. How many godly parents do you know who have lost their children to peers or ungodly influences? Sadly it is often easier to count those who haven't gone astray rather than those who have.

Strong families make strong churches. Good training in the family will result in a strong church as each father embraces his role of shepherding and discipleship and this overflows into the local church in his own maturing and his children's growth in the Lord. As the mother learns to love her husband and children and guide the house, she also prepares herself for dealing with the poor, widows, and orphans, and opening her mouth with wisdom rather than slander. By her example, she disciples younger single women to become help meets to the young men in the assembly who are simultaneously being trained to become visionary and godly leaders by older men.

The normative scriptural goal of our young people should be to marry early rather than remain in prolonged singleness and to raise godly children (Prov. 5:8, Mal. 2:15, Ps. 127:4). Our youth should be redeeming time rather than wasting it in selfish pursuits. Even if single, there is much work to be done in the Lord's work. Our elderly should not have the attitude of retirement from the Lord's work, but realize that their godly input and discipleship is needed by the next and subsequent generations.

REVIVAL IN THE HOME

Reformation must start somewhere! Reformation is not just for leaders, it is for grass-roots Christianity. It is for every believer which makes up the church of God. Scripture memorization and family devotion is not just for families of those "in the ministry", it is for every family where parents seek to raise their children in the nurture and admonition of the Lord. If you haven't begun on that road of reformation, it's time to start. For those of us who are on it, let's not become complacent—every reformation has a start but no reformation has an end.

Chapter 4

REVIVAL IN THE CHURCH

WHAT DO I mean by revival in the church? A healthy church is one in which there is:

- The preaching of the gospel and genuine conversions
- A multigenerational vision of discipleship with genuine and meaningful relationships between the oldest and youngest believers
- Fervent and meaningful corporate prayer
- A clear growth of young believers into mature believers who are encouraged to exercise their God-given gifts according to Ephesians 4 and 1 Corinthians 11 and 14
- Worship that is God-centered and not man-centered
- Believers who enjoy sweet fellowship and hospitality with one another without the destruction of gossip and backbiting
- A biblical and relevant equipping of the saints to live godly in this perverse and crooked generation
- Sound expository and topical doctrine

No local church this side of glory will be perfect but a local church can certainly become predominately mature and spiritual rather than carnal in its reputation.

REVIVAL IN THE CHURCH

In this chapter I will look at exactly what the church is, its function, and its methods of accomplishing that function. Again, we must take the desert island challenge in defining all of these things rather than man's tradition. In seeking to do this, I will consider the following points:

- What is the church?
- What is the church's role?
- How should it be structured?
- What is the biblical pattern for its public worship?
- How is it to be kept pure?
- What is its jurisdiction?
- What about tithes and offerings?
- What can we learn from the seven churches of Revelation 2 and 3?

4.1 What Is the Church?

What exactly is the church? Today it would seem like a gathering of people governed by a hierarchical structure headed by a man or woman that engages in "worship," "evangelism," and "good works in the community." What does the Bible say? Who are the church's members? What is the church's role? In what activities should the church be engaged? Is what the modern church calls "worship" biblical?

The word *church* comes from the Greek word *ekklesia* or "called-out assembly." From its usage it appears God is the one who calls out each believer. The universal church, or simply "the church," is made up of all believers since the day of Pentecost until the rapture. The Israelites who wandered in the wilderness were also referred to as "the church in the wilderness" (see Acts 7:38) but this is not to be confused with the New Testament assembly, which the apostle Paul declared as a revealed mystery or secret (see Rom. 16:25, 1 Cor. 2:7, Eph. 1:9, 3:1-12).

THE SUFFICIENCY OF SCRIPTURE

> *For this cause I Paul, the prisoner of Jesus Christ for you Gentiles, If ye have heard of the dispensation of the grace of God which is given me to you-ward: How that by revelation he made known unto me the mystery; (as I wrote afore in few words, Whereby, when ye read, ye may understand my knowledge in the mystery of Christ) Which in other ages was not made known unto the sons of men, as it is now revealed unto his holy apostles and prophets by the Spirit; That the Gentiles should be fellowheirs, and of the same body, and partakers of his promise in Christ by the Gospel: Whereof I was made a minister, according to the gift of the grace of God given unto me by the effectual working of his power. Unto me, who am less than the least of all saints, is this grace given, that I should preach among the Gentiles the unsearchable riches of Christ; And to make all men see what is the fellowship of the mystery, which from the beginning of the world hath been hid in God, who created all things by Jesus Christ: To the intent that now unto the principalities and powers in heavenly places might be known by the church the manifold wisdom of God, According to the eternal purpose which he purposed in Christ Jesus our Lord: In whom we have boldness and access with confidence by the faith of him.*
> (Eph. 3:1-12)

The universal church must not be confused with the ecumenical church. The universal church consists of all believers in the "faith once delivered unto the saints" (see Jude 1:3 and Eph. 4:4-5), whereas the ecumenical church is the bringing together of many manmade religions (see Rev. 13:8, 1 Tim. 4:1, 2 Tim. 3:1-5). There are absolutes in the universal church, but in the ecumenical church there are no absolutes. It is clear from the Scriptures that God has no equal! The almighty God says, "I am the LORD: that is my name: and my glory will I not give to another, neither my praise to graven images" (Isa. 42:8).

The local church is an independent gathering of believers in a particular area who meet together and fulfill the role of the church in that specific locality. We see the difference between the universal church and the local church in the way it is addressed. The book of Acts speaks of God adding to the universal church daily, such as those who were being saved, while many of the epistles were written to "the church at" a particular place (e.g., to the church at Corinth, to the seven churches in Asia, etc.), which demonstrates the local church.

Christ is the founder, head, and builder of the church (see Matt. 16:18, Eph. 5:23, Col. 1:18, Acts 2:47). From Matthew 16:18 we note that at the time of Christ's earthly ministry, the New Testament church was still a future entity and this is why we should not confuse it with the church in the wilderness mentioned in Acts 7:38. This is further confirmed by Ephesians 2:20, where the teaching of the apostles and prophets is said to form the foundation of this spiritual building.

> *And I say also unto thee, That thou art Peter, and upon this rock I will build my church; and the gates of hell shall not prevail against it.*
> *(Matt. 16:18)*

The Lord was careful to use two related but distinct words to differentiate the roles of Himself and Peter. When the Lord said, "thou art Peter", He used the word for Peter being "Petros" meaning a stone or small piece of rock. However, when He said, "upon this Rock I will build my church", He used the word "Petra" which is the word for a massive rock, not unlike the contrast between the famous Ayers' Rock in Australia and a pebble lying nearby. Christ clearly is the "Rock of Ages", the foundation and founder of the church, whereas Peter and all believers are "living stones" built into his church. (1 Pet. 2:5-8). This destroys the concept of apostolic succession and the myth that Peter is the head of the church as taught by Roman Catholicism.

Christ is also known as the cornerstone, and the teaching of the apostles and prophets forms the foundation as mentioned (see Eph. 2:20). It is clear that no other foundation can be laid—that is, no new teaching or revelation should be expected (see 1 Cor. 3:11, Heb. 1:2, 2 Peter 2:1). This destroys the claims of many denominations which claim that God still reveals new truth today.

THE SUFFICIENCY OF SCRIPTURE

The church is also known as the "body of Christ" (see 1 Cor. 12:27). Each member of His body (a living stone built on the foundation), the church, has a function or purpose in the local gathering. The church is God's dwelling place (see Eph. 2:21). Though there are elders who have responsibilities to shepherd the flock, they are not over the flock but "among them" (see 1 Peter 5:1-3). As members of Christ's body, we then work together to accomplish the will of the Head, Christ.

4.2 What Is the Church's Role?

The role of the church (and in particular the local church) is to:

1. Preach the gospel of the Lord Jesus Christ to the lost (see 2 Cor. 5:18-20 and Matt. 28:19-20).
2. Baptise believers as did the early church by immersion in water in obedience to the Lord's command. (Note: Not a sprinkling of infants, which is a false doctrine of men.) (Matt 28:19-20 Acts 8:37-38 Acts 10:47-48).
3. Disciple believers in the faith through non-age segregated exemplary living. Age-segregated activities as already discussed in the section on education are a humanistic concept and foreign to the Scriptures (see Titus 2:4; 1 Tim. 4:12; Deut. 29:10-12, 31:12; Josh. 8:35; 2 Chron. 20:13; Ezra 10:1; Neh. 8:1-3; Matt. 14:21, 15:38). The goal of discipleship is to equip the saints for godliness (see Eph. 4:15).
4. Be salt and light, in the world, but not of it (see Matt. 5:13-14, Phil. 2:15, Rom. 12:1-2, John 15:19, 17:16).
5. Demonstrate God's manifold wisdom to the principalities and powers in heavenly places (see Eph. 3:10, 1 Cor. 11:10, 1 Tim. 3:15) by our conduct as the body of Christ in corporate worship.
6. Meet together to remember the Lord's death in the breaking of bread until He comes (see 1 Cor. 11:23-26 and Acts 20:7).
7. Pray together (see Acts 12:5, Eph. 6:18, Col. 4:2, 1 Thess. 5:17).

8. Provoke one another to love and good works (see Heb. 10:24-25, 1 Thess. 5:11, 1 Cor. 14:5, 14:12, 14:26).
9. Study God's Word together and proclaim it as truth by preaching it and living it (see 2 Tim. 2:15, 2 Tim. 4:2, Matt. 28:19-20, Rom. 12:1-2, Ezra 7:10).
10. Take care of widows, orphans, and those with needs in the local church (see Acts 6:1-7, 1 Tim. 5:3, James 1:27, Luke 14:13).
11. Collect funds to support other believers in need (see 1 Cor. 16:1-4, 2 Cor. 9:6-15, Est. 10:3).
12. Share in fellowship outside the corporate worship and breaking of bread through hospitality (see Acts 2:46, Rom. 12:13, 1 Tim. 3:2, Titus 1:8, 1 Peter 4:9).

Notice there are no official programs above such as Sunday school, women's Bible studies, youth groups, etc. The church gatherings in the Bible were always as families. This is as true of the Old Testament church in the wilderness as it was of the crowds who followed and listened to the Lord Jesus as it also was of the house churches that followed the Lord's ascension, as I pointed out earlier.

One complaint leveled against the first edition of this book was that I had argued from silence to support my claims that the early church didn't age segregate children and adults, that is, the Scriptures do not speak of such childrens' programs, womens' groups etc therefore we shouldn't have them. We must be very careful not to fall back to refuting something simply because we believe the Scriptures are silent on an issue. It is true that on some issues, the Scriptures may appear to be silent at first, that is, until one takes other patterns, precepts and principles to their logical conclusion. In logic, if p implies q and q implies r then p implies r, even if it is not explicitly stated that p implies r. Also, p and (not p) cannot both be true. To support our argument that the early church did not have age segregated programs, we only need to consider all of the Scriptures to the contrary, i.e. which state that throughout the entire Scriptures, children were present during public worship, teaching and the discussion of the law, including during the Lord's earthly ministry (as we have already done). Therefore, since the pattern is to not age segregate, and that this pattern was well established, regardless of whether or not the Scriptures are silent on whether the new testament church segregated children or not, the contrary view has already been proven. When attempting to argue that Scripture is silent on a matter, we must be very careful that our argument is not nullified by another direct pattern or principle. We must be careful not to superimpose our current humanistic methodologies and mind set on the historical Biblical record. We must be careful to respect proven historical wisdom rather than arogantly assuming that our modern godless research can improve on such wisdom. Finally, we should not use an isolated exception to argue against a normative pattern. In response to this particular issue, if we do choose to still allow such age segregated programs in our church life, we should be honest enough to acknowledge that they are the inventions of man and not Scripturally sanctioned. We should also regularly assess whether they are really accomplishing the goals for which they were created and be willing to give them up when they cease to do so. Most importantly, we should ensure that they are not abused, resulting in individuals shirking their responsibilities to their own families.

4.3 What Is the Local Church's Biblical Structure?

As I already mentioned, the head of the church is Christ, not the queen of England, the Pope, priest or pastor. The one-pastor system is also foreign to the Scriptures. I want to spend some time demonstrating this from Scripture because fighting against the status quo is difficult when we have years of manmade traditions that have overridden the Scriptures on this matter. The Scriptures speak of a plurality of elders and deacons. The New Testament uses the term bishop (episkopos), elders (presbuteros), and presbyters interchangeably. The role was that of overseer—a mature believer qualified to guide, teach, and otherwise set an example for the flock to emulate (1 Tim. 3:2-7, 4:14, 5:17;

Titus 1:7-9; 1 Pet. 5:1-3, etc). Note below how pastors fit into the structure as a gift to the church rather than an office:

And when they had ordained them elders in every church, and had prayed with fasting, they commended them to the Lord, on whom they believed. (Acts 14:23)
(elders plural/church singular, i.e., local church)

And when they were come to Jerusalem, they were received of the church, and of the apostles and elders, and they declared all things that God had done with them. (Acts 15:4)
(church singular/elders plural)

Then pleased it the apostles and elders, with the whole church, to send chosen men of their own company to Antioch with Paul and Barnabas; namely, Judas surnamed Barsabas, and Silas, chief men among the brethren. (Acts 15:22)
(church singular/elders plural)

And from Miletus he sent to Ephesus, and called the elders of the church. (Acts 20:17)
(elders plural/church singular)

Is any sick among you? let him call for the elders of the church; and let them pray over him, anointing him with oil in the name of the Lord. (James 5:14)
(church singular/elders plural)

And he gave some, apostles; and some, prophets; and some, evangelists; and some, pastors and teachers. (Eph. 4:11)
(Pastor is a gift to the church, not an office—again, even these appear to be plural)

Paul and Timotheus, the servants of Jesus Christ, to all the saints in Christ Jesus which are at Philippi, with the bishops and deacons. (Phil. 1:1)

(Bishop means the same as elder, not pastor—again plural at the church at Philippi. At least in the early church, there was only one church in each city—see Rev. 2-3.)

This is a true saying, If a man desire the office of a bishop, he desireth a good work. (1 Tim. 3:1)
(bishop described as an office/pastor as a gift)

A bishop then must be blameless, the husband of one wife, vigilant, sober, of good behaviour, given to hospitality, apt to teach. (1 Tim. 3:2)
(note a bishop, not the bishop)

Take heed therefore unto yourselves, and to all the flock, over the which the Holy Ghost hath made you overseers, to feed the church of God, which he hath purchased with his own blood. (Acts 20:28)
(note church singular/overseers [elders] plural)

Let the elders that rule well be counted worthy of double honour, especially they who labour in the word and doctrine. (1 Tim. 5:17)
(elders plural)

The elders which are among you I exhort, who am also an elder, and a witness of the sufferings of Christ, and also a partaker of the glory that shall be revealed. (1 Peter 5:1)
(elders again plural)

It is not that the apostle Paul is loose in his choice of the word church or churches, he is careful to distinguish between individual local churches in a region and the church universal when discussing eldership. Some have taken his words to mean that he meant that there were multiple elders in a region but not necessarily in each local church. When Paul speaks of local churches he means churches and when he refers to a single local church he chooses his words carefully (see Acts 9:31, 15:41, 16:5; Rom. 16:4, 16:16; 1 Cor. 7:17, 11:16, 14:33-34, 16:1; etc.).

REVIVAL IN THE CHURCH

There is not a single verse in the New Testament describing a head pastor, senior pastor, single pastor, etc. The only offices mentioned are elders and deacons, both in the plural as demonstrated. The only head of the church is Christ (see Eph. 5:23). If you took the desert island challenge, with only the Bible to guide you, you would not find a single Scripture supporting the modern church model of a single pastor system.

The elders' role as described in Acts 6:4 is to labor in God's Word and prayer. The deacons' role is described as the hands and feet (see Acts 6:2-3). Pastors are simply those who have a pastoral gift or a God-given gift of nurturing and discipling other believers, just as others have a specific gift of evangelism, although none of us are exempt from always being ready to give an answer for the hope that is within us (see 1 Peter 3:15).

> *Wherefore he saith, When he ascended up on high, he led captivity captive, and gave gifts unto men. ... And he gave some, apostles; and some, prophets; and some, evangelists; and some, pastors and teachers; For the perfecting of the saints, for the work of the ministry, for the edifying of the body of Christ.*
>
> *(Eph. 4:8, 11-12)*

Let's consider the definition of the word edify.
Strong's Definition 3619 οικοδομη oikodome
feminine (abstract) of a compound of 3624 and the base of 1430; n f
AV-edifying 7, building 6, edification 4, wherewith (one) may edify 1; 18
1. (the act of) building, building up
2. metaph. edifying, edification
2a. the act of one who promotes another's growth in Christian wisdom, piety, happiness, holiness
3.a building (i.e. the thing built, edifice)

One can only be built up if they remain long enough in a local church to be discipled. While I do not advocate staying in an apostate church, many Christians today tend to move on too hastily for the wrong reasons.

THE SUFFICIENCY OF SCRIPTURE

So we, being many, are one body in Christ, and every one members one of another. Having then gifts differing according to the grace that is given to us, whether prophecy, let us prophesy according to the proportion of faith; Or ministry, let us wait on our ministering: or he that teacheth, on teaching; Or he that exhorteth, on exhortation: he that giveth, let him do it with simplicity; he that ruleth, with diligence; he that sheweth mercy, with cheerfulness.

(Rom. 12:5-8)

The Lord Jesus hated the Nicolaitans' doctrine and deeds (see Rev. 2:6, 2:15). We understand from this word's origin and interpretation that the Nicolaitans were those who ruled by force over God's people, forming a clergy-laity distinction. The early church did not have this distinction. There were, as we have already seen, mature believers acting as elders but all men participated in the worship and all women were active in the Lord's service through their practical work in the home, church, and community. This clergy-laity distinction was never really shaken off during the reformation and has served to reinforce the separation of secular and sacred, an error inherited from Roman Catholicism. All believers are priests unto God though public expression of this priesthood must be governed by Scriptures such as 1 Cor. 14:34, 1 Tim. 2:12 etc.

But ye are a chosen generation, a royal priesthood, an holy nation, a peculiar people; that ye should shew forth the praises of him who hath called you out of darkness into his marvellous light.

(1 Peter 2:9)

And from Jesus Christ, who is the faithful witness, and the first begotten of the dead, and the prince of the kings of the earth. Unto him that loved us, and washed us from our sins in his own blood, And hath made us kings and priests unto God and his Father; to him be glory and dominion for ever and ever.

(Rev. 1:5-6)

REVIVAL IN THE CHURCH

The Lord Jesus clearly was against this clergy-laity distinction, even during His earthly ministry. He said, "But be not ye called Rabbi: for one is your Master, even Christ; and all ye are brethren. And call no man your father upon the earth: for one is your Father, which is in heaven. Neither be ye called masters: for one is your Master, even Christ" (Matt. 23:8-10). We are also told His name is "holy and reverend " (Ps. 111:9b). The titles of *Father* or *Reverend* do not belong to any clergyman in the Lord's church.

The biblical qualifications for elders and deacons are clearly defined in the following verses:

A bishop then must be blameless, the husband of one wife, vigilant, sober, of good behaviour, given to hospitality, apt to teach; Not given to wine, no striker, not greedy of filthy lucre; but patient, not a brawler, not covetous; One that ruleth well his own house, having his children in subjection with all gravity; (For if a man know not how to rule his own house, how shall he take care of the church of God?) Not a novice, lest being lifted up with pride he fall into the condemnation of the devil. Moreover he must have a good report of them which are without; lest he fall into reproach and the snare of the devil. Likewise must the deacons be grave, not doubletongued, not given to much wine, not greedy of filthy lucre; Holding the mystery of the faith in a pure conscience. And let these also first be proved; then let them use the office of a deacon, being found blameless.

(1 Tim. 3:2-10)

If these qualifications were taken much more seriously when recognizing an elder, rather than a man's charisma, it would go far toward bringing revival to our churches. I specifically want to draw your attention to the apostle Paul's admonition when he, by the Holy Spirit, wrote that an elder must be "one that ruleth well his own house, having his children in subjection with all gravity; (For if a man know not how to rule his own house, how shall he take care of the church of God?)." As I already explained in the chapter on family, the family is the training ground for the Lord's service, which includes eldership.

THE SUFFICIENCY OF SCRIPTURE

4.4 What Is the Biblical Pattern for the Public Meeting of the Local Church?

I have been astounded over the years when I've asked believers if the Scriptures set forth a pattern for the local church to be told emphatically no. It would be rather incredible if the Lord Jesus Christ, the builder and Head of the church, did not leave us with some guidance as to the structure, role, and exercise of this most important manifestation of His presence on earth. Indeed, the Scriptures are not silent on this most important matter, and in fact they set forth an unmistakable pattern any student of God's Word can clearly see if they have not yet been prejudiced by Rome's traditions, which are still taught in most Bible colleges today.

4.4.1 OPEN WORSHIP

Today it would seem that the pattern for the local church's public worship is that of a song leader directing an auditorium full of singers in a few spiritual songs with a verse or two read by way of introduction. In many churches this takes the form of a rock concert. If, however, we return to Sola Scriptura, we find a very different pattern. The pattern in Scripture is a gathering in which all men were able to participate, not all in one meeting, but several as the Holy Spirit led. They were to lead the rest of the assembly in worship through the reading of a Psalm, the singing of a hymn or spiritual song, and the praying of a prayer. Women covered their heads and remained silent. After the men took turns in edifying the assembly, one of the men, typically but not necessarily an elder, would preach from the Scriptures. The center of the meeting was the breaking of bread to remember the Lord Jesus Christ.

> Consider all of the Scriptures below that set forth this pattern.
> *How is it then, brethren? when ye come together, every one of you hath a psalm, hath a doctrine, hath a tongue, hath a revelation, hath an interpretation. Let all things be done unto edifying. If any man speak in an unknown tongue, let it be by two, or at the most by three, and that*

by course; and let one interpret. But if there be no interpreter, let him keep silence in the church; and let him speak to himself, and to God. Let the prophets speak two or three, and let the other judge. If any thing be revealed to another that sitteth by, let the first hold his peace. For ye may all prophesy one by one, that all may learn, and all may be comforted. And the spirits of the prophets are subject to the prophets. For God is not the author of confusion, but of peace, as in all churches of the saints. Let your women keep silence in the churches: for it is not permitted unto them to speak; but they are commanded to be under obedience, as also saith the law. And if they will learn any thing, let them ask their husbands at home: for it is a shame for women to speak in the church.

(1 Cor. 14:26-35)

But I suffer not a woman to teach, nor to usurp authority over the man, but to be in silence.

(1 Tim. 2:12)

Speaking to yourselves in psalms and hymns and spiritual songs, singing and making melody in your heart to the Lord.

(Eph. 5:19)

Let the word of Christ dwell in you richly in all wisdom; teaching and admonishing one another in psalms and hymns and spiritual songs, singing with grace in your hearts to the Lord.

(Col. 3:16)

Till I come, give attendance to reading, to exhortation, to doctrine.

(1 Tim. 4:13)

And they, continuing daily with one accord in the temple, and breaking bread from house to house, did eat their meat with gladness and singleness of heart, Praising God, and having favour with all the people. And the Lord added to the church daily such as should be saved.

(Acts 2:46-4)

THE SUFFICIENCY OF SCRIPTURE

Note carefully that in 1 Corinthians 14:26, the apostle Paul says, "Every one of you hath a psalm, hath a doctrine." That means all the men came prepared to share, although not all necessarily took part (see 1 Cor. 14:29, 14:34; 1 Tim. 2:12). All men were permitted to do so, however, as the apostle Paul's encouragement demonstrated: "For ye may all prophesy one by one, that all may learn, and all may be comforted" (1 Cor. 14:31, also see 14:24). This actually reinforces the Old Testament principle that no priest should appear before God empty (see Ex. 23:15, 34:20; 1 Chron. 16:29; Heb. 13:15). It is a sad result of the clergy-laity distinction that many of our churches are full of biblically illiterate pew warmers and the ministry is left to the leaders. This was never the intent for the church body, as we have already seen. We must be reformed.

Also note in 1 Corinthians 14:26 that the references to tongues must be taken in the context of the spiritual gifts that have ceased:

> *Charity never faileth: but whether there be prophecies, they shall fail; whether there be tongues, they shall cease; whether there be knowledge, it shall vanish away. For we know in part, and we prophesy in part. But when that which is perfect is come, then that which is in part shall be done away.*
>
> (1 Cor. 13:8-10)

Also, *prophesy* can mean both foretelling and forth-telling, i.e., preaching.

Strong's Definition 4395 προφητευω propheteuo
from 4396; v
AV-prophesy 28; 28
1. to prophesy, to be a prophet, speak forth by divine inspirations, to predict
1a. to prophesy

1b. with the idea of foretelling future events pertaining esp. to the kingdom of God
1c. to utter forth, declare, a thing which can only be known by divine revelation
1d. to break forth under sudden impulse in lofty discourse or praise of the divine counsels
1d1. under like prompting, to teach, refute, reprove, admonish, comfort others
1e. to act as a prophet, discharge the prophetic office

This was the pattern of the meeting of the local church and should be our pattern if we want to nurture an environment ripe for revival and spiritual maturity. This is because men are forced to be diligent in their own spiritual lives in order to come prepared for the Lord's Day meeting. Also, as I have personally experienced, the Holy Spirit often is able to emphasize a common theme even though there has been no prearrangement, a blessing God uses to further encourage and bring home truths for the edification of all gathered.

It is important to take a moment to look at 1 Corinthians 14:34 where the apostle Paul, by the Holy Spirit, commands the women not to speak but to be silent in the public meeting of the church. The meaning of these words are as follows:

Strong's Definition 2980 λαλεω laleo
a prolonged form of an otherwise obsolete verb; TDNT-4:69,505; v
AV-speak 244, say 15, tell 12, talk 11, preach 6, utter 4, misc 3, vr speak 1; 296
1. to utter a voice or emit a sound
2. to speak
2a. to use the tongue or the faculty of speech
2b. to utter articulate sounds
3. to talk

4. to utter, tell
5. to use words in order to declare one's mind and disclose one's thoughts
5a. to speak

Strong's Definition 4601 σιγαω sigao
from 4602; v
AV-hold (one's) peace 4, keep silence 3, keep close 1, keep secret 1; 9
1. to keep silence, hold one's peace
2. to be kept in silence, be concealed

Many commentaries say that women were simply chattering in the meeting and that this was a prohibition on such disruption. The definitions indicate that the prohibition is much more encompassing than that. The context of this prohibition is also in prophesy and audible participation in the public meeting of the church. A woman was to be "concealed" in public worship, i.e. it was not permitted to her to speak at all. While we may not like the fact that God made the family, church and nation patriarchal, and that the Lord Jesus chose twelve male disciples, this is His choice and design and we are not at liberty to change it. Having said this, this doesn't mean that women are inferior to men or to be treated as such, as already pointed out. All I am demonstrating from Scripture is that the role of the man and the woman in the family and church are distinct and complementary and that God is a God of order and that defying God's creation order has serious consequences.

Returning to the verses which demonstrate the pattern of the public gathering of the local church, we come to the apostle Paul's teaching on the Lord's Supper. While this is often dealt with in depth in terms of the actual bread and cup, I want to draw your attention to the chastening which results from taking God's patterns, precepts and commands lightly.

REVIVAL IN THE CHURCH

For I have received of the Lord that which also I delivered unto you, That the Lord Jesus the same night in which he was betrayed took bread: And when he had given thanks, he brake it, and said, Take, eat: this is my body, which is broken for you: this do in remembrance of me. After the same manner also he took the cup, when he had supped, saying, This cup is the New Testament in my blood: this do ye, as oft as ye drink it, in remembrance of me. For as often as ye eat this bread, and drink this cup, ye do shew the Lord's death till he come. Wherefore whosoever shall eat this bread, and drink this cup of the Lord, unworthily, shall be guilty of the body and blood of the Lord. But let a man examine himself, and so let him eat of that bread, and drink of that cup. For he that eateth and drinketh unworthily, eateth and drinketh damnation to himself, not discerning the Lord's body. For this cause many are weak and sickly among you, and many sleep. For if we would judge ourselves, we should not be judged. But when we are judged, we are chastened of the Lord, that we should not be condemned with the world. Wherefore, my brethren, when ye come together to eat, tarry one for another.
                                                                (1 Cor. 11:23-33)

We are so ignorant of God's holiness and His Word today that God very well might be chastening us and we don't even know it because of our disobedience and indifference to the pattern set forth for the breaking of bread and public gathering.

Of course we can easily get tangled up solely with methodology and forget the rest of the practical interaction of the body. Having said that, though, we should not discard the pattern simply because we fail in some other aspect of our practical obedience (see Matt. 23:23-28). Yet others covet the spiritual gifts so much that they forget the methodology. First Corinthians 12 and 13 outline this working of the body and emphasize that love without pretension must be the binding force, not just the exercise of spiritual gifts or methodology.

Note: While those who gathered to the name of the Lord Jesus, sometimes known as *brethren* (see Matt. 23:8, 12:48-50), rediscovered these truths in the 1800s, it is by no means exclusive to their gatherings.

THE SUFFICIENCY OF SCRIPTURE

If all we had were the Scriptures and no tradition of man, this is all we would know about the public meeting of the local church.

Since Christians are members of Christ's body, and since the Christian life is a full-time job, most of our activities in evangelism, encouragement, prayer, and living out His Word should occur during the rest of the week through family-based hospitality (according to the season of one's life). The problem with a lot of churches is that we cram all of this into Sunday and forget about the rest of the week. As members of the local church, our daily responsibility to Christ is to fulfill our function and use our gifts as He provides the opportunity, strength, and discernment. We should pray for each other, provide for each other's needs, and be subject to one another—that is, esteem others as more important than ourselves in our attitudes and dealings (Philippians 2:3).

As for our weekly gathering, what should it be like? What should be accomplished during this short time? As it is written (see Eph. 3:1-12): The mystery of the church was not known in the past but was revealed to the apostles and prophets in the interim while God temporarily put His dealings with Israel on hold (see Rom. 11:2). The church's purpose is to be a display of God's manifold wisdom to the principalities and powers in heaven (see Eph. 3:10). This is why our conduct is so important. The method and reason for our gathering is of great significance—if it were not so, Christ wouldn't have founded it. We should, therefore, treat our gathering with great respect, for there is nowhere else in creation that God can demonstrate this mystery except in the church. If He could, He wouldn't have created the church.

What exactly is it that we are showing to the principalities? How God in Christ reconciled us to Himself and how we respond in adoration and remembrance. Our response to God's grace is therefore extremely important. Our time of worship should be filled with Christ-centered expression and not self-centered activities. We do not come to just receive a blessing from God as so many churches teach but we come to remember Christ, to thank Him, and to pour out our hearts as we center our thoughts on Him and His character. Worship must be in spirit and truth (see John 4:23-24 and Rev. 1:10). This is an intimate communication between our spirit and God, expressing deep adoration, gratitude, dependence, and reverence. This may or may not involve our emotions, and if it does, it may be an indication of our inability to grasp God's greatness and mercy, but it is never an indication of how spiritual or great the service is. We do not gather on our terms to feel good but on His terms to give Him what is due Him regardless of our emotional or physical state (see 1 Chron. 16:29 and Heb. 13:15). We must avoid the temptation of thinking we need other trimmings to worship God. Jacob simply worshipped leaning on the top of his staff (see Heb. 11:21).

Let's consider the true meaning of worship:

Strong's Definition 4352 προσκυνεω proskuneo
from 4314 and a probable derivative of 2965 (meaning to kiss, like a dog licking his master's hand); v
AV-worship 60; 60
1. to kiss the hand to (towards) one, in token of reverence
2. among the Orientals, esp. the Persians, to fall upon the knees and touch the ground with the forehead as an expression of profound reverence
3. in the NT by kneeling or prostration to do homage (to one) or make obeisance, whether in order to express respect or to make supplication
3a. used of homage shown to men and beings of superior rank
3a1. to the Jewish high priests
3a2. to God
3a3. to Christ
3a4. to heavenly beings
3a5. to demons

It is very wrong of us to bring the elements of the world into our worship and remembrance service. When we do so, we rob God of His rightful glory. It is very wrong to change our operation to accommodate unbelievers. After all, we are setting an example to them and not them to us. Our evangelism and explanation of worship and remembrance must be done outside of this time as this time is the Lord's. If one comes into our meeting off the street and sees our manner of worship, the person will know of a truth that God is among us (see 1 Cor. 14:24-25). By accommodating the world in our manner of worship, we are proclaiming that the world's ways and idols are acceptable. Some of the idols that rob God during this time are entertaining music, rousing speeches to whip up emotion, self-centered songs that talk about "me," etc. It is clear from Scripture that Paul never used cunning devices to proclaim truth. He spoke with simplicity and only used God's Word (see 2 Cor. 4:1-6 and 1 Cor. 2:1-5).

It is also interesting to note that the only time praise and worship are mentioned together is in Psalm 138:2, and here we see that worship is first, and then praise (i.e., worship and praise, not praise and worship). This is significant because praise can really only be given when we approach God with a worshipful and reverent attitude first.

It is important to reiterate that the primary purpose of the public meeting of the local church on the first day of the week was to worship and remember the Lord Jesus Christ in the breaking of bread as He himself commanded (Mat. 26:26-28).

> *And upon the first day of the week, when the disciples came together to break bread, Paul preached unto them, ready to depart on the morrow; and continued his speech until midnight.*
>
> *(Acts 20:7)*

The primary reason for gathering was to break bread and remember the Lord as He instructed. The secondary reason for gathering was to grow in the knowledge of the Lord through the hearing of God's Word. In today's churches, the focus is on the message and the real purpose for gathering has been lost. The remembrance of the Lord Jesus Christ's death and atonement for sins by the breaking of bread and taking of the cup is to be done regularly. The pattern is set forth as "upon the first day of the week" and only "until He comes" (see Acts 20:7). This is then a reminder of our blessed hope, His return (see 1 Thess. 4:13-18 and John 14:1-3), and our responsibility to "occupy" until He comes (see Luke 19:13). We are forgetful creatures so this continual remembrance is necessary!

Note that this part of the meeting is clearly described in the second half of 1 Corinthians 11, after the first half, which is conveniently ignored in so many modern churches today. In this passage we are taught to examine ourselves before participating in this remembrance, as not discerning the emblems' significance is a serious offense that caused some in the Corinthian church to fall sick and even die (see 1 Cor. 11:30-32).

How do we appear to the principalities and heavenly powers? Do they see God's order? Do they acknowledge God's manifold wisdom when they see our response to His grace? Have we allowed the world to permeate our worship and remembrance to obscure our focus on God's character, holiness, righteousness, love, and future plan? Do we examine ourselves adequately before taking the bread and cup? Do we truly see our sin in its absolute filthiness and the immense and unwarranted pardon accomplished for us in the Lord Jesus Christ's shed blood?

May our everyday prayer and desire be to take seriously our place in the church as members of Christ's body so our gathering for worship will truly reflect His Lordship over our lives.

4.4.2 A Note on the Spiritual Song and Music in Worship

Let the word of Christ dwell in you richly in all wisdom; teaching and admonishing one another in psalms and hymns and spiritual songs, singing with grace in your hearts to the Lord.

(Col. 3:16)

Much could be said about today's treatment of hymns and spiritual songs. On the one hand we have those who almost exalt hymns to the level of the Scriptures themselves, and on the other we have self-centered choruses sung to rock music. Again, the Scriptures alone should be our guide as to what constitutes a hymn or spiritual song. I can assure you that the disdain some folks feel at modern-day choruses would very

THE SUFFICIENCY OF SCRIPTURE

well have been felt by some when hymns were introduced in the 1800s (and which are now exalted to Psalm status). The truth is that time is the friend of deceit, and time alone does not give weight to the validity of something as being acceptable. There are just as many hymns in the most traditional of hymnbooks that are as unscriptural as the choruses chanted to the rock music of today. The problem is that our favorites often remain our favorites because of a pleasant melody or sentimental words regardless of the song's scriptural accuracy. We do not in any way want to discourage a new believer who loves to sing a shallow chorus that expresses his love of the Lord Jesus, but it is up to the mature believer to gently guide and teach on this most important subject.

We all know music is one of the most powerful expressions of the human existence and words put to music are most easily remembered. It is therefore vitally important that the songs we sing by habit express Scriptural truths that are both biblically sound and rigorously reverent. Too often we learn faulty doctrine from the hymns we sing. Consider, for instance, the many hymns that sentimentally plead with Jesus to "abide with us." This teaches the false doctrine that somehow we must plead with God for His presence when in reality the Bible promises His presence and commands us to abide in Him, not for us to plead that He abide with us.

> *Now ye are clean through the word which I have spoken unto you. Abide in me, and I in you. As the branch cannot bear fruit of itself, except it abide in the vine; no more can ye, except ye abide in me. I am the vine, ye are the branches: He that abideth in me, and I in him, the same bringeth forth much fruit: for without me ye can do nothing. If a man abide not in me, he is cast forth as a branch, and is withered; and men gather them, and cast them into the fire, and they are burned.*
>
> (John 15:3-6)

> *And, lo, I am with you always, even unto the end of the world. Amen.*
>
> (Matt. 28:20)

REVIVAL IN THE CHURCH

Let your conversation be without covetousness; and be content with such things as ye have: for he hath said, I will never leave thee, nor forsake thee. So that we may boldly say, The Lord is my helper, and I will not fear what man shall do unto me.

(Heb. 13:5-6)

Why is this so important? It is the very understanding of God's promise to be with us continuously that gives us confidence as Christians. If, however, we sing such hymns, it reinforces a faulty view that God somehow leaves us to flounder and that we must plead with Him to look on our helplessness as if He doesn't care. This is just one example of many such fallacies expressed in our hymnbooks. Sadly also, in most church meetings we spend much more time in the hymnbook or chorus book than in God's Word itself, which will by nature cause us to memorize such fallacies more than we remember the truths of God's Word.

I do not want to outline a formula for the hymn or spiritual song—that would be just as unscriptural. What I do want to do is draw your attention to this most important subject, that we dare to reform what we have come to love sometimes as much as the Holy Bible and sadly sometimes even more so. I'd like to simply draw your attention to the four most basic prerequisites for a hymn or spiritual song:

- its music
- its audience
- its scriptural accuracy
- its reverence

Its music should not be that which was rooted in the pagan culture of rebellion from which rock music sprang forth, but be that which is rooted in the hearts of men who were moved to express God's own heavenly music through their deep love of and desire to be like Him. Music is not neutral. Music, like education, reflects the culture that gave rise to it.

THE SUFFICIENCY OF SCRIPTURE

It is fitting to warn against the idolatry of music in worship. While the pattern of worship being accompanied by music is certainly found in the Old Testament and in heaven itself, it was not the focal point of the worship (see 1 Chron. 15:16, 16:42; 2 Chron. 5:13, 7:6, 34:12; Neh. 12:36; Rev. 5:8, 14:2, 15:2).

We also do not read about the Lord Jesus bringing His orchestra around with Him, nor do we read of the New Testament church or any of the apostles referring to musical instruments in their worship. Since God allowed music in worship in the Old Testament and will allow it in heaven, we cannot say it is strictly forbidden in the church, but it was never the focus or subject of discussion. It should thus be much lower on our priority list than it often is today.

In the prior section I alluded to our dependence on music in order to worship God. Music in worship has become as important as the stained-glass windows and lofty architecture of the Roman cathedrals. While these things in and of themselves may not be wrong, they quickly lead to an unhealthy dependence on such symbols for worship, which too often results in idolatry. Remember the words of the Lord Jesus, "But the hour cometh, and now is, when the true worshippers shall worship the Father in spirit and in truth: for the Father seeketh such to worship him. God is a Spirit: and they that worship him must worship him in spirit and in truth" (John 4:23-24). To worship God in spirit and truth means that our spirit communes with God, expressing adoration, appreciation, and reverence. If this were so common, God would not have to "seek" such worshippers (see John 4:23).

Satan appears to have been connected to worship in heaven prior to his fall from pride. The references to viols, pipes and tabrets, all musical instruments, indicates this connection. It is no surprise then that Satan often uses music to rob God of the glory it is supposed to be giving Him, as the music, or the musician, becomes the focus of the meeting.

Thy pomp is brought down to the grave, and the noise of thy viols: the worm is spread under thee, and the worms cover thee. How art thou fallen from heaven, O Lucifer, son of the morning! how art thou cut down to the ground, which didst weaken the nations! For thou hast said in thine heart, I will ascend into heaven, I will exalt my throne above the stars of God: I will sit also upon the mount of the congregation, in the sides of the north: I will ascend above the heights of the clouds; I will be like the most High.

(Isa. 14:11-14)

Thou hast been in Eden the garden of God; every precious stone was thy covering, the sardius, topaz, and the diamond, the beryl, the onyx, and the jasper, the sapphire, the emerald, and the carbuncle, and gold: the workmanship of thy tabrets and of thy pipes was prepared in thee in the day that thou wast created. Thou art the anointed cherub that covereth; and I have set thee so: thou wast upon the holy mountain of God; thou hast walked up and down in the midst of the stones of fire. Thou wast perfect in thy ways from the day that thou wast created, till iniquity was found in thee.

(Ezek. 28:13-15)

The connection between music and idolatry is not just conjecture (see Amos 5:23-24, 6:1-7, particularly verse 5, and Dan. 3:4-18).

Because music was never the focal point of worship, we must ensure that both musicians and music are not given higher priority or adoration than they are given in the Scriptures. I am not saying that the Scriptures forbid music in worship, I am only warning against the idolatrous worship of music or the musicians who play or sing in our worship meetings.

It is clear from Scripture that our singing of spiritual songs is to be worship and praise to the Lord and not simply singing to each other (see Col. 3:16 and Heb. 13:15). If a song is self-centered it is neither worship nor praise nor edifying of the church as a whole.

A hymn or spiritual song should most certainly not contradict the Scriptures. As I already pointed out, songs are generally what we remember most, which is why Psalms were sung throughout the ages in many of the saints' meetings.

THE SUFFICIENCY OF SCRIPTURE

The spiritual song must not be irreverent in its treatment of the name above all names! Again, habits are most easily formed, and singing songs that treat the name of the Lord with a familiarity with which we would not address an earthly dignitary only serve to reinforce irreverence in how we treat the Lord of Glory. A study of the Gospels and epistles demonstrates that when a disciple used the name of the Lord Jesus Christ to address Him, as compared to God as the author of a narrative, His disciples almost always called Him "Lord" or "Master" unless they were specifically addressing His humanity. The Lord Himself says, "Ye call me Master and Lord: and ye say well; for so I am." (John 13:13). The apostle Paul says, "…yea, though we have known Christ after the flesh, yet now henceforth know we him no more." (2 Cor. 5:16). He is saying that as born again believers, we no longer know Jesus as just a man, but as the Lord of Glory.

4.4.3 Headship and Creation Order

Let's consider the issue of a woman's head covering. Many today argue that this was a cultural practice that is no longer relevant. The truth is that women have kept this practice throughout history up until less than a hundred years ago. Interestingly, there are only four words in the Bible that tell us not to steal (see Ex. 20:15), yet there is half a chapter on this important lost doctrine. There is also ample evidence from historical records and pictures of women recognizing and keeping this commandment.[65] The catacombs depict Christian women with their heads covered. The writings of Irenaeus (120-202 AD), Tertullian (150-225 AD), Clement of Alexandria (153-217 AD), Hippolytus (170-236 AD), John Chrysostom (340-407 AD), Jerome (345-429 AD), Augustine (354-430 AD), John Knox (1505-1572), and John Calvin (1509-1564), all refer to the veiling of a woman's head when discussing 1 Corinthians 11:1-17. While history is not necessarily proof of a practice's truth, if it confirms the Scriptures then it is obvious this was the accepted interpretation up until very recently. In any case, let the Scriptures speak rather than man's tradition. The significance of head covering is a truth long lost in this day of modern theology. I would like to show you from Scripture why this is not a trivial topic and why it should be duly considered.

> *These things write I unto thee, hoping to come unto thee shortly: But if I tarry long, that thou mayest know how thou oughtest to behave thyself in the house of God, which is the church of the living God, the pillar and ground of the truth.*
>
> *(1 Tim. 3:14-15)*

> *Be ye followers of me, even as I also am of Christ. Now I praise you, brethren, that ye remember me in all things, and keep the ordinances, as I delivered them to you. But I would have you know, that the head of every man is Christ; and the head of the woman is the man; and the head of Christ is God. Every man praying or prophesying, having his head covered, dishonoureth his head. But every woman that prayeth or prophesieth with her head uncovered dishonoureth her head: for that is even all one as if she were shaven. For if the woman be not covered, let her also be shorn: but if it be a shame for a woman to be shorn or shaven, let her be covered. For a man indeed ought not to cover his head, forasmuch as he is the image and glory of God: but the woman is the glory of the man. For the man is not of the woman; but the woman of the man. Neither was the man created for the woman; but the woman for the man. For this cause ought the woman to have power on her head because of the angels. Nevertheless neither is the man without the woman, neither the woman without the man, in the Lord. For as the woman is of the man, even so is the man also by the woman; but all things of God. Judge in yourselves: is it comely that a woman pray unto God uncovered? Doth not even nature itself teach you, that, if a man have long hair, it is a shame unto him? But if a woman have long hair, it is a glory to her: for her hair is given her for a covering. But if any man seem to be contentious, we have no such custom, neither the churches of God.*
>
> *(1 Cor. 11:1-16)*

Note that verse 3 does not imply inequality but order—alphabetical order does not mean A is more important than Z. Also, verse 4 indicates that a man who dishonors his literal head dishonors his figurative head, Christ. So it follows that of a woman dishonors her literal head as well as her figurative head, man, she in turn dishonors Christ.

This covering does not refer to the woman's hair as it does not make sense to compare uncovered with shaven if uncovered means no hair. Why compare no hair with shaven? It is a literal covering as the Greek demonstrates (see verse 6).

Strong's Definition 2619 κατακαλυπτω katakalupto
from 2596 and 2572; v
AV - cover 3; 3
A. to cover up
B. to veil or cover one's self

The "if" in verse 6 is not asking a question for which we have the prerogative of answering but is really saying that because it is a shame for a woman to be shorn or shaven, and because being shorn or shaven is as bad as having her head uncovered, if she is uncovered then she may as well be shorn or shaven. The meaning of shorn is to cut one's hair short. Thus if a woman doesn't cover her hair with a veil, she may as well cut it short or shave it off which God says is shameful.

A woman praying or prophesying—this cannot contradict Scripture (see 1 Cor. 14:34 and 1 Tim. 2:12-13). As the whole of Corinthians demonstrates, this church was extremely carnal, but Paul graciously deals with each problem in turn. If women are to keep silent then how are they supposed to pray and prophesy? (see 1 Cor. 12:26). When one member prays audibly, all members share in that prayer silently. In terms of prophecy, Philip the evangelist had four daughters who prophesied, but according to the context this was at home and not in the public meeting of the church (Acts 21:8-9). These verses do not indicate the audience, however it is always important to compare scripture with scripture rather than taking isolated verses out of context. They may well have preached to other women. The apostle Paul's repeated injunction for women to be silent in the church, however, is the rule within the church meeting. Taking this isolated verse out of context is like using the example of Deborah as a woman judge as permission for women to rule over men (see Judg. 4:4-9). Isaiah 3:12, like other verses, however, indicates this was not the normal pattern, and rather indicated judgment of a people who did what was right in their own eyes (see Judg. 17:6 and Prov. 14:12, 16:25).

Man is the image and glory of God and woman is the glory of man, thus a man covering his head covers God's glory while a woman who represents man's glory with her head uncovered reveals man's glory. No flesh should glory in His presence (see 1 Cor. 1:29). You can see why this is much more than a trivial case of to cover or not to cover. The apostle Paul writes of the church, "To the intent that now unto the principalities and powers in heavenly places might be known by the church the manifold wisdom of God" (Eph. 3:10, also see 1 Peter 1:12).

Verses 8 and 9 speak of creation order, not equality, though equality does not mean that men and women were created to fulfill the same roles.

In verse 10, the word *power* should be understood as authority. Again, the reason is given: because of the angels.

In verses 11-12, the woman is of the man but man is by the woman—they are not independent but complementary.

Verse 13 poses another rhetorical question, not one we have the prerogative of answering, except by Scripture itself.

Verse 14 says that even nature itself teaches us that long hair on a man is a shame. God's order in nature does not change like the fads and fashions of man. Meanwhile in verse 15 we find that a woman's long hair is her glory, given to her as a covering or vesture/veil. If this is given to women as a glory then why should men have women's glory? Just as long hair on a man is a shame, short hair on a woman is also a shame (see verse 6).

Strong's Definition 4018 περιβολαιον peribolaion
from a presumed derivative of 4016; n
AV - covering 1, vesture 1; 2

A. a covering thrown around, a wrapper
B. a mantle
C. a veil

Ah, but one might say a woman's head covering is her hair. When we compare scripture with scripture, we see that although hair is a covering for her, it is not a covering of man's glory but is her glory. The word *covering* used in verse 15 is a different Greek word from that used in verses 6 and 7. In verses 6 and 7 the word katakalupto means "to cover up" or "veil oneself" (i.e., to put something on), whereas the word for *cover* in verse 15, peribolaion, means a veil, vesture, or mantle thrown around. The difference is that one is placed over the other. If this is not enough, we must remember verses 4 to 7, which clearly show that a woman's hair is not what is meant by the covering of verse 6. Again, why compare a shaven head to an uncovered head if they are the same thing?

Also, why would the apostle Paul go to such lengths to set this in order instead of just telling the women in a few words to keep their hair long? As I mentioned earlier, up until recently there was no dispute about this interpretation and history bears it out through the ample evidence of pictures depicting Christian women covering their heads. The fact is, it is God's glory that must be visible in the church meeting, not man's, because no flesh should glory in His presence (see 1 Cor. 1:29). Since woman's head represents man's glory, it must be covered, and so must her own glory (i.e., her hair).

This covering should not be a fashion statement, for that is another artificial glory. It should simply be a plain piece of fabric that covers her head and hair and does not enhance the woman's glory.

Verse 16 is the most misunderstood verse. Many claim that Paul is saying that churches of God have no such custom. If this was the case, why did he write half a chapter about it and why was he so emphatic about the importance of this doctrine, especially when he said in verse 2 and 3 that he praised them for following his teaching except on this point? The answer is simple: Have you not heard someone say, "There is no such hymn as 'How Great Thou Art'"? Perhaps even right after saying how beautiful the words and majestic the melody? The word *such* in verse 16 does not mean "non-existent" but rather that this custom is unlike any other in the churches of God—it is unique.

> Strong's Definition 5108 τοιουτος toioutos
> (including the other inflections)
> from 5104 and 3778; adj
> AV - such 39, such thing 11, such an one 8, like 1, such a man 1, such a fellow 1; 61
> 1. such as this, of this kind or sort.

Even if you take the "such" of verse 16 to mean that there was no *existing* custom in the churches of God, this couldn't mean that there was no such custom of head covering, after the apostle Paul had just forcefully set in order what was appropriate. It instead referred to a woman not covering her head. The apostle Paul was in effect saying, I've just presented all the evidence as to why a woman should veil herself in the public meeting of the church, don't be contentious about this, none of the churches of God allow such a custom of a woman praying or prophesying with her head unveiled. It would be like me saying, "You shouldn't cohabit before marriage, we have no such custom, neither the churches of God." Would anyone interpret this to mean that cohabitation is wrong but we have no such rule in the church and in fact allow it? No, you would interpret it to mean that we have no such custom of allowing cohabitation in any church of God. So too, the interpretation of this half chapter has for the most part been unanimous throughout history up until our "modern" era, that the woman should cover her head in the public meeting of the church and that the veil was something other than her own hair.

This is an important warning to men. As we look around and see the covered heads of our sisters in Christ, it is a solemn warning that our glory is covered and that no flesh should glory in God's presence.

THE SUFFICIENCY OF SCRIPTURE

This is why silent covered women are an essential part of the worship meeting and their obedience to this doctrine is as important as the men's participation in the open worship.

In spite of the controversy which has arisen in recent years over 1 Corinthians 11:1-16, one thing which should be clear from this text is the importance of God's creation order and His declaration of man's authority and headship. A woman who covers her head in the meeting of the saints, yet does not submit to her husband at home, has failed to understand the significance of the symbol she is instructed to wear. One of the passages used to justify women speaking or taking up positions of leadership in the church is, "There is neither Jew nor Greek, there is neither bond nor free, there is neither male nor female: for ye are all one in Christ Jesus" (Gal. 3:28). The context of that verse is clearly salvation and equality before the Lord, not roles, which is what headship is about. Man's abdication of his role as leader and the rule of feminism have to a very large extent obscured this important doctrine and our families, churches and nations are reaping the consequences.

In today's modern meetings, instead of the world thinking that the church's spiritual symbols are foolishness (see 1 Cor. 2:14), they see familiarity and similarity. Instead of God's glory they see man's glory. Instead of the cross's foolishness they see man's wisdom. If we are to glorify God and not the flesh, then our worship meetings should be such that man's glory is covered and God's is uncovered. The meeting should be such that if the Lord Jesus Christ stood among us as pictured in the apostle John's vision on the isle of Patmos, we would not be ashamed (see Rev. 1:9-18).

4.5 Tithing vs Freewill Offering

Tithing, or contributing a tenth part of the increase of one's produce was the means by which the children of Israel supplied for the provision of the priests and their families (Lev. 27:30-34; Num. 18:26-31; 2 Chr. 31:5-19; Neh. 10:38-39; Mal. 3:8-10; Mat. 23:23; Luke 11:42; Heb. 7:5-28.) There was also a special tithe to be used for the family's own rejoicing before the Lord at the physical location where the Lord placed His name (the physical temple). (Deut. 14:22-29, cp Deut 12:5-7 and John 4:21.)

Since this earthly priesthood ceased at the crucifixion of the Lord Jesus, when the veil of the temple was torn in two (Mat. 27:51), tithing as under the old covenant is not directly applicable. It was rather replaced with something much more profound. We are all now a royal priesthood and are bodies the temple of the living God (1 Pet. 2:9; 1 Cor 6:19-20, 2 Cor 16:16; John 4:21-24.) Rather than a tenth, all of what we are and own belongs to the Lord (Rom. 12:1; 1 Pet. 2:5; 1 Chron. 29:14b; 1 Cor. 7:22; Rom. 7:4, 8:9-14).

Some have argued that since tithing is first mentioned before the Levitical priesthood when Abraham gave tithes to Melchizedek (Gen. 14:20), that it predates the Mosaic covenant and thus is not terminated by its fulfilment in Christ. Though Melchizedek is a type of the Lord Jesus Christ (Ps. 110:4; Heb. 7:1-28), and the bread and the wine which he brought forth prefigured the Lord's supper, the Lord did not command tithing in His ministry but did command the breaking of bread in remembrance of Himself (Mat. 26:26; 1 Cor. 11:23-30.) Some may cite Matthew 23:23 and Luke 11:42 as evidence that the Lord sanctioned the continuation of the tithe. This tithe however referred to the Levitical tithe which only had relevance when there was a Levitical priesthood and temple, both of which ceased at the Lord's crucifixion. I say relevance because the usage of these tithes was specifically outlined, being mostly for the upkeep of the priesthood and their families, and since there is no longer a physical temple or Levitical priesthood, it would require assumption on our part to correctly appropriate any tithe now. It should be noted that Abraham was not commanded to give a tenth of the spoil to Melchizedek but willingly gave it, which concurs with the idea of freewill offerings outside the context of the Mosaic law. We should not assume that the use of the word tithe in Genesis 14:20 Is the same thing as the Levitical tithe, since the Levitical priesthood had not yet been established nor its commands revealed, just like the reference to the word baptism does not automatically mean water baptism (e.g. 1 Cor. 10:2, 12:13). Abraham's tithe referred merely to the amount he willingly gave, i.e. a tenth, rather than the special command given to the children of Israel to tithe, which was also a tenth. In any case, if you interpret Scripture to imply the continuance of the tithe, well and good for the Lord's work. I don't want to be side-tracked as to the relevance of tithing so much as bring the Christian back to the understanding that the Lord's work is to be financed by His people, regardless of whether it be by commanded tithe or freewill offering.

It is important to be reminded that it is not merely the dollars that count when giving to God but the motive and faith with which it is given.

> *And Jesus sat over against the treasury, and beheld how the people cast money into the treasury: and many that were rich cast in much. And there came a certain poor widow, and she threw in two mites, which make a farthing. And he called unto him his disciples, and saith unto them, Verily I say unto you, That this poor widow hath cast more in, than all they which have cast into the treasury: For all they did cast in of their abundance; but she of her want did cast in all that she had, even all her living.*
> *(Mark 12:41-44)*

> *Now concerning the collection for the saints, as I have given order to the churches of Galatia, even so do ye. Upon the first day of the week let every one of you lay by him in store, as God hath prospered him, that there be no gatherings when I come. And when I come, whomsoever ye shall approve by your letters, them will I send to bring your liberality unto Jerusalem.*
> *(1 Cor. 16:1-3)*

> *But this I say, He which soweth sparingly shall reap also sparingly; and he which soweth bountifully shall reap also bountifully. Every man according as he purposeth in his heart, so let him give; not grudgingly, or of necessity: for God loveth a cheerful giver.*
> *(2 Cor. 9:6-7)*

REVIVAL IN THE CHURCH

As we have therefore opportunity, let us do good unto all men, especially unto them who are of the household of faith.
(Gal. 6:10; also see Rom. 12:11-13, 15:25-27)

Let the elders that rule well be counted worthy of double honour, especially they who labour in the word and doctrine. For the scripture saith, Thou shalt not muzzle the ox that treadeth out the corn. And, The labourer is worthy of his reward.
(1 Tim. 5:17-18. Also see 1 Cor. 9:13-14)

Honour the LORD with thy substance, and with the firstfruits of all thine increase: So shall thy barns be filled with plenty, and thy presses shall burst out with new wine.
(Proverbs 3:9-10)

Note that there was no paid pastoral position described in the New Testament local church, however if elders or other mature believers dedicated themselves to the labour of preaching, such that they were unable to also support themselves via other paid labour, the assembly was to support such workers.
(1 Tim. 5:17-18; 1 Cor. 9:13-14)

I do not think the Apostle Paul envisaged that the freewill offering of a heart overflowing with gratitude for one's unmerited salvation would be less generous than that which was tithed by commandment under the old covenant. Indeed if we truly took this seriously, there would be no believer in need anywhere, nor would there be any workers struggling to keep their various ministries or charities afloat as is the case in the current climate of selfish materialism. Revival in the church will only come when Christians put the gospel's work before personal peace and affluence. Money talks, and where we place our physical riches says a lot about our priorities for God's work. Yes, we absolutely must provide for our own as already discussed, and a good man leaves an inheritance to his children's children (see Prov. 13:22,

2 Cor. 14:12b, 1 Tim. 5:8), but even if all Christians willingly gave at least 10 percent of their increase to the Lord's work, much could be done to increase the potency of the church's salt and light in the community. Being salt and light is more than just moral excellence, it is also about setting an example to the unbelieving world in family relationships, children's education as well as science, medicine, literature, mathematics, and every other field under God as I discussed earlier. One might argue that God can work through people without money, but as we have learned, God gives people the power to get wealth for a purpose: to establish His covenant or to take dominion of the world for His glory (see Deut. 8:18, Gen. 1:28, Matt. 28:18-20). There are still physical costs to doing God's physical work.

While the following verses were spoken in the context of the physical house of God, yet the practical principles can surely be applied to the neglect of the work of the Lord today:

> *Now therefore thus saith the LORD of hosts; Consider your ways. Ye have sown much, and bring in little; ye eat, but ye have not enough; ye drink, but ye are not filled with drink; ye clothe you, but there is none warm; and he that earneth wages earneth wages to put it into a bag with holes. Thus saith the LORD of hosts; Consider your ways. Go up to the mountain, and bring wood, and build the house; and I will take pleasure in it, and I will be glorified, saith the LORD. Ye looked for much, and, lo it came to little; and when ye brought it home, I did blow upon it. Why? saith the LORD of hosts. Because of mine house that is waste, and ye run every man unto his own house.*
>
> (Hag. 2:5-9)

4.6 Hospitality

Hospitality in the church today is becoming a lost art. A young family visiting our church once told us when we invited them for a meal that it was the first time in ten years that anyone had asked them for a meal. I too could concur as in the many years of attending church, there were really only a handful of families who offered us hospitality. This is truly a sad indictment on the household of faith.

There are two kinds of hospitality in which God's church is commanded to engage—one to members of the household of faith and the second to strangers. The first is described in the following three passages:

A bishop then must be blameless, the husband of one wife, vigilant, sober, of good behaviour, given to hospitality, apt to teach.
(1 Tim. 3:2)

For a bishop must be blameless, as the steward of God; not selfwilled, not soon angry, not given to wine, no striker, not given to filthy lucre; But a lover of hospitality, a lover of good men, sober, just, holy, temperate.
(Titus 1:7-8)

Use hospitality one to another without grudging.
(1 Peter 4:9)

Strong's Definition 5382 φιλοξενος philoxenos
from 5384 and 3581; adj
AV-given to hospitality 1, lover of hospitality 1, use hospitality 1; 3
1. hospitable, generous to guests

The second, to strangers, is described in the following verse:

Distributing to the necessity of saints; given to hospitality.
(Rom. 12:13)

Strong's Definition 5381 φιλοξενια philoxenia
from 5382; n f
AV-hospitality 1, lover of strangers 1; 2
1. love to strangers, hospitality

The first form of hospitality is between believers and is to edify and show practical love to one another. The second is outreach to unbelievers, to bring them into our homes to share with them the Lord Jesus Christ's glorious gospel and to show them God's way through our families' testimonies.

It is crucial to point out also that while hospitality is for all believers, it is not for all believers at all times of their lives. There are seasons in which illness, the care of children, or focusing on getting one's house in order when a family may not be able to host visitors. "To every thing there is a season, and a time to every purpose under the heaven" (Ecc. 3:1). Those who are able should give due diligence to this lost art in the church today without expectation of reciprocation. They should also be conscious of those with special needs, such as the elderly, infirmed, families with young children, visitors, traveling preachers or missionaries, etc. Elders particularly should ensure that they do not neglect this important function of the church nor neglect to encourage those who are able to fulfill this ministry.

> *Then said he also to him that bade him, When thou makest a dinner or a supper, call not thy friends, nor thy brethren, neither thy kinsmen, nor thy rich neighbours; lest they also bid thee again, and a recompence be made thee. But when thou makest a feast, call the poor, the maimed, the lame, the blind: And thou shalt be blessed; for they cannot recompense thee: for thou shalt be recompensed at the resurrection of the just.*
> (Luke 14:12-14)

With the encouragement to hospitality there also comes a warning: "Withdraw thy foot from thy neighbor's house; lest he be weary of thee, and so hate thee" (Prov. 25:17). The apostle Paul also warns us, "And withal they learn to be idle, wandering about from house to house; and not only idle, but tattlers also and busybodies, speaking things which they ought not" (1 Tim. 5:13). This is generally not an issue in today's churches where hospitality is neglected, but if this practice is revived, these warnings become applicable. Each family is still its own entity and needs space to fulfill its God-given functions. Revival, though, truly has been greatest when believers share in each other's lives outside the Lord's Day worship meeting.

4.7 How Is the Church to Be Kept Pure?

Yet another command that has largely gone by the way in today's church, and which must be rediscovered if we want revival, is the command to hold believers accountable for their behavior, to discipline wayward believers, and to publicly address issues so others are warned. It is, of course, important to follow the scriptural pattern for this process—too often this does not occur.

> *Moreover if thy brother shall trespass against thee, go and tell him his fault between thee and him alone: if he shall hear thee, thou hast gained thy brother. But if he will not hear thee, then take with thee one or two more, that in the mouth of two or three witnesses every word may be established. And if he shall neglect to hear them, tell it unto the church: but if he neglect to hear the church, let him be unto thee as an heathen man and a publican. Verily I say unto you, Whatsoever ye shall bind on earth shall be bound in heaven: and whatsoever ye shall loose on earth shall be loosed in heaven.*
>
> (Matt. 18:15-18)

> *Them that sin rebuke before all, that others also may fear.*
>
> (1 Tim. 5:20)

> *But when I saw that they walked not uprightly according to the truth of the Gospel, I said unto Peter before them all.*
>
> (Gal. 2:14)

> *It is reported commonly that there is fornication among you, and such fornication as is not so much as named among the Gentiles, that one should have his father's wife. And ye are puffed up, and have not rather mourned, that he that hath done this deed might be taken away from among you. ... But now I have written unto you not to keep company, if any man that is called a brother be a fornicator, or covetous, or an idolater,*

or a railer, or a drunkard, or an extortioner; with such an one no not to eat. For what have I to do to judge them also that are without? do not ye judge them that are within?

(1 Cor. 5:1-2, 11-12)

Discipline's goal is always to bring the disciplined to repentance, not apostasy.

One might ask why it really matters if we dot our i's and cross our t's when it comes to how we run our personal, family, or church lives. Can't revival happen if we pray a lot, love God, and love others? What does it mean to love God according to God's own Word? Is it a warm, fuzzy feeling of happiness? Is it simply getting contentment from doing good works? Is it singing emotional songs? Let the Scriptures speak for themselves:

The Lord Jesus said, "If ye love me, keep my commandments."

(John 14:15)

For this is the love of God, that we keep his commandments: and his commandments are not grievous.

(1 John 5:3)

The prophet Samuel said, "Hath the LORD as great delight in burnt offerings and sacrifices, as in obeying the voice of the LORD? Behold, to obey is better than sacrifice, and to hearken than the fat of rams."

(1 Sam. 15:22)

The apostle Paul wrote to Timothy, "That thou mayest know how thou oughtest to behave thyself in the house of God, which is the church of the living God, the pillar and ground of the truth."

(1 Tim. 3:15)

For God is not the author of confusion, but of peace, as in all churches of the saints.

(1 Cor. 14:33)

REVIVAL IN THE CHURCH

What does it mean to love others? Is it simply tolerating each other's carnality? Again, let the Scriptures speak for themselves:

Charity suffereth long, and is kind; charity envieth not; charity vaunteth not itself, is not puffed up, Doth not behave itself unseemly, seeketh not her own, is not easily provoked, thinketh no evil; Rejoiceth not in iniquity, but rejoiceth in the truth Beareth all things, believeth all things, hopeth all things, endureth all things.

(1 Cor. 13:4-7)

While much is preached on this most important passage, it is good to remember that kindness is best practiced on those who are unkind, patience on those who are impatient, and not being easily provoked when there is much provocation against you. Love is best learned in the family and in the local church, yet how quickly Christians move on when they are tested in any of these areas in which we must demonstrate love! The apostle Paul exhorts Timothy to "be thou an example of the believers ... in charity" (1 Tim. 4:12).

We must also realize that an important aspect of love and life is the aspect of correction.

For the commandment is a lamp; and the law is light; and reproofs of instruction are the way of life.

(Prov. 6:23)

God corrects us (see Ps. 89:30-33, 94:12; Prov. 3:11; Deut. 8:5; 1 Cor. 11:32; Heb. 13:6-11), the state bears the sword to correct lawbreakers (see Rom. 13:3-5), we are to correct our children, as we saw in the previous chapter, and there is to be correction in the local church.

Preach the word; be instant in season, out of season; reprove, rebuke, exhort with all longsuffering and doctrine.

(2 Tim. 4:2)

THE SUFFICIENCY OF SCRIPTURE

This witness is true. Wherefore rebuke them sharply, that they may be sound in the faith.

(Titus 1:13)

These things speak, and exhort, and rebuke with all authority. Let no man despise thee.

(Titus 2:15)

For there are many unruly and vain talkers and deceivers, specially they of the circumcision: Whose mouths must be stopped, who subvert whole houses, teaching things which they ought not, for filthy lucre's sake.

(Titus 1:10-11)

Ephesians 4:15 tells us to speak the truth in love. Yes, loving others has a very practical aspect of correction just as God chastens those who disobey His Word, as I have already discussed. The Lord Jesus sanctifies, cleanses, and keeps His church pure by the washing of the water of the Word, as described in Ephesians 5:26. This is achieved by the exercise of biblical church discipline through the application of the doctrine of the sufficiency of Scripture.

The importance of obedience, faith, works, and love for the Christian cannot be understated. Faith without works is dead (see James 2:18-26), works without love is a noisy gong (see 1 Cor. 13:1-3), and obedience must always come before the sacrifice of works (see 1 Sam. 15:22). We must be so careful not to disobey God in our zeal to serve him in some sacrificial work. Understanding the priority of these three Christian virtues is paramount to revival in our personal lives, our families, and the local church. We would do well to heed the wise words of King Artaxerxes when he wrote, "Whatsoever is commanded by the God of heaven, let it be diligently done for the house of the God of heaven: for why should there be wrath against the realm of the king and his sons?" (Ezra 7:23).

REVIVAL IN THE CHURCH

4.8 What Is the Local Church's Jurisdiction?

A local church only has jurisdiction over those who are "within," according to 1 Corinthians 5:11-12. This implies that a local church has a membership and is borne out by the following verses:

And so were the churches established in the faith, and increased in number daily. (Acts 16:5)
(Each church had a known number.)

Let not a widow be taken into the number under threescore years old, having been the wife of one man. (1 Tim. 5:9)
("Take into the number" implies that there is a known number.)

Else when thou shalt bless with the spirit, how shall he that occupieth the room of the unlearned say Amen at thy giving of thanks, seeing he understandeth not what thou sayest? (1 Cor. 14:16)
("The room of the unlearned" implies a place where unbelievers observed the meeting's proceedings.)

It is also obvious that one cannot be separated for discipline if there is no concept of membership and accountability. It appears from Matthew 16:19 and 18:19 that each local church is independent of other local churches and that God upholds what one binds on earth in terms of discipline or freedom.

The church is a separate entity from the family and is never given the role of educating one's children. This is borne out by Ephesians 6:4, where the father is commanded to educate his children, as I already discussed. The church and the family are complementary rather than conflicting. The rod is given to the father to train his children, the sword of God's Word is given to the church to train its members, and the physical sword is given to the state to uphold God's law in the nation (see Rom. 13:1-7). The Scriptures govern the jurisdiction of each of these entities and each of these entities are complementary rather than conflicting.

Today we live in a statist society that has taken over the jurisdiction of the family and church as well. It was never the state's role to provide for widows, orphans, the poor, the elderly, or the infirmed. As Christians we must stand our ground and stop giving over our role to the state, lest we end up like the Israelites who didn't even have the power to sharpen their own swords but had to go to the Philistines to do so (see 1 Sam. 13:19-22). This can be achieved (as I already discussed in section 4.5) through the appropriation of believers' pooled free-will offerings.

4.9 The Sabbath vs The Lord's Day

Yet another confusion in the church today is the topic of the Sabbath. On the one hand we have those who worship on the seventh day known as Sabbath Keepers, and on the other we have those who claim that the first day of the week is the Christian Sabbath. Let us go to the Scriptures to see the relevance of the Sabbath today.

4.9.1 THE SABBATH DECLARED

> *And on the seventh day God ended his work which he had made; and he rested on the seventh day from all his work which he had made. And God blessed the seventh day, and sanctified it: because that in it he had rested from all his work which God created and made.*
>
> *(Genesis 2:2-3)*

God declares the Sabbath day as holy and sanctified, for in it He rested. He does not command anyone else to do likewise here.

4.9.2 THE SABBATH CODIFIED IN THE MOSAIC LAW

> *Remember the sabbath day, to keep it holy. Six days shalt thou labour, and do all thy work: But the seventh day is the sabbath of the LORD thy God: in it thou shalt not do any work, thou, nor thy son, nor thy daughter, thy manservant, nor thy maidservant, nor thy cattle, nor thy stranger that is within thy gates: For in six days the LORD made heaven and earth,*

> *the sea, and all that in them is, and rested the seventh day: wherefore the LORD blessed the sabbath day, and hallowed it.*
>
> *(Exod. 20:8-11)*

> *Wherefore the children of Israel shall keep the sabbath, to observe the sabbath throughout their generations, for a perpetual covenant.*
>
> *(Exod. 31:16)*

> *And remember that thou wast a servant in the land of Egypt, and that the LORD thy God brought thee out thence through a mighty hand and by a stretched out arm: therefore the LORD thy God commanded thee to keep the sabbath day.*
>
> *(Deut. 5:15)*

The "therefore" in the above verse is very important. It tells us why God gave the Sabbath as a sign to the children of Israel, namely because of how He rescued them from under the yoke of the Egyptians.

4.9.3 The Principle of Rest and Delight in the Lord

> *Six days thou shalt labour, and do all thy work: But the seventh day is the sabbath of the LORD thy God: in it thou shalt not do any work, thou, nor thy son, nor thy daughter, nor thy manservant, nor thy maidservant, nor thine ox, nor thine ass, nor any of thy cattle, nor thy stranger that is within thy gates; that thy manservant and thy maidservant may rest as well as thou.*
>
> *(Deut. 5:13-14)*

> *If thou turn away thy foot from the sabbath, from doing thy pleasure on my holy day; and call the sabbath a delight, the holy of the LORD, honourable; and shalt honour him, not doing thine own ways, nor finding thine own pleasure, nor speaking thine own words: Then shalt thou delight thyself in the LORD; and I will cause thee to ride upon the high places of the earth, and feed thee with the heritage of Jacob thy father: for the mouth of the LORD hath spoken it.*
>
> *(Isa. 58:13-14)*

THE SUFFICIENCY OF SCRIPTURE

Even strangers of the house of Israel were to honour the Sabbath and benefit from the declared rest.

(Isa. 56:6-7)

And he said unto them, The sabbath was made for man, and not man for the sabbath: Therefore the Son of man is Lord also of the sabbath.

(Mark 2:27-28)

4.9.4 PAUL'S TEACHING ON THE SABBATH

Let no man therefore judge you in meat, or in drink, or in respect of an holyday, or of the new moon, or of the sabbath days: Which are a shadow of things to come; but the body is of Christ.

(Colossians 2:16-17)

One man esteemeth one day above another: another esteemeth every day alike. Let every man be fully persuaded in his own mind. He that regardeth the day, regardeth it unto the Lord; and he that regardeth not the day, to the Lord he doth not regard it.

(Romans 14:5-6a)

The writer of Hebrews says the following.

Let us therefore fear, lest, a promise being left us of entering into his rest, any of you should seem to come short of it. For unto us was the gospel preached, as well as unto them: but the word preached did not profit them, not being mixed with faith in them that heard it. For we which have believed do enter into rest, as he said, As I have sworn in my wrath, if they shall enter into my rest: although the works were finished from the foundation of the world. For he spake in a certain place of the seventh day on this wise, And God did rest the seventh day from all his works. And in this place again, If they shall enter into my rest. Seeing therefore it remaineth that some must enter therein, and they to whom it was first preached entered not in because of unbelief: Again, he limiteth a certain day, saying in David, To day, after so long a time; as it is said, To day if ye will hear his voice, harden not your hearts. For if Jesus (Joshua) had given them rest, then would he not afterward have spoken of another day.

There remaineth therefore a rest to the people of God. For he that is entered into his rest, he also hath ceased from his own works, as God did from his.
(Heb. 4:1-10)

The Apostle Paul never exhorted the gentile Christians to keep the Sabbath. On the contrary, he taught the church to not judge one another as to whether they observed any Sabbaths as there were more Sabbaths than simply the seventh day of the week. He did not teach that the church replaced Israel but on the contrary distinguished the three groups in his teachings when he said, "Give none offence, neither to the Jews, nor to the Gentiles, nor to the church of God" (1 Cor. 10:32.) The Apostle Paul taught us that the Sabbath (among other pictures) is a shadow of heavenly things to come.
(Col 2:17; Heb. 4:1-10)

The Apostle Paul provides us the most church doctrine out of all of the new testament authors. Indeed without his epistles we would know very little about the operation of the new testament church. It is thus significant that the keeping of the Sabbath is the only commandment which the Apostle Paul does not affirm in his church doctrine (and neither does any other New Testament writer).

Commandment	Reference in Mosaic Law	Reference in Paul's Church Epistles
+ 1 & 2 Idolatry	Ex. 20:3-5	Gal. 5:20; 1 Cor. 6:9; 1 Cor. 10:7, 16:22, 8:4-12, 10:19-31
+ 3 Blasphemy	Ex. 20:7	Titus 2:5; 1 Tim. 1:20
- 4 Keeping of Sabbath	Ex. 20:8-11	Col. 2:16-17; Heb. 4:9-10; Rom. 14:5-6
+ 5 Honouring parents	Ex. 20:12	Eph. 6:2
+ 6 Murder	Ex. 20:13	Gal. 5:21
+ 7 Adultery	Ex. 20:14	Gal. 5:19
+ 8 Theft	Ex. 20:15	Rom. 13:9; Eph. 4:28
+ 9 Bearing false witness	Ex. 20:16	Rom. 13:9
+ 10 Covetousness	Ex. 20:17	Rom 1:29, 13:9; Eph. 5:3; Col. 3:5

THE SUFFICIENCY OF SCRIPTURE

4.9.5 THE EARLY CHURCH MET ON THE FIRST DAY OF THE WEEK

And upon the first day of the week, when the disciples came together to break bread, Paul preached unto them, ready to depart on the morrow; and continued his speech until midnight.

(Acts 20:7)

Upon the first day of the week let every one of you lay by him in store, as God hath prospered him, that there be no gatherings when I come.

(1 Cor. 16:2)

I was in the Spirit on the Lord's day, and heard behind me a great voice, as of a trumpet.

(Rev. 1:10)

Early Christians met not on the Sabbath but on the first day of the week, presumably to celebrate Christ's resurrection. It appears from Revelation 1:10 that this became known as The Lord's Day.

4.9.6 PRINCIPLES FOR THE CHURCH

What we learn then are the following principles:

1. The principle of rest for one holy day of the week was given prior to the Mosaic law, (Gen. 2:2-3).
2. While the church is not under the Mosaic law, we must learn from the principles which the Mosaic law was intended to teach the children of Israel (Deut. 4:5-10). While we are not directly subject to the penalty of breaking the Sabbath both because it was a sign between the children of Israel and God (Exod. 31:16) and because nowhere is the church described as having replaced Israel (1 Cor. 10:32), yet, one day of rest and reflection on the Lord is both beneficial and demonstrated by practise in the early church albeit on the first day of the week rather than

the seventh. Just as we are not commanded to give our fields rest for one year every seven, we would do well to learn from the practicality of this law given to the children of Israel in our own farming practises, just as we would do well to rest one day a week from our regular labours in order to come together to worship the Lord as His body.

3. The church is taught that Sabbaths (among other ordinances) are a shadow of heavenly things and not the ends in themselves (Col. 2:16-17; Heb. 4:1-10, Rom. 14:5-6.) We are clearly taught that the spiritual aspect of the Sabbath rest is fulfilled in Christ. While we would do well to recognize the sensibility of a physical day of rest one day a week, we should not judge those who regard all days alike (Rom. 14:5-6.) We should however acknowledge that the early church treated the first day of the week as holy unto the Lord, coming together to break bread and fellowship. It is apparent from history that this first day, the Lord's day, was their day of rest from their other labours. This is abundantly clear in every culture based on Biblical values where we have had, up until very recently, a maximum of a six day working week, something foreign in other cultures.

4.10 He That Hath an Ear, Let Him Hear What the Spirit Saith unto the Churches

In considering revival in the church, it would be remiss of us not to consider what the Head of the church, the Lord Jesus Christ, had to say about the seven churches in Revelation 2 and 3. While these churches were literal, historical churches, they are also representative of the types of churches throughout history. The warnings they were given must be heeded if we want to see revival. If we do not heed these warnings, the death of a local church might result because the Lord who walks among the candlesticks removes its testimony by extinguishing its light. This section is by no means comprehensive but should serve as a starting point for examining the vital lessons we must learn from these seven literal, yet representative, churches.

The church at Ephesus (see Rev. 2:1-7) was characterized by works, endurance, diligent labor, and abhorrence of evil. They also demonstrated discernment between the true and false apostle. In a sense they sound much like the fundamental churches of today that speak against apostasy. Their big problem, from which they had to repent to save themselves, however, was leaving their first love (see Rev. 2:1-6). In spite of their good fruit, the leaving of their first love was enough for the dire warning to repent, lest all their good virtues be worthless.

The church at Smyrna (see Rev. 2:8-11) was characterized by works, tribulation, and physical poverty, yet the Lord described them as rich. The Lord speaks of the blasphemy of those who claim to be Jews when instead they are the synagogue of Satan. Although this had specific application to that local church, I think the application can be made today for those who claim that the church has replaced God's chosen people but in truth will never replace the apple of His eye (see Zech. 2:8, Jer. 31:35-37, Rom. 11). The Lord warns them of the pending tribulation but encourages their hearts with the promise of the reward of the crown of life for endurance. Smyrna is one of only two churches that are not told to repent. This demonstrates something that has proven throughout history to be true, namely that persecution is an environment in which fruit and revival flourish. Persecution casts us in utter dependence on God.

The church at Pergamos (see Rev. 2:12:17) was also characterized by works and loyalty to the Lord's name, even though it was situated in the heart of Satan's territory. The Lord, however, begins with a reminder of that great two-edged sword of His Word. He warns them to repent of their tolerance of false doctrine, a departure from His Word. The false doctrines to which some of them held were Balaam and that of the Nicolaitans.

The doctrine of Balaam was subtle. Rather than an outright contradiction of established truths, the doctrine of Balaam lead people astray through an indirect appeal to their carnality so they would fall of their own accord as they were enticed by their own lusts (see James 1:13-14, 4:1-6). Balaam taught Balac to cast a stumbling block before the Children of Israel (see Num. 31:16). Churches today cast stumbling blocks before God's people by using worldly methods and profaning God's scriptural commands, patterns, and precepts in their methodology. They cast stumbling blocks before God's people by condoning what God hates, teaching tolerance and acceptance of sin rather than repentance from it. They cast stumbling blocks before God's people when they do not speak against the surrounding cultural influences but rather invite them into their churches. Then when God's people see their teachers condone and accept what God hates, even arguing away scriptural teaching on a matter, the flock are lead astray as they drown in the surrounding culture, pulled under the waves by the very ones who should be setting the example (see Heb. 13:17, 1 Pet. 5:2-3). The reports of churches in which idolatry and fornication are rife are staggering beyond belief, but more unbelievable is the leadership's tolerance and even condoning of such behavior!

I already addressed the doctrine of the Nicolaitans, that of rule by force of a clergy over laity, so I won't elaborate on that again here.

The church of Thyatira (see Rev. 2:18-29) was known for its works, charity, service, faith, and patience. The great sin of this church was their allowance of a woman who called herself a prophetess to teach and seduce His servants. Her teaching was liberal and, again, idolatry and fornication both were accepted and condoned. This is so typical of many churches today. It is no accident that the Lord drew attention to the woman leading His flock. It is simply not tolerable.

The difference between the churches of Thyatira and Pergamos was leadership. Both taught doctrine that lead to fornication and idolatry, but the church of Thyatira was one step further in apostasy, allowing a woman to usurp authority over the man. The Lord refers to this doctrine as "the depths of Satan" (see Rev. 2:24) so it cannot be underestimated in its severity (see Isa. 3:12, 1 Tim. 2:12, 1 Cor. 14:34-35). In Thyatira there was a remnant who were faithful to God's Word and did not agree with the doctrine being taught.

Interestingly, both the churches at Ephesus and Thyatira were praised for their great works, faith, and patience. Their sin, however, overshadowed their works, which is a solemn reminder that departure from our first love or departure from the sufficiency of Scripture, unless repented, will lead to the removal of that church's candlestick in spite of all its good fruit. There is no room for pride if, for instance, we come from a church like that of Ephesus. When considering a church like that of Thyatira, we, like they, will lose our lamp stand of testimony if we do not repent and rekindle our first love.

The church in Sardis (see Rev. 3:1-6) had the reputation for being vibrant and alive yet the Lord said it was almost dead. Even in Sardis as in Thyatira there was a remnant of true believers (a few names) who were faithful to God's Word. We get the impression that this church was so carnal and deceived that the Lord didn't even elaborate on the sins needing repentance.

The church at Philadelphia (see Rev. 3:7-13), like Smyrna, had little physical strength but great spiritual fortitude. Their great spiritual strength was their close adherence to God's Word and reverence to the Lord's name. Not denying the Lord's name means much more than denying His deity. Denying His name is denying all His name represents, His character, and His Word. Good works also characterized the church at Philadelphia. From the statement that the Lord is the one who opens and closes doors, it appears they had a lot of opposition and were encouraged that God Himself had given them the opportunity to be faithful and fruitful in their work. He reminded them, in effect, that He is the one building His church in spite of the opposition (see Matt. 16:18) through their faithful adherence to His Word and love of His name. The reference to the false Jews and the pronouncement that those liars will know that the Lord loves churches who discern their falsehood tells us much of

God's heart for the true Jewish people. The church at Philadelphia is the other church for which the Lord had no rebuke. It is interesting to note that both the churches at Smyrna and Philadelphia discerned God's heart for the Jew and both had no rebuke.

In both the sections on Smyrna and Philadelphia, I mentioned the error of replacement theology where people teach that the church has replaced the Jewish nation, becoming spiritual Israel. It is clear from Romans 11 that the church on earth is a temporal parenthetical arrangement and that the Lord will again deal with the nation of Israel. The Lord through His servant Jeremiah makes it clear that the Jewish people will not cease to be a physical nation before Him as long as the ordinances of heaven remain. He said, "Thus saith the LORD, which giveth the sun for a light by day, and the ordinances of the moon and of the stars for a light by night, which divideth the sea when the waves thereof roar; The LORD of hosts is his name: If those ordinances depart from before me, saith the LORD, then the seed of Israel also shall cease from being a nation before me for ever. Thus saith the LORD; If heaven above can be measured, and the foundations of the earth searched out beneath, I will also cast off all the seed of Israel for all that they have done, saith the LORD" (Jer. 31:35-37). He also said through His servant Zechariah, "For thus saith the LORD of hosts; After the glory hath he sent me unto the nations which spoiled you: for he that toucheth you toucheth the apple of his eye" (Zech. 2:8).

The apostle Paul also maintains this distinction between the three groups when he says, "Give none offence, neither to the Jews, nor to the Gentiles, nor to the church of God" (1 Cor. 10:32). The apostle Paul makes God's plan for physical Israel clear in Romans 11. He says, "For I would not, brethren, that ye should be ignorant of this mystery, lest ye should be wise in your own conceits; that blindness in part is happened to Israel, until the fulness of the Gentiles be come in" (Rom. 11:25). The Lord's promise to bless those who bless Israel and curse those who curse Israel made to Abraham and his physical seed still stands (see Gen. 12:3). This is critical because Israel as a nation continues to be in the news, usually the target of Islamic hatred, and how we as other nations treat her will either result in national blessing or national judgment as we defend her or defend her enemies. We will never have national revival while we curse the apple of God's eye.

The church at Laodicea (see Rev. 3:14-22) is characterized by total apostasy. Their works are lukewarm yet they have the reputation, like the church at Sardis, of being vibrant and alive. The Lord's warning is dire, He says, "Because thou sayest, I am rich, and increased with goods, and have need of nothing; and knowest not that thou art wretched, and miserable, and poor, and blind, and naked" (Rev. 3:17). They are totally deceived into thinking they have what really counts yet they have nothing. They are the antithesis of the church at Smyrna.

What we learn from these seven churches is that the foundation of a good church depends on the sufficiency of Scripture and a deep love for the Lord Jesus Christ, tempered with tribulation, endurance, and good works. The downfall was compromise of His Word, complacency, lack of love for the Lord, and materialism. Let's take heed of these things lest the Lord stand outside our churches, knocking patiently for someone—one of the faithful few names—to open up and let Him in. Over and over in Revelation—seven times—the Lord pleads with us, "He that hath an ear, let him hear what the Spirit saith unto the churches" (2:7, 2:11, 2:17, 2:29, 3:6, 3:13, 3:22).

As many as I love, I rebuke and chasten: be zealous therefore, and repent. Behold, I stand at the door, and knock: if any man hear my voice, and open the door, I will come in to him, and will sup with him, and he with me. To him that overcometh will I grant to sit with me in my throne, even as I also overcame, and am set down with my Father in his throne. He that hath an ear, let him hear what the Spirit saith unto the churches.

(Rev. 3:19-22)

Chapter 5

REVIVING CHRISTIAN INFLUENCE IN THE GOVERNING OF THE NATION

LIKE MANY ISSUES in the church today, Christians are divided over whether we should be involved in the civil sphere. At one end of the scale we are taught that Christians should not be involved at all in any form of worldly governance, and at the other, men have tried to convert a nation by making Christianity the national religion. In this chapter I appeal to the commands, patterns and principles of Scripture to speak for themselves. While one's eschatological view of end times seems to determine which camp one belongs to, I encourage you to think outside the mold you may have been forced into by this view and instead look at Scripture alone to know God's heart on this vitally important matter. For whether we anticipate the Lord returning today or in a thousand years, the principle of occupying until He comes as salt and light, retarding the effects of moral decay in society, should be the same. After all, besides the transformation of salvation accomplished by the preaching of the gospel, the Holy Spirit also works through the indwelling of Christians in the world to restrain evil amongst the unbelieving. (2 Thes. 2:7; Rom. 13:3-4.)

One of the major reasons why Western civilization became so prosperous—which led to the freedoms we enjoyed at the height of its

THE SUFFICIENCY OF SCRIPTURE

zenith—was that its laws were taken directly from the Holy Scriptures. England, Australia, and the U.S. in particular initially had legal systems rooted in biblical law—not just the Ten Commandments, but in biblical wisdom gleaned from the entire counsel of the only wise God. Such principles undergirded property law, family law, financial law, business law, etc.

The founders of these nations realized that God's law was essential to the nations' prosperity, and not just to Christians or to govern worship. Founding a nation upon God's law did not make the citizens Christians, but it did create a culture conducive to the spread of the gospel and which helped to restrain evil through this salt and light in governance. To understand the critical importance of a nation having a Judeo-Christian foundation, one only need compare the freedom and prosperity of such nations at the height of their respect for Christianity to the pagan nations around them in terms of the resultant value systems which were manifested in their culture.[66] We have taken for granted the ease at which we have been able to run a business because we could generally trust the word of a fellow citizen. We expected the law to uphold justice and be free of corruption which meant there was relative safety on our streets after dark. Flagrant immorality such as open homosexuality, prostitution, blatant promiscuity and easy divorce was shunned by society generally and condemned by the government. We believed the truthfulness of news reporters and even the research results of scientists. This is seldom the case in a nation not founded upon such Christian values as truth. In our own nation which now treats Christianity as inferior to other worldviews, there is now open promotion of moral abomination by government, common corruption in the justice system, lies in the media, suspicion in business, and rampant materialism as we work ourselves into the ground having discarded our weekly day of rest (which most other pagan cultures never had). We often lament the loss of such values, though society has rejected their source. What we enjoyed at our peak was not only due to the average citizen respecting Christianity even if they themselves weren't Christian, but also because Christians ensured

REVIVING CHRISTIAN INFLUENCE IN THE GOVERNING OF THE NATION

those values were codified at every level of government. In recent years, however, Christians have shrunk back from the civil sphere, because they have been convinced that Christianity and politics don't mix, because they believe that the Lord Jesus forbade them to participate in the ruling of earthly kingdoms, or, as already pointed out earlier, they have separated secular and sacred and reduced Christianity to a sentimental sing-song for Sunday. The argument that Christianity and politics don't mix because church and state are separate jurisdictions is true in the sense that the role of the civil sphere and the role of the church are distinct, but, just as we saw with the family, God's creation order and moral law must be the foundation of every institution over which God has made man steward if it is to enjoy the blessing and fruit God intended.

As Christians have retreated from the civil sphere, secular humanists have stepped up to seize control. Our laws now reflect their evil agenda, and God's judgment has begun to fall as a consequence. There is no neutrality in life—anyone who tells you that politicians do not bring their religious views into the policy room is deceived. Our worldview directly impacts our thinking and thus our policies. A secular humanist's religion impacts the values that undergird that person's policies, just as a Christian's should.

Revival of our nation must thus come from a three-pronged approach. First, we Christians must take raising godly seed very seriously by returning our families to the biblical pattern as already discussed in this book. Second, we must preach the true and full gospel—not just an "express ticket to heaven" but the full message of repentance, regeneration, and ongoing sanctification. We must teach that once a sinner is regenerated, he or she must walk in newness of life and be the salt and light of which the Lord Jesus spoke (Matt. 5:13-14; Mark 9:50). Third, we must revive our influence in the civil sphere to retard the decay of God's moral law, to maintain an environment conducive to the spread of the gospel, and to support the biblical family. This chapter will deal with the third of these prongs since the first two have already been covered in earlier chapters.

THE SUFFICIENCY OF SCRIPTURE

5.1 The Role of Civil Government

First, let's consider civil government's role as God defines it in the New Testament. The apostle Paul, under the Holy Spirit's direction, said, "For rulers are not a terror to good works, but to the evil. Wilt thou then not be afraid of the power? do that which is good, and thou shalt have praise of the same: For he is the minister of God to thee for good. But if thou do that which is evil, be afraid; for he beareth not the sword in vain: for he is the minister of God, a revenger to execute wrath upon him that doeth evil" (Rom. 13:3-4).

The apostle Peter wrote, "Submit yourselves to every ordinance of man for the Lord's sake: whether it be to the king, as supreme; Or unto governors, as unto them that are sent by him for the punishment of evildoers, and for the praise of them that do well" (1 Peter 2:13-14).

Civil government's main role is to enforce law and protect its citizens. Enforcing law is, of course, not arbitrary. The apostle notes that they are to punish evil and reward good, which are defined by God, not man. We are not at liberty to make up our own arbitrary laws such that what God calls evil we call good, or vice versa (Isa. 5:20).

Rulers are under God's authority to enforce His moral law. Twice in Romans 13:4 a ruler is referred to as a "minister of God." When there are no righteous men in authority, arbitrary and wicked laws are enacted—after all, what do the godless care about evil and good? God has used unrighteous rulers to chasten His people throughout history when they have fallen into idolatry (Neh. 9:6-38), but His will is that we have righteous leaders who uphold His moral law. We are told that God delights in righteousness and judgment being exercised in the earth (Jer. 9:23-24).

We also learn from the Psalms and Proverbs that, "The wicked walk on every side, when the vilest men are exalted" (Ps. 12:8); and that "Righteousness exalteth a nation: but sin is a reproach to any people" (Prov. 14:34). Proverbs goes on to say, "When the righteous are in authority, the people rejoice: but when the wicked beareth rule, the people mourn" (Prov. 29:2). How can the righteous be in authority if

REVIVING CHRISTIAN INFLUENCE IN THE GOVERNING OF THE NATION

the Lord Jesus does not permit them to participate in the civil sphere in which they may exercise that authority?

On the contrary, Proverbs makes it abundantly clear that "A righteous man falling down before the wicked is as a troubled fountain, and a corrupt spring." (Proverbs 25:26.) If the righteous man capitulates to the wicked, he is like a polluted spring or fountain. A polluted spring does not give life but death. It is a mirage which appears to promise life-giving refreshment and hope in the heat of war, but instead, they which wearily arrive at it to drink are weakened and left poisoned. All those who look to the righteous for justice and judgment are similarly disillusioned when he surrenders to the wicked. It is absurd to think that we should desire godly governance in the family and the church, yet leave the governance of the state to the unbelieving. The Scriptures are consistently clear, except when a nation is under judgment, it is the will of God that the righteous actively take the lead in a nation, especially a nation which is founded upon Judeo-Christian values.

5.2 Temporary Dual Citizenship

While our citizenship is in heaven (Phil. 3:20), we currently live on this earth. Citizenship in heaven doesn't mean we are not citizens of an earthly kingdom now. We must pay our taxes (Luke 20:25), obey the law when it doesn't contradict God's law (Titus 3:1; Heb. 13:17; Acts 5:29), and, when opportunity arises, be salt and light even in this realm as God's ministers (Rom. 13:4).

The apostle Paul of all people did not just lie down and die without appealing to the civil government. If he had understood the words of the Lord Jesus to mean that he should just turn the other cheek and let the Romans beat him again and kill him, would the following have been recorded for our learning?

> *And when it was day, the magistrates sent the serjeants, saying, Let those men go. And the keeper of the prison told this saying to Paul, The magistrates have sent to let you go: now therefore depart, and go in peace.*

THE SUFFICIENCY OF SCRIPTURE

But Paul said unto them, They have beaten us openly uncondemned, being Romans, and have cast us into prison; and now do they thrust us out privily? nay verily; but let them come themselves and fetch us out. And the serjeants told these words unto the magistrates: and they feared, when they heard that they were Romans. And they came and besought them, and brought them out, and desired them to depart out of the city.
(Acts 16:35-39)

For if I be an offender, or have committed any thing worthy of death, I refuse not to die: but if there be none of these things whereof these accuse me, no man may deliver me unto them. I appeal unto Caesar.
(Acts 25:11)

We know that the apostle Paul approved of fellow Christians in the civil sphere by the way he fondly greets Erastus, who was the chamberlain of the city, in Romans 16:23 (also see Acts 19:22 and 2 Tim. 4:20), and sends greetings from the saints in Caesar's household in Phil. 4:22. Sergius Paulus, the deputy of the country of Paphos, was converted under Barnabas and Paul's ministry (see Acts 13:7-12). There is no record of the apostle Paul telling any of these believers to leave their positions of authority.

5.3 Imposing Morality on the Unbeliever

The principle Amos spoke to Israel is just as applicable for us today, he said, "Hate the evil, and love the good, and establish judgment in the gate: it may be that the Lord God of hosts will be gracious" (Amos 5:15). While it is true that every citizen's heart must be regenerated for a nation to know complete revival, it is also true that even in a nation of unbelievers, God expects His moral law to be both taught and upheld (Ezra 7:25-27a; Matt. 28:19-20.)

For those who think we cannot impose morality on the unbeliever, consider the red traffic light. Even enforcing that drivers stop at a red

REVIVING CHRISTIAN INFLUENCE IN THE GOVERNING OF THE NATION

traffic light is imposing morality on all citizens, whether they believe in stopping at it or not.

A lawless nation will disintegrate into chaos very rapidly. John the Baptist imposed God's moral law on Herod, who was clearly not a Jew,[67] when he rebuked Herod for committing adultery (see Luke 3:19 and Mark 6:17-18). Under the Mosaic Law, strangers living with Jews were also expected to observe the Jews' law (Exod. 12:19, 12:48; Deut. 1:16, 5:14, etc.). While we live on this earth, we are all subject to God's moral law, as Romans 2:14-16 explains.

King David wrote of the purpose for raising godly seed when he said, "Lo, children are an heritage of the Lord: and the fruit of the womb is his reward. As arrows are in the hand of a mighty man; so are children of the youth. Happy is the man that hath his quiver full of them: they shall not be ashamed, but they shall speak with the enemies in the gate" (Ps. 127:3-5). The gate is a position of authority and leadership in a city. Our children are to be raised to potentially take such opportunities to be salt and light, even in civil leadership.

If a Christian has opportunity to influence his nation through participating in civil government—thereby preserving God's moral law—and does not do so, he is actually abetting sin. As the apostle James wrote, "Therefore to him that knoweth to do good, and doeth it not, to him it is sin" (James 4:17).

David, Solomon, Josiah, Joseph, Daniel, and Nehemiah are just a few godly men who were either kings or servants in the civil sphere. God also used Esther mightily to save her people as queen alongside a pagan king. Some, however, argue that this was under the old covenant and that things changed when the Lord Jesus came to earth.

5.4 The Lord Jesus' Teaching in Context

Some people use the passage below to argue that Christians are forbidden to have authority over other Christians, thus disallowing them from having positions of authority in the civil sphere.

THE SUFFICIENCY OF SCRIPTURE

And he said unto them, The kings of the Gentiles exercise lordship over them; and they that exercise authority upon them are called benefactors. But ye shall not be so: but he that is greatest among you, let him be as the younger; and he that is chief, as he that doth serve.

(Luke 22:25-26)

The Lord Jesus does not forbid being chief or having a position of authority over others, only that the position is not exercised despotically, maliciously, or for personal gain. He said, "He that is" not "don't be chief" or "there is no such one as the greatest in authority." The truth revealed in Scripture is that God has ordained a hierarchical authority structure starting with God at the top and three spheres under Him: civil, church, and family. Each has its ministers. In the family it is the father and then the mother (1 Cor. 11:3; Col. 3:20; Eph. 6:1-4), in the church it is the elders (1 Tim. 5:17; 1 Peter 5:1-3; 1 Cor. 5:9-12), and in the civil sphere it is those who enforce God's moral law (Rom. 13:4). In each case, the authority should be exercised with godly fear and humility and with a servant attitude—but it nevertheless must be exercised.

As to the assertion (often gleaned from the following verse) that we now belong solely to a spiritual kingdom and thus have no place participating in this earth's physical kingdoms, pay attention to what the Lord Jesus actually says: "And I appoint unto you a kingdom, as my Father hath appointed unto me; That ye may eat and drink at my table in my kingdom, and sit on thrones judging the twelve tribes of Israel" (Luke 22:29-30). This is a future physical kingdom in which certain members of the Lord's saints will rule over the twelve physical tribes of Israel. This cannot be a spiritual kingdom because there are no twelve spiritual tribes mentioned anywhere in God's Word, only physical tribes.

The following verse is also quoted often to justify not participating in earthly kingdoms:

REVIVING CHRISTIAN INFLUENCE IN THE GOVERNING OF THE NATION

Jesus answered, My kingdom is not of this world: if my kingdom were of this world, then would my servants fight, that I should not be delivered to the Jews: but now is my kingdom not from hence.

(John 18:36)

Of course the Lord Jesus' kingdom is not of this world—He created it. He does not derive His authority from our kingdom but we derive our authority from Him. We too are in the world but not of it, which is why we speak against moral decay and any worldly philosophy that opposes God's Word. As already demonstrated, however, this verse does not mean that we do not participate in the kingdoms of the world, only that the Lord Jesus' destiny to go to the cross was ordained of His father and not from the government of the day.

Some may argue that we are to pray for those in authority but not be one in authority. Yes, indeed, we must pray for those in authority as the Scriptures command (see 1 Tim. 2:1-4). No verse, however, commands us not to be one in authority, only that if we are, we should exercise that authority with humility and a servant attitude.

Still others say that the apostle Paul taught that Christians are not to be involved with the affairs of this world, which include participation in the civil sphere, when he wrote, "No man that warreth entangleth himself with the affairs of this life; that he may please him who hath chosen him to be a soldier" (2 Tim. 2:4). The apostle Paul teaches here that Christians should arm themselves to be focused on the Lord's work as a good soldier focuses on his role of defense. If part of his role of defense is truth itself, he cannot allow the wicked to enact laws that contradict God's law. Rather, he teaches that as good soldiers we are not to be entangled with the godless culture, the latest fads, fashions, movies, social gossip, etc. We are instead to be focused on fulfilling God's will in every area of our interaction with people in life, our families, our churches, and our nation, and we are to do so with the rigor and discipline of a soldier who endures hardness (2 Tim. 2:3).

5.5 Today's Battles: Socialism, Islam and Environmentalism

And he charged them, saying, Take heed, beware of the leaven of the Pharisees, and of the leaven of Herod.

(Mark 8:15)

The Lord Jesus told His disciples to "take heed" and "beware" of two very serious dangers: manmade religion and the philosophies of the state. These warnings are also relevant to us in our context. Leaven totally permeates a lump of dough, just like man's philosophies totally permeate a culture. "The leaven of Herod" represents philosophies the state preached to control people. For too long, the church has concentrated solely on the enemy of the roaring lion, totally blinded to the other two enemies: the leaven of Herod (statist philosophies) and the enemy of the wolves in sheep's skin who have crept into our churches.

One such form of leaven of which many Christians are unaware is socialism. Socialism has been deliberately and openly undermining Christianity to destroy morality in our society, making women discontent with God's ordained role for them in the home, teaching men to relinquish their headship to the state, and educating our children on social justice and environmentalism rather than how to analyze and think for themselves and to be moral citizens with integrity. Socialism's foundation is far from just. Its foundation is threefold:

- Atheism
- No private property
- Government control of everything

Its final goal is communism. At each point, socialism is anti-God. First, it presupposes no God and that man is inherently good or at least neutral. Second, it goes against the scriptural teaching of private property and ownership—"thou shalt not steal" and "thou shalt not covet thy neighbor's goods" implies private ownership. Third, it takes from those willing to work hard and gives to those who will not work,

REVIVING CHRISTIAN INFLUENCE IN THE GOVERNING OF THE NATION

effectively sharing poverty rather than distributing wealth. The larger the government, the more it spends, and it spends our money, not its own. It then teaches our children moral relativism, and dumbs down the education system to cause society to depend on big government.

Most Christians are ignorant of Satan's relentless agenda. Here are just a few of the 45 goals of Socialism which are being, or have already been, accomplished through ungodly governance, and deliberate infiltration of the education system, both "secular" and "Christian." These are taken from The Naked Communist, by Cleon Skousen, Ensign Publishing Company, 1958. The full list of these communist goals was read into the Congressional Record by U.S. Congressman Albert S. Herlong, Jr. of Florida, on January 10, 1963.

- Get control of the schools. Use them as transmission belts for socialism and current Communist propaganda. Soften the curriculum. Get control of teachers' associations. Put the party line in textbooks.
- Gain control of all student newspapers.
- Infiltrate the press. Get control of book-review assignments, editorial writing, policymaking positions.
- Gain control of key positions in radio, TV, and motion pictures.
- Control art critics and directors of art museums. "Our plan is to promote ugliness, repulsive, meaningless art."
- Eliminate all laws governing obscenity by calling them "censorship" and a violation of free speech and free press.
- Break down cultural standards of morality by promoting pornography and obscenity in books, magazines, motion pictures, radio, and TV.
- Present homosexuality, degeneracy and promiscuity as "normal, natural, healthy."
- Infiltrate the churches and replace revealed religion with "social" religion. Discredit the Bible and emphasize the need for intellectual maturity which does not need a "religious crutch."

THE SUFFICIENCY OF SCRIPTURE

- Discredit the family as an institution. Encourage promiscuity and easy divorce.
- Emphasize the need to raise children away from the negative influence of parents. Attribute prejudices, mental blocks and retarding of children to suppressive influence of parents.

The Bible clearly teaches that the role of government is only twofold: to enforce God's law and to protect its citizens (Rom. 13:4-8). Anything beyond that encroaches on the jurisdiction of the family or the church.

Consider the catch cry in the media today: "Rights, rights, rights!" When we think of these rights—for example, the right to abortion, euthanasia, government housing, public education, whatever—we first are implying that anything and everything is a right, regardless of its morality. Second, we are saying that we have a right to obtain something we did not earn by denying someone else the right to what he or she did earn. The Bible calls that stealing. (Charity and the care of the poor is to be a voluntary service of Christians, not an enforced burden upon all, see Rom. 15:26; Gal 2:10; 2 Cor. 9:7.)

The definition of "social justice" taught in our public education system today is not the care of the poor, elderly or disabled—they fight for legal euthanasia for that purpose—but equality of value systems and religions. This definition implies that homosexuality is equal to Biblical marriage, that all religions are equal to Christianity, and that a culture decides its own moral law rather than morality being revealed by God in the Holy Bible.

As socialist politicians seek to annihilate Christianity in society, they embrace anyone who will help, including, of course, Islam, which has its own agenda to destroy Christianity and is on a steady increase around the world.

Hirsi Ali (once a Muslim) is now an atheist, and counts British atheist campaigner Richard Dawkins as a close friend. But she believes

REVIVING CHRISTIAN INFLUENCE IN THE GOVERNING OF THE NATION

Christianity can combat the rise of conservative Islam. "Churches should do all in their power to win this battle for the souls of humans in search of a compassionate God, who now find that a fierce Allah is closer to hand," she writes in Nomad.[68]

These are the words and recognition of an atheist who knows Islam's agenda firsthand. Even as an atheist, she recognizes that not all "religions" are equal and calls on Christianity to combat Islam.

Environmentalism is yet another doctrine uniting evolutionist and pantheist alike, which Satan is successfully using to undermine Christianity. This evil doctrine has permeated many churches through the public education system. It threatens the family, the economy, and the world. Good stewardship of God's creation is not what environmentalism teaches. At its core is the worship of the creature above the creator, the reduction of the value of human life to that of an earthworm, and the control of the world's resources through global governance using false science, as already noted in the chapter on the family.

Why am I talking about socialism, Islam, environmentalism, and the war against God? The apostle Paul wrote in 2 Corinthians 2:11, "Lest Satan should get an advantage of us: for we are not ignorant of his devices." Are we ignorant of his devices? Some might argue that by doing anything at all we just delay the Lord's return—why would we want to do that? That would be like saying, "Let's just accelerate evil to cause God's judgment to fall sooner." The Lord Jesus in the parable of the nobleman told us to "occupy till I come" (Luke 19:13), not sit back and just wait for His return. Regardless of one's eschatological view, we must all spend our lives being the Lord's ambassadors upon this earth (2 Cor. 5:20).

What are Christians doing? At one extreme they are enjoying themselves, being entangled with the affairs or culture of this world, and being like the godless culture around them in the name of Christian liberty. At the other end of the scale they retreat from the world, shun other true Christians and even divide within themselves, and engage in Bible study after Bible study without applying the Bible to the day's issues.

THE SUFFICIENCY OF SCRIPTURE

What does the Bible say about abortion, euthanasia, socialism, atheism, environmentalism, etc.? We need to think about the consequences of abandoning biblical application to all of life. We must not sit back and allow the infiltration of our homes, churches, schools, and communities without a word, lest Satan will get an advantage over us through our ignorance of his devices.

5.6 The Wise Master Builder

> *For we are labourers together with God: ye are God's husbandry, ye are God's building. According to the grace of God which is given unto me, as a wise masterbuilder, I have laid the foundation, and another buildeth thereon. But let every man take heed how he buildeth thereupon. For other foundation can no man lay than that is laid, which is Jesus Christ. Now if any man build upon this foundation gold, silver, precious stones, wood, hay, stubble; Every man's work shall be made manifest: for the day shall declare it, because it shall be revealed by fire; and the fire shall try every man's work of what sort it is. If any man's work abide which he hath built thereupon, he shall receive a reward. If any man's work shall be burned, he shall suffer loss: but he himself shall be saved; yet so as by fire.*
> (1 Cor. 3:9-15)

Take careful note of the apostle Paul's words: "But let every man take heed how he buildeth thereupon." It is assumed that every man will build. Build what? We are co-laborers with God—our job is to build strong families that in turn build strong churches and a strong nation founded on God's moral law (also see 1 Peter 2:5, 2:9). Are we careful how we build? Are we deliberate in our strategy for raising our family? Contributing to our local church? Being salt and light in our community? The apostle Paul likens himself to a "wise masterbuilder." A wise master-builder doesn't haphazardly throw his building together—he plans it, carefully choosing the materials and planning ahead. Then he purposefully, thoughtfully, diligently, and persistently builds on a good foundation with a vision to accomplish his final goal.

REVIVING CHRISTIAN INFLUENCE IN THE GOVERNING OF THE NATION

Are we as strategic and persistent as the socialists? Are we as zealous as the Muslims? Are we as influential as the environmentalists? Let's learn from the words of Isaiah, who wrote, "justice standeth afar off: for truth is fallen in the street, and equity cannot enter. Yea, truth faileth; and he that departeth from evil maketh himself a prey: and the LORD saw it, and it displeased him that there was no judgment. And he saw that there was no man, and wondered that there was no intercessor" (Isa. 59:14-16). Surely God is just as displeased today as He was in Isaiah's day at the lack of righteous men to stand for truth and exercise godly judgment in the earth.

5.7 Concluding Thoughts on Christians in the Civil Sphere

In conclusion, throughout the Scriptures, God expects man to exercise justice, judgment, and equity in the earth as His ministers. Whether in the family, the church, or civil sphere, each authority is God-ordained and is to be exercised with humility, fear, and a servant attitude, being directly accountable to God, who is over all. As wise master-builders, we must take heed how we build, being co-laborers with God to accomplish His purposes. We must not be ignorant of Satan's devices but understand the times in which we live (1 Chron. 12:32) that we may apply the Scriptures appropriately.

Revival of our nation will only come when Christianity has the influence on culture that it once had: when its families are built according to the Scriptures, when its churches uncompromisingly preach the whole counsel of God, when its laws are firmly founded on God's law, and when Christian values form the warp and woof of society's fabric.

Chapter 6

THE ROLE OF PRAYER IN REVIVAL

6.1 The Attributes of Biblical Prayer

MANY HAVE POINTED out that each great revival has been directly attributed to prayer. Fervent and consistent prayer indeed is fundamentally essential and we cannot minimize its absolute power. Prayer, however, must be accompanied by action. Since many books have already been devoted to the importance of prayer in revival, I will not dwell on it except to say that prayer must be:

- Fervent (1 Thess. 5:17, 2 Tim. 1:3, Rom. 1:9, Acts 12:5, James 5:17-18)
- With thankfulness (1 Thes. 5:18; Col. 4:2; Php. 4:6)
- Insistent (Luke 11:5-10, 18:1-7; Gen. 18:23-33)
- Expectant (John 15:7, 1 John 5:14-15)
- In agreement (Matt. 18:19)
- Specific (John 14:13, 16:23; James 1:6)
- In accordance with God's will and Word (James 4:3)
- Accompanied by obedience and action (Micah 3:4, Jer. 7:9-18, Isa. 59:2, Ps. 34:15, 1 Peter 3:12, James 5:16)
- Unhindered by a bad relationship with our spouse (1 Peter 3:7)

- Accompanied by fasting in certain situations (1 Sam. 7:5-6, 2 Sam. 12:16, 2 Chron. 20:3, Judg. 20:26, Ezra 8:21, Neh. 1:4, Est. 4:16, Jer. 36:9, Joel 1:14, Jonah 3:5, Matt. 6:16, 9:15, Luke 5:35, Acts 13:2-3, 27:9)

6.2 God Will Not Do For Us What He Has Commanded Us To Do

It is very important to understand what to pray for. God will not do for us what we ourselves must do. He will only do what is impossible for us to accomplish. We see this time and again in the Scriptures. One such time was when the Lord Jesus commanded that His disciples roll the stone from Lazarus's tomb and to untie him once He had called him forth from the dead (see John 11:39-44). We do not need to pray for what God has already commanded us to do, only to ensure that we are doing what God indeed has commanded, and to do it with the right motive. We may then pray that He would make what we are doing fruitful for His own glory and name's sake. Praying for revival without action and in disobedience is like standing in front of that tomb refusing to roll the stone from its mouth after being directly commanded to do so, then, when God does raise someone from the dead spiritually, we leave the poor man shackled in his old grave clothes rather than untying him and discipling him to true freedom and maturity in the Lord.

6.3 Pray With Humble Expectation

When we pray earnestly for something such as revival, we must pray expectantly. We laugh at the account of Rhoda who left the apostle Peter knocking at the door while the whole gathering prayed for him, presumably for his release (see Acts 12:5-16), but how often are we just as astonished at God's answers to prayer or secretly think people are crazy when they report that God has answered their requests? God is indeed merciful in our unbelief!

THE SUFFICIENCY OF SCRIPTURE

> *Peter therefore was kept in prison: but prayer was made without ceasing of the church unto God for him. And when Herod would have brought him forth, the same night Peter was sleeping between two soldiers, bound with two chains: and the keepers before the door kept the prison. And, behold, the angel of the Lord came upon him, and a light shined in the prison: and he smote Peter on the side, and raised him up, saying, Arise up quickly. And his chains fell off from his hands. And the angel said unto him, Gird thyself, and bind on thy sandals. And so he did. And he saith unto him, Cast thy garment about thee, and follow me. And he went out, and followed him; and wist not that it was true which was done by the angel; but thought he saw a vision. When they were past the first and the second ward, they came unto the iron gate that leadeth unto the city; which opened to them of his own accord: and they went out, and passed on through one street; and forthwith the angel departed from him. And when Peter was come to himself, he said, Now I know of a surety, that the Lord hath sent his angel, and hath delivered me out of the hand of Herod, and from all the expectation of the people of the Jews. And when he had considered the thing, he came to the house of Mary the mother of John, whose surname was Mark; where many were gathered together praying. And as Peter knocked at the door of the gate, a damsel came to hearken, named Rhoda. And when she knew Peter's voice, she opened not the gate for gladness, but ran in, and told how Peter stood before the gate. And they said unto her, Thou art mad. But she constantly affirmed that it was even so. Then said they, It is his angel. But Peter continued knocking: and when they had opened the door, and saw him, they were astonished.*
> *(Acts 12:5-16)*

Take careful note also how the angel did not escort the apostle Peter to Mary's house but left him in the street to contemplate and use his judgment and wisdom to decide what to do. The angel only did for the apostle what he could not do for himself.

I take great comfort from the reminder that "Elias was a man subject to like passions as we are, and he prayed earnestly that it might not rain: and it rained not on the earth by the space of three years and six months.

And he prayed again, and the heaven gave rain, and the earth brought forth her fruit" (James 5:17-18). The key to his prayer was earnestness, righteousness, and obedience. We are promised that "the effectual fervent prayer of a righteous man availeth much" (James 5:16b).

6.4 Fasting May Be Appropriate

Throughout the Scriptures we learn that prayer should be accompanied by fasting for major requests where the impact of a wrong decision or event may be detrimental to one's own life, family, church, or nation. Fasting demonstrates to God that one is serious enough about his request to forgo basic needs or pleasures such as food or marital intimacy (see 1 Cor. 7:5). Fasting humbles us and reminds us to whom we owe all and for whom we do all things. Fasting will, however, be fruitless if one has not confessed known sin or harbors bitterness against one's wife (see Jer. 14:12, 1 Peter 3:7).

6.5 Comprehend The Meaning of Praying In the Name of The Lord Jesus

One very important guide to our prayer is understanding what it means to pray in the name of the Lord Jesus. What we are really saying is that He would totally sanction our prayer and that we are simply making a request on His behalf. The simple test: Would the Lord of glory really ask this in *this* way? Praying in the name of the Lord Jesus is not some mystical incantation. It rather appeals to the absolute authority of the Lord Jesus who has given us bold (not flippant) access to the throne of grace through His substitutionary death in our stead (Heb. 4:16, 10:19). The Lord of glory does not promise to give us anything we ask for, but anything we ask for in His name, according to His will. This rightly understood means that desiring and knowing the will of the father will result in us asking for things which would please Him, not us.

THE SUFFICIENCY OF SCRIPTURE

The Lord Jesus words in context are, "If ye abide in me, and my words abide in you, ye shall ask what ye will, and it shall be done unto you. Herein is my Father glorified, that ye bear much fruit; so shall ye be my disciples."
(John 14:7-8)

There is a condition to us asking and receiving, that we not only abide in His Word, but that we bear much fruit which in turn glorifies God. Nowhere in Scripture does God promise to unconditionally give us what we want outside the context of accomplishing His will and glory. (Also see John 14:16; Mat. 7:8-11; Ps. 37:4-5; James 4:2-8.)

Some may appeal to Mark 11:24 which seems to indicate unconditional granting of arbitrary requests.

And Jesus answering saith unto them, Have faith in God. For verily I say unto you, That whosoever shall say unto this mountain, Be thou removed, and be thou cast into the sea; and shall not doubt in his heart, but shall believe that those things which he saith shall come to pass; he shall have whatsoever he saith. Therefore I say unto you, What things soever ye desire, when ye pray, believe that ye receive them, and ye shall have them.
(Mark 11:22-24)

In context, we see that the opening phrase in verse 22 places the request in verse 23 and 24 on a particular foundation, namely faith in God. Putting this more strongly, faith in the character, will, authority and power of the Almighty God of the universe. When we understand in whom we are placing our faith, it should moderate the kind of request to one which could be made in good conscience by one who fears the Lord. It will however also give us the confidence to believe that we will receive the desired request since we trust it aligns with His will.

6.6 Prayer Is Not An Excuse For Inaction

Prayer is often an excuse for inaction. I've been in meetings where revival has been prayed for earnestly and yet the congregation is riddled

THE ROLE OF PRAYER IN REVIVAL

with open sin, with which neither the elders nor individuals were willing to deal. I'm sure revival would have come without prayer if the sins in the congregation had been dealt with scripturally and all of the members were willing to obey the Lord, get their families in order, and confess and forsake their individual sins. Then, if this had happened along with the fervent prayer, God would have blessed their efforts tremendously! It is sobering to be reminded of how Achan's sin affected the whole congregation of Israel (see Josh. 7), and so too the sin of individuals in our local congregations today (see 1 Cor. 5:6, 11:30). In summary, we must obey, then pray.

While it may appear that I am being rather harsh toward those who pray without action, this must be put in its context. While visiting a very respected elderly gentleman in hospital recently, I asked if he had been able to get out to meetings in recent days. He told me, "No, but I've been able to pray, able to pray for all of the precious seed that has been planted and watered over my able years." This is the key. This man had faithfully preached the gospel for more than fifty years. Now, as he lay in his bed of infirmity, still preaching to my children and me with a smile in his voice, even as we sat beside his bed he could pray. He could pray for all of the seed that had been sown that it might yet bring forth fruit. The work had been done. He had planted, he had watered, and now, as he prayed believing, God will even yet bring the increase, I am certain. Often we are so focused on the reaping that we forget that preparing the soil, sowing, and watering are just as important a focus as the actual reaping of the harvest.

Chapter 7

THE SPIRITUAL BATTLE

7.1 Not "If" But "When"

ONE AREA THAT often can hinder our efforts for personal, family, or church revival is spiritual warfare. This is usually underestimated. It is not that Satan is equal and opposite to God—God is almighty and rules over all. Satan does, however, attempt to oppose God's work and we must be prepared for this opposition and call on God to overcome it. We must not flinch in the face of persecution or trial. We cannot cast off our faith in the heat of testing. God allows and uses testing to see what we're really made of. Do not believe anyone who tells you that the victorious Christian life is without difficulty. The Scriptures are clear, and the sooner a Christian understands this, the better. Our opposition is from the world, our own flesh, and Satan.

> *These things I have spoken unto you, that in me ye might have peace. In the world ye shall have tribulation: but be of good cheer; I have overcome the world.*
>
> (John 16:33)

If the world hate you, ye know that it hated me before it hated you.
(John 15:18)

Beloved, think it not strange concerning the fiery trial which is to try you, as though some strange thing happened unto you: But rejoice, inasmuch as ye are partakers of Christ's sufferings; that, when his glory shall be revealed, ye may be glad also with exceeding joy. If ye be reproached for the name of Christ, happy are ye; for the spirit of glory and of God resteth upon you: on their part he is evil spoken of, but on your part he is glorified.
(1 Peter 4:12-14)

Wherein ye greatly rejoice, though now for a season, if need be, ye are in heaviness through manifold temptations: That the trial of your faith, being much more precious than of gold that perisheth, though it be tried with fire, might be found unto praise and honour and glory at the appearing of Jesus Christ.
(1 Peter 1:6-7)

For godly sorrow worketh repentance to salvation not to be repented of: but the sorrow of the world worketh death.
(2 Cor. 7:10)

But let none of you suffer as a murderer, or as a thief, or as an evildoer, or as a busybody in other men's matters. Yet if any man suffer as a Christian, let him not be ashamed; but let him glorify God on this behalf.
(1 Peter 4:15-16)

7.2 The Eternal Perspective

The key to handling difficulty in our Christian lives is to keep it in perspective no matter how difficult it is. As the apostle Paul puts it, "For our light affliction, which is but for a moment, worketh for us a far more exceeding and eternal weight of glory; While we look not at the things which are seen, but at the things which are not seen: for the things which are seen are temporal; but the things which are not seen are eternal" (2 Cor. 4:17-18). He certainly knew persecution at its worst (see 2 Cor. 11:23-31).

The writer of Hebrews reminds us where our inner gaze must remain, he writes, "Wherefore seeing we also are compassed about with so great a cloud of witnesses, let us lay aside every weight, and the sin which doth so easily beset us, and let us run with patience the race that is set before us, Looking unto Jesus the author and finisher of our faith; who for the joy that was set before him endured the cross, despising the shame, and is set down at the right hand of the throne of God. For consider him that endured such contradiction of sinners against himself, lest ye be wearied and faint in your minds. Ye have not yet resisted unto blood, striving against sin" (Heb. 12:1-4).

> *Wherefore gird up the loins of your mind, be sober, and hope to the end for the grace that is to be brought unto you at the revelation of Jesus Christ.*
>
> *(1 Pet. 1:13)*

7.3 The Enemy and the Armour

> *Finally, my brethren, be strong in the Lord, and in the power of his might. Put on the whole armour of God, that ye may be able to stand against the wiles of the devil. For we wrestle not against flesh and blood, but against principalities, against powers, against the rulers of the darkness of this world, against spiritual wickedness in high places. Wherefore take unto you the whole armour of God, that ye may be able to withstand in the evil day, and having done all, to stand. Stand therefore, having your loins girt about with truth, and having on the breastplate of righteousness; And your feet shod with the preparation of the Gospel of peace; Above all, taking the shield of faith, wherewith ye shall be able to quench all the fiery darts of the wicked. And take the helmet of salvation, and the sword of the Spirit, which is the word of God: Praying always with all prayer and supplication in the Spirit, and watching thereunto with all perseverance and supplication for all saints.*
>
> *(Eph. 6:10-18)*

THE SPIRITUAL BATTLE

Wherefore we would have come unto you, even I Paul, once and again; but Satan hindered us.

(1 Thess. 2:18)

Fear none of those things which thou shalt suffer: behold, the devil shall cast some of you into prison, that ye may be tried; and ye shall have tribulation ten days: be thou faithful unto death, and I will give thee a crown of life.

(Rev. 2:10)

And the God of peace shall bruise Satan under your feet shortly. The grace of our Lord Jesus Christ be with you. Amen.

(Rom. 16:20)

7.4   Are We Ignorant Of His Devices?

Lest Satan should get an advantage of us: for we are not ignorant of his devices.

(2 Cor. 2:11)

We in the West particularly underestimate the spiritual realm and are ignorant of Satan's devices, about which the apostle Paul spoke. In many countries and cultures, however, the people are very aware of the spirit world. Not being aware of it does not diminish its presence or power. So often spiritual forces hamper our efforts and we are oblivious to the cause of the resistance. At the same time, we also are oblivious to the Lord's ministering spirits He sends to aid us in our battles (see Heb. 1:14). When the Lord Jesus dwelt amongst us in the flesh, demonic activity was very common. What makes us think it has somehow disappeared just because we live in the twenty-first century in a Western nation? The Lord Jesus often talked of this spiritual realm and we too need to be aware of its presence.

Some of Satan's devices include:

THE SUFFICIENCY OF SCRIPTURE

Device	Scripture Reference	Armor
Deception	2 Thess. 2:9-12, 2 Cor. 11:14, John 8:44, 2 Tim. 2:26, Rev. 20:7-10	Helmet of salvation and belt of truth
Doubt	Gen. 3:1	Shield of faith
Fear	2 Tim. 1:7, 1 John 4:18	Helmet of salvation
Temptation in our weakest areas	Matt. 4:1-4	Breastplate of righteousness
Misuse of the Scriptures	Matt. 4:6-7	Sword of the Spirit
Offering of glory and power	Matt. 4:8-10	Helmet of salvation
A repentant sinner's unforgiveness	2 Cor. 2:8-11	Sword of the Spirit
Persecution	Rev. 2:10	Whole armor
Pride	1 Tim. 3:6	Helmet of salvation
Fiery darts of discouragement or discredit	Eph. 6:16	Shield of faith
Depression, vexation, and bondage	Matt. 15:22, Luke 8:29, Acts 10:38	Whole armor
Stealing away God's Word from one's understanding	Luke 8:12	Sword of the Spirit
Bad thoughts	John 13:2, Acts 5:3	Helmet of salvation
Direct opposition (through people or circumstance)	Acts 13:8-10, 1 Thess. 2:18	Whole armor

Device	Scripture Reference	Armor
Snare (perhaps an unbreakable habit or false doctrine leading to cultic entrapment)	1 Tim. 3:7, 2 Tim. 2:26	Whole armor
Bitter envying and strife	James 3:14-16	Helmet of salvation
Anger	Eph. 4:26-27	Whole armor

When we don't recognize that Satan masquerades as an angel of light, and his ministers as ministers of righteousness, we are unprepared to meet his manifestations. We don't recognize the sugarcoated death pills or the wolf in sheep's clothing in the midst of our assembly. We somehow expect him to look like an impish devil from the fairy tales of our childhood. Whether the well-dressed preacher, the elderly piano teacher whispering words of contradiction into our children's ears, or the modestly dressed but slanderous young lady, Satan will choose the least likely means of attack. He will not use the method against which you're fortified. Be warned.

And no marvel; for Satan himself is transformed into an angel of light. Therefore it is no great thing if his ministers also be transformed as the ministers of righteousness; whose end shall be according to their works.
(2 Cor. 11:14-15)

7.5 The Spiritual Realm

Consider the following verses together to get a glimpse into the spiritual realm:

And when the servant of the man of God was risen early, and gone forth, behold, an host compassed the city both with horses and chariots. And

THE SUFFICIENCY OF SCRIPTURE

his servant said unto him, Alas, my master! how shall we do? And he answered, Fear not: for they that be with us are more than they that be with them. And Elisha prayed, and said, LORD, I pray thee, open his eyes, that he may see. And the LORD opened the eyes of the young man; and he saw: and, behold, the mountain was full of horses and chariots of fire round about Elisha.

(2 Kings 6:15-17)

Ye are of God, little children, and have overcome them: because greater is he that is in you, than he that is in the world.

(1 John 4:4)

Be sober, be vigilant; because your adversary the devil, as a roaring lion, walketh about, seeking whom he may devour: Whom resist stedfast in the faith, knowing that the same afflictions are accomplished in your brethren that are in the world.

(1 Peter 5:8-9)

Submit yourselves therefore to God. Resist the devil, and he will flee from you. Draw nigh to God, and he will draw nigh to you. Cleanse your hands, ye sinners; and purify your hearts, ye double minded.

(James 4:7-8)

And it came to pass, as we went to prayer, a certain damsel possessed with a spirit of divination met us, which brought her masters much gain by soothsaying: The same followed Paul and us, and cried, saying, These men are the servants of the most high God, which shew unto us the way of salvation. And this did she many days. But Paul, being grieved, turned and said to the spirit, I command thee in the name of Jesus Christ to come out of her. And he came out the same hour.

(Acts 16:16-18)

For the weapons of our warfare are not carnal, but mighty through God to the pulling down of strong holds.

(2 Cor. 10:4)

THE SPIRITUAL BATTLE

The Bible is clear that not all of our battles are against the flesh or the world. It reminds us that we wrestle not with flesh and blood but against principalities, against powers, against the rulers of the darkness of this world, and against spiritual wickedness in high places. It also reminds us that the weapons for such battles are not carnal. The apostle Paul tells us we must stand with the armor of God in place—that is, wearing the helmet of salvation; holding the shield of faith (not wavering in our trust in God's ability to save), the breastplate of righteousness (having confessed known sin), the belt of truth (knowing on what grounds we stand as being the truth of God's Word), and the sword of the Word (having studied it to apply any wisdom to the current situation); and wearing the shoes of the preparation of the gospel (prepared to follow the Lord's direction). Then we must submit ourselves to God and resist the Devil in the name of the Lord Jesus Christ. We are promised that Satan will flee from us (for a season). We must not underestimate this area of the battle for revival in our personal, family, or church life.

Chapter 8

COMPLACENCY

ONE OF THE greatest enemies of revival is complacency. Complacency will prevent revival and will quickly destroy the fruit of revival.

The definition of complacency according to dictionary.com is "a feeling of quiet pleasure or security, often while unaware of some potential danger, defect, or the like; self-satisfaction or smug satisfaction with an existing situation, condition, etc."[69]

> *And when the people saw that Moses delayed to come down out of the mount, the people gathered themselves together unto Aaron, and said unto him, Up, make us gods, which shall go before us; for as for this Moses, the man that brought us up out of the land of Egypt, we wot not what is become of him. And Aaron said unto them, Break off the golden earrings, which are in the ears of your wives, of your sons, and of your daughters, and bring them unto me. And all the people brake off the golden earrings which were in their ears, and brought them unto Aaron. And he received them at their hand, and fashioned it with a graving tool, after he had made it a molten calf: and they said, These be thy gods, O Israel, which brought thee up out of the land of Egypt. And when Aaron saw it, he built an altar before it; and Aaron made proclamation, and said, To morrow is*

COMPLACENCY

a feast to the LORD. And they rose up early on the morrow, and offered burnt offerings, and brought peace offerings; and the people sat down to eat and to drink, and rose up to play.

(Ex. 32:1-6)

Then Peter said unto him, Lord, speakest thou this parable unto us, or even to all? And the Lord said, Who then is that faithful and wise steward, whom his lord shall make ruler over his household, to give them their portion of meat in due season? Blessed is that servant, whom his lord when he cometh shall find so doing. Of a truth I say unto you, that he will make him ruler over all that he hath. But and if that servant say in his heart, My lord delayeth his coming; and shall begin to beat the menservants and maidens, and to eat and drink, and to be drunken; The lord of that servant will come in a day when he looketh not for him, and at an hour when he is not aware, and will cut him in sunder, and will appoint him his portion with the unbelievers. And that servant, which knew his lord's will, and prepared not himself, neither did according to his will, shall be beaten with many stripes.

(Luke 12:41-47)

Also see Matthew 21:33-41 for a similar story.

Complacency is one of the greatest dangers to a Christian. We are warned of it and thus should endeavor to avoid it. Why is it so bad? Let's consider some of its results.

8.1 The Dangers of Complacency

8.1.1 Our View of God Is Diminished

Complacency leads us to forget God's works and think that gods of gold and silver can replace the all powerful, all knowing, all providing, holy and just God who has provided our every need to this point, including the greatest need of salvation. Carefully note this part of Exodus 32:1: "Make us gods, which shall go before us." How could we manufacture something to replace God? How could any golden god part the Red Sea's waters? Give them water from a rock? Feed them manna? Guide them in their physical journey? Ensure that their clothes and footwear didn't wear out? Yet they wanted gods of gold instead.

More specifically, complacency leads us to trust in material things rather than in the sovereign God's providence. While we may think the Israelites' response to delay was ludicrous, we are no different. The power God demonstrated in the past so quickly loses its impact and our trust diminishes to the point of idolatry.

While the following admonition was written to the children of Israel, its principle is very much applicable to Christians today who so readily forsake the Fountain of Living Water to embrace dumb idols. A browse of many shops today will amply yield our passion for idolatry, even if we don't physically bow down to the statues—yet we'll readily welcome them to "grace" our houses and yards. Many Christians also think they can engage in yoga and other pagan practices without offending God. The children of God should not engage in taekwondo, karate, kung fu, or similar martial arts that originate from pagan spiritism (see 2 Cor. 6:14-18). The Lord God asks, "Consider diligently, and see if there be such a thing. Hath a nation changed their gods, which are yet no gods?" (Jer. 2:10-11). In all of history God has said it is unheard of for a nation to cast away its belief in its idols except to serve the living God, and yet the Lord says of those who worship the true God, "But my people have changed their glory for that which doth not profit" (Jer. 2:11). Can you imagine Buddhist nations giving up Buddhism, or Islamic nations giving up Islam? Yet Christians in the West have forsaken the true God to embrace these very idols and other pagan practices, just like the children of Israel. Let the words of the prophet Jeremiah sink deep into our hearts.

> *Thus saith the LORD, What iniquity have your fathers found in me, that they are gone far from me, and have walked after vanity, and are become vain? Neither said they, Where is the LORD that brought us up out of the land of Egypt, that led us through the wilderness, through a land of*

COMPLACENCY

deserts and of pits, through a land of drought, and of the shadow of death, through a land that no man passed through, and where no man dwelt? And I brought you into a plentiful country, to eat the fruit thereof and the goodness thereof; but when ye entered, ye defiled my land, and made mine heritage an abomination. The priests said not, Where is the LORD? and they that handle the law knew me not: the pastors also transgressed against me, and the prophets prophesied by Baal, and walked after things that do not profit. Wherefore I will yet plead with you, saith the LORD, and with your children's children will I plead. For pass over the isles of Chittim, and see; and send unto Kedar, and consider diligently, and see if there be such a thing. Hath a nation changed their gods, which are yet no gods? but my people have changed their glory for that which doth not profit. Be astonished, O ye heavens, at this, and be horribly afraid, be ye very desolate, saith the LORD. For my people have committed two evils; they have forsaken me the fountain of living waters, and hewed them out cisterns, broken cisterns, that can hold no water."

(Jer. 2:5-13)

Moses warned them against this very sin:

For the LORD thy God bringeth thee into a good land, a land of brooks of water, of fountains and depths that spring out of valleys and hills; A land of wheat, and barley, and vines. ... A land wherein thou shalt eat bread without scarceness. ... When thou hast eaten and art full, then thou shalt bless the LORD thy God for the good land which he hath given thee. Beware that thou forget not the LORD thy God. ... Lest when thou hast eaten and art full, and hast built goodly houses, and dwelt therein ... and thy silver and thy gold is multiplied, and all that thou hast is multiplied ... and thou forget the LORD thy God. ... And thou say in thine heart, My power and the might of mine hand hath gotten me this wealth.

(Deut. 8:7-17)

Moses also wrote by the Word of the Lord, "And in all things that I have said unto you be circumspect: and make no mention of the name of other gods, neither let it be heard out of thy mouth" (Ex. 23:13). He also said, "Take heed to thyself that thou be not snared by following them ... and that thou enquire not after their gods, saying, How did these nations serve their gods?" (Deut. 12:30).

8.1.2 Our Respect of Authority Is Diminished

Complacency caused the children of Israel to forget how they previously respected and held in high esteem the servant of the Lord. Carefully note Exodus 32:1: "For as for this Moses, the man that brought us up out of the land of Egypt, we wot not what is become of him." Compare this with Exodus 11:3: "Moreover the man Moses was very great in the land of Egypt, in the sight of Pharaoh's servants, and in the sight of the people." Also compare it with Exodus 14:31: "And Israel saw that great work which the LORD did upon the Egyptians: and the people feared the LORD, and believed the LORD, and his servant Moses."

Complacency leads us to dishonor and usurp authority as we forget our place. Note that the people gathered themselves to Aaron, not to inquire of him, not to ask him to inquire of the Lord, not to ask him to send a search party after Moses, but to abandon all that had sustained them to that point.

8.1.3 Weak Leaders Bow to the People's Whims

Complacency causes weak leaders to give in to the people's whims rather than leading them to what is good for them. Note Exodus 32:2-4, where the people gathered themselves to Aaron and demanded of him, and he gave them their desires. Aaron never challenged them to wait patiently, never inquired of the Lord, and never rebuked them for their request—he simply gave in.

Aaron failed to point the people to God. He easily succumbed to their negative pressure rather than being the strong leader. It is interesting also to note that Moses blamed him directly for the people's sin: "And Moses said unto Aaron, What did this people unto thee, that thou hast brought so great a sin upon them?" (Ex. 32:21).

COMPLACENCY

8.1.4 We Become Distracted

Complacency leads to distraction from the primary task and leads to mistreatment of others and selfish indulgence. As Luke 12:45 says, people "shall begin to beat the menservants and maidens, and to eat and drink, and to be drunken." Also see Exodus 32:6: "And the people sat down to eat and to drink, and rose up to play."

8.1.5 We Must Be Chastened

Complacency leads to discipline, destruction, and the delaying or even falling short of the accomplishment of the original goal (compare with Ezra 7:10):

> *And that servant, which knew his lord's will, and prepared not himself, neither did according to his will, shall be beaten with many stripes.*
> (Luke 12:47)

8.1.6 We Are Eventually Blinded to the Truth

If we do not repent, complacency eventually leads to blindness.

> *I know thy works, that thou art neither cold nor hot: I would thou wert cold or hot. So then because thou art lukewarm, and neither cold nor hot, I will spue thee out of my mouth. Because thou sayest, I am rich, and increased with goods, and have need of nothing; and knowest not that thou art wretched, and miserable, and poor, and blind, and naked.*
> (Rev. 3:15-17)

8.1.7 We Become Unteachable

Finally, complacency leads to an unteachable spirit.

> *And Samuel told all the words of the LORD unto the people that asked of him a king. And he said, This will be the manner of the king that shall reign over you: He will take your sons, and appoint them for himself, for his chariots, and to be his horsemen; and some shall run before his*

> *chariots. And he will appoint him captains over thousands, and captains over fifties; and will set them to ear his ground, and to reap his harvest, and to make his instruments of war, and instruments of his chariots. And he will take your daughters to be confectionaries, and to be cooks, and to be bakers. And he will take your fields, and your vineyards, and your oliveyards, even the best of them, and give them to his servants. And he will take the tenth of your seed, and of your vineyards, and give to his officers, and to his servants. And he will take your menservants, and your maidservants, and your goodliest young men, and your asses, and put them to his work. He will take the tenth of your sheep: and ye shall be his servants. And ye shall cry out in that day because of your king which ye shall have chosen you; and the LORD will not hear you in that day. Nevertheless the people refused to obey the voice of Samuel; and they said, Nay; but we will have a king over us; That we also may be like all the nations; and that our king may judge us, and go out before us, and fight our battles.*
>
> (1 Sam. 8:10-20)

This is really a replay of Exodus 32:1—God was diminished in the children of Israel's eyes to the point that they thought a man could be substituted for God. It led to an unteachable spirit.

This issue alone should be a grave concern to us—that is, the diminishing of our appreciation and total dependence and subjection to the Lord of glory to the point of substitution of material possessions. This is such a false sense of security. From there it is just downhill.

8.2 How Can We Recognize Complacency?

Here is a list of the symptoms of complacency:

1. We begin to lose faith in God's sovereign ability to act.
2. We begin to lose respect for those whom we once admired.
3. We become discontented and begin to show a desire for things other than God and godliness.

4. We no longer have a feeling of awe when we think of God's works or don't think about God much at all.
5. The testimony to God's saving grace no longer excites us.
6. Doing God's work becomes a chore.
7. Time passes without any event to challenge us.
8. We become unteachable.
9. We are ungrateful.

8.3 Antidote to Complacency

8.3.1 Diligent Observation

The key to wisdom is receiving personal instruction through observation.

I went by the field of the slothful, and by the vineyard of the man void of understanding; And, lo, it was all grown over with thorns, and nettles had covered the face thereof, and the stone wall thereof was broken down. Then I saw, and considered it well: I looked upon it, and received instruction. Yet a little sleep, a little slumber, a little folding of the hands to sleep: So shall thy poverty come as one that travelleth; and thy want as an armed man.
(Prov. 24:30-34)

Be thou diligent to know the state of thy flocks, and look well to thy herds.
(Prov. 27:23)

But watch thou in all things, endure afflictions, do the work of an evangelist, make full proof of thy ministry.
(2 Tim. 4:5)

Therefore let us not sleep, as do others; but let us watch and be sober.
(1 Thess. 5:6)

Watch ye, stand fast in the faith, quit you like men, be strong.
(1 Cor. 16:13)

> *Therefore watch, and remember, that by the space of three years I ceased not to warn every one night and day with tears.*
>
> *(Acts 20:31)*

> *Remember therefore how thou hast received and heard, and hold fast, and repent. If therefore thou shalt not watch, I will come on thee as a thief, and thou shalt not know what hour I will come upon thee.*
>
> *(Rev. 3:3)*

Note that the very first qualification of an elder is vigilance (see 1 Tim. 3:2). I believe that quite often elders fail to be vigilant in this very area of complacency.

8.3.2 Prayer

Throughout the Scriptures we are repeatedly encouraged to watch and pray that we don't fall into temptation.

> *Watch and pray, that ye enter not into temptation: the spirit indeed is willing, but the flesh is weak.*
>
> *(Matt. 26:41)*

> *Continue in prayer, and watch in the same with thanksgiving.*
>
> *(Col. 4:2)*

> *But the end of all things is at hand: be ye therefore sober, and watch unto prayer.*
>
> *(1 Peter 4:7)*

8.3.3 Diligent and Earnest Heed to God's Word

> *Therefore we ought to give the more earnest heed to the things which we have heard, lest at any time we should let them slip. For if the word spoken by angels was stedfast, and every transgression and disobedience received a just recompence of reward; How shall we escape, if we neglect*

so great salvation; which at the first began to be spoken by the Lord, and was confirmed unto us by them that heard him.
(Heb. 2:1-3)

But take diligent heed to do the commandment and the law, which Moses the servant of the LORD charged you, to love the LORD your God, and to walk in all his ways, and to keep his commandments, and to cleave unto him, and to serve him with all your heart and with all your soul.
(Josh. 22:5)

And whatsoever ye do, do it heartily, as to the Lord, and not unto men.
(Col. 3:23)

8.4   Final Thoughts on Complacency

Complacency's starting ingredient is time—time without strong leadership, time away from God, time without action. Time is the friend of deceit. All of us are at risk of complacency because we all have been left here while our Lord prepares a place for us (see John 14:1-6). Let's be warned and diligent, and let's take the more earnest heed to the things we have heard lest we let them slip (see Heb. 2:1). Complacency is the enemy of true revival.

Chapter 9

CONCLUSION

IT'S EASY TO read a book like this, put it down, and then forget all you read. As I am reminded each day when I see my own character flaws reflected in my children or the fruit of my own selfishness grieving my precious bride, we have a constant battle with self and a great responsibility to apply what we have learned. Let's heed the warnings of the apostle James, who said, "Be ye doers of the word, and not hearers only, deceiving your own selves. For if any be a hearer of the word, and not a doer, he is like unto a man beholding his natural face in a glass: For he beholdeth himself, and goeth his way, and straightway forgetteth what manner of man he was. But whoso looketh into the perfect law of liberty, and continueth therein, he being not a forgetful hearer, but a doer of the work, this man shall be blessed in his deed" (James 1:22-25). He also said, "To him that knoweth to do good, and doeth it not, to him it is sin" (James 4:17).

God through the prophet Isaiah said, "I have not spoken in secret, in a dark place of the earth" (Isa. 45:19). And Moses, the Lord's servant, wrote, "For this commandment which I command thee this day, it is not hidden from thee, neither is it far off. It is not in heaven, that thou shouldest say, Who shall go up for us to heaven, and bring it unto us,

CONCLUSION

that we may hear it, and do it? Neither is it beyond the sea, that thou shouldest say, Who shall go over the sea for us, and bring it unto us, that we may hear it, and do it? But the word is very nigh unto thee, in thy mouth, and in thy heart, that thou mayest do it" (Deut. 30:11-14).

If we keep ignoring the call to return to the Lord's Word with a repentant heart, the Lord's Word given to Jeremiah will also be our judgment:

> *To whom shall I speak, and give warning, that they may hear? behold, their ear is uncircumcised, and they cannot hearken: behold, the word of the LORD is unto them a reproach; they have no delight in it. Therefore I am full of the fury of the LORD; I am weary with holding in: I will pour it out upon the children abroad, and upon the assembly of young men together: for even the husband with the wife shall be taken, the aged with him that is full of days. And their houses shall be turned unto others, with their fields and wives together: for I will stretch out my hand upon the inhabitants of the land, saith the LORD. For from the least of them even unto the greatest of them every one is given to covetousness; and from the prophet even unto the priest every one dealeth falsely. They have healed also the hurt of the daughter of my people slightly, saying, Peace, peace; when there is no peace. Were they ashamed when they had committed abomination? nay, they were not at all ashamed, neither could they blush: therefore they shall fall among them that fall: at the time that I visit them they shall be cast down, saith the LORD. Thus saith the LORD, Stand ye in the ways, and see, and ask for the old paths, where is the good way, and walk therein, and ye shall find rest for your souls. But they said, We will not walk therein. Also I set watchmen over you, saying, Hearken to the sound of the trumpet. But they said, We will not hearken. Therefore hear, ye nations, and know, O congregation, what is among them. Hear, O earth: behold, I will bring evil upon this people, even the fruit of their thoughts, because they have not hearkened unto my words, nor to my law, but rejected it.*
>
> *(Jer. 6:10-19)*

THE SUFFICIENCY OF SCRIPTURE

I must reiterate that this book is not about bringing the believer under law for salvation. Salvation is a free, unmerited gift of God, by grace, through faith in the name of the Lord Jesus Christ. This is rather about our ongoing sanctification once saved, applying the wisdom of God in our lives. Christians often talk about the fundamentals and non-essentials of the faith, as if there is a body of revelation which we can optionally ignore. Grace has been misunderstood to the extent that we often seek the bear minimum in order to get by as a Christian, rather than being so awestruck with God that we can't apply enough of His wisdom to our lives (1 John 5:3; Rom. 3:31; Ps. 1:2, 19:7.) There is nothing revealed of God which is non-essential otherwise He wouldn't have revealed it for our learning (Mat. 4:4.) Thus, once saved, we should glean all we can from the pages of God's revelation to mankind in order to live our lives in such a manner that would glorify Him and reflect the sensibility and wisdom of His immutable counsel to the unbelieving world around us.

This book was written as a corrective to a liberal Christian culture that has lost sight of the critical importance of God's written revelation to man-kind. Grace is not a license for a free-for-all. Salvation is not merely an escape route from hell. What God loved and hated under the old covenant, He still loves or hates today. The true Christian walk is a relational walk with God by faith in the totally sufficient and completed work of the Lord Jesus Christ, directed by God's forever-settled revealed wisdom, patterns, precepts and commandments (Ps. 119:89). It is evidenced by the fruit of the Holy Spirit (Gal. 5:22), and willing, humble submission under His Lordship.

> *Jesus answered and said unto him, If a man love me, he will keep my words: and my Father will love him, and we will come unto him, and make our abode with him. He that loveth me not keepeth not my sayings: and the word which ye hear is not mine, but the Father's which sent me. (John 14:23-24). Ye are my friends, if ye do whatsoever I command you.*
> *(John 15:14)*

CONCLUSION

Your application of Scripture may vary in your context, but the intent to seek and act upon God's written revelation with a humble and willing heart is ultimately how we demonstrate our submission to Christ's Lordship once saved. Whether you agree with every point raised in this book is not important to me. What is important is that you have sought wisdom from the Lord in His revealed Word and in prayer, rather than arriving at your convictions by default. If I have challenged you as I am constantly challenged, to know what and why you believe what you do, if I have helped you see that much of what is practiced in Christendom today is not based upon God's revelation but the traditions of men, and if I have encouraged you to return and trust the sufficiency of Scripture for all of life, then this book has served its purpose. This book is no substitute for studying the Word of God for yourself. I pray it merely serves as a starting point to help you in your pilgrim journey.

I'd like to conclude by recalling one of my favorite accounts in the history of God's people—the recovery of a truth not taught for hundreds of years!

> *And on the second day were gathered together the chief of the fathers of all the people, the priests, and the Levites, unto Ezra the scribe, even to understand the words of the law. And they found written in the law which the LORD had commanded by Moses, that the children of Israel should dwell in booths in the feast of the seventh month: And that they should publish and proclaim in all their cities, and in Jerusalem, saying, Go forth unto the mount, and fetch olive branches, and pine branches, and myrtle branches, and palm branches, and branches of thick trees, to make booths, as it is written. So the people went forth, and brought them, and made themselves booths, every one upon the roof of his house, and in their courts, and in the courts of the house of God, and in the street of the water gate, and in the street of the gate of Ephraim. And all the congregation of them that were come again out of the captivity made booths, and sat under the booths: for since the days of Jeshua the son of*

THE SUFFICIENCY OF SCRIPTURE

Nun unto that day had not the children of Israel done so. And there was very great gladness.

(Neh. 8:13-17)

Notice the phrase "for since the days of Jeshua the son of Nun unto that day had not the children of Israel done so." They had rediscovered a truth not obeyed for literally hundreds of years. Did they continue to disobey it with the excuse that no one had done it for generations? No, they obeyed it and there was great gladness! A study of history from Josiah's time to this account of Nehemiah to the reformation of the 1600's to the awakenings of the 1800's clearly demonstrates that revival always begins with a return to God's Word, repentance, and then vision to apply the sufficiency of Scripture to all of faith and practice. Let's rediscover the commands, principles, and patterns God has revealed in His Word, repent from our disobedience, and bring revival to our lives, families, churches, and nation—even if some of these things haven't been done for generations!

ENDNOTES

1. Sir Robert Anderson, *Misunderstood Texts of the New Testament*, 25.
2. A Third of SA Women Will Abort by Elissa Doherty http://www.theadvertiser.com.au accessed on 21 May 2006.
3. http://www.adelaidenow.com.au/news/south-australia/shock-teen-abortion-rate/story-e6frea83-1111115251719.
4. John Hudson Tiner, *Exploring the History of Medicine*, Master Books, 1999, 13.
5. John Hudson Tiner, *Exploring the History of Medicine*, Master Books, 1999, 68-74.
6. "Our young aren't marrying. Here's Y not" by LISA CORNISH, News Limited Network, January 04, 2013.

    YOUNG Australians are putting marriage and children on the backburner, as they concentrate on their careers and travel. Social researchers are warning the result could be a generation who have fewer children and less time to spend with those they have.

    "Starting families later means less kids," Mark McCrindle, director of McCrindle Research, said. "Parents may be more established in their careers and have double income, but they are also busier and have less time for activities and volunteering." Mr McCrindle said with parents getting older and kids living at home longer, there is concern that Australians will be retiring while still supporting their adult children at home.

7. "The biological clock and the career clock are in total conflict with one another: Total and complete conflict," MarketWatch reports the PepsiCo chief Indra Nooyi as saying during an Ideas Festival in Aspen, Colorado. "We cannot have it all". (by MarketWatch, News Corp Australia Network, July 04, 2014.)

"Infertility third most serious health problem after cancer and heart disease" by SUE DUNLEVY, NATIONAL HEALTH REPORTER, News Corp Australia, April 01, 2014.

This article cites Professor Robert Norman from the Robinson Institute in Adelaide as attributing high infertility to factors such as couples marrying later in life and work pressures, a direct result of women being encouraged to seek a career rather than motherhood. This is generally not much different in Christian circles.

"Landmark Australian research pinpoints birth defect issues linked to IVF" by Heather Kennett, Sunday Mail (SA), May 05, 2012.

IVF is often made necessary because of the deferral of children due to career or further study.

"85% of affairs begin in the workplace" (http://www.good-therapy.org/blog/truths-workplace-affair/ Accessed on 7 July 2014.)

While divorce rates are less than the general population amongst Bible believing Christians, they are almost identical amongst nominal conservative Christians according to the Barner research Group in their Marriage and Divorce Statistics Released March 31, 2008, (https://www.barna.org/barna-update/article/15-familykids/42-new-marriage-and-divorce-statistics-released#.U7nxMU2KAiQ Accessed on 7 July 2014).

"Divorce is costing the Australian economy $14 billion a year" by Lauren Wilson and Lisa Cornish, News Corp Australia, July 05, 2014.

ENDNOTES

8. "Report shows 59pc of married women are in the workforce" by Sue Dunlevy, The Advertiser, April 10, 2010.

    THE sole male breadwinner is a dying breed according to a study that found 59 per cent of married women with children are in the workforce. A hundred years ago, our wage system was built around the base pay a man needed to support his family, but over the past 30 years the number of men participating in the workforce has fallen from 79 to 72 per cent. More women (59 per cent) than men (41 per cent) are completing university degrees.

    "WOMEN will outnumber men in the workforce within a decade, business experts predict" by Candice Keller, The Advertiser, January 02, 2010.

9. "Men, Who Needs Them?" by GREG HAMPIKIAN, New York Times, August 24, 2012.

    This article asserts that with expanding reproductive choices, we can expect to see more women choose to reproduce without men entirely. "... women are both necessary and sufficient for reproduction, and men are neither. From the production of the first cell (egg) to the development of the fetus and the birth and breast-feeding of the child, fathers can be absent. ..."

10. Muhammad boys' prove 'Islam will enter every house in Europe' by Aaron Klein www.worldnetdaily.com accessed on December 19, 2007.
11. John 19:1-3.
12. Isa. 50:6; Mat. 27:30.
13. Mat. 27:29.
14. Mat. 27:35.
15. Mark 3:25.
16. Gen. 2:24.
17. Matt. 19:6.
18. Eph. 5:22.
19. Eph. 5:25.
20. Prov. 4:23.
21. 1 Cor. 12:26.

22. Eph. 5:23-29.
23. 1 Peter 3:7.
24. Col. 3:19.
25. Gen. 2:18.
26. 1 Peter 3:6.
27. Prov. 14:1.
28. Prov. 31:10-12, 26.
29. Prov. 31:30.
30. Prov. 21:19.
31. Prov. 26:21.
32. Prov. 27:15.
33. James 1:20.
34. Heb. 13:4.
35. Mal. 2:15.
36. 1 Peter 3:4; Prov. 31:10-31.
37. 1 Cor. 16:13.
38. Charles D Provan, *The Bible and Birth Control*, 1989.
39. www.globalwarmingglobalgovernance.com.
40. Ps. 127:3-5, 128:1-4; Gen. 17:6, 17:20, 24:60, 28:3, 41:52, 49:25; Deut. 7:13.
41. Jer. 32:35; Lev. 18:21; R. J. Rushdoony, *The Philosophy of the Christian Curriculum*, 112-113, describes the essence of the worship of Moloch as Statism.
42. Matt. 19:14; Mark 10:14; Luke 18:16.
43. Prov. 10:4, 12:24, 13:4, 22:29; 2 Thess. 3:10.
44. Ps. 37:25.
45. Luke 23:29.
46. Gen. 1:28, 9:1, 9:7, 35:11.
47. A Google search for "overpopulation myth" will result in numerous articles exposing this satanic lie.
48. Ex. 1:9-20.
49. R. J. Rushdoony, *The Philosophy of the Christian Curriculum*, 3-4.
50. A Common Faith, John Dewey, page 51, Yale University Press, 1934.

ENDNOTES

51. The Calvinistic Concept of Culture (Philadelphia, PA: Presbyterian and Reformed, 1959, 1972), p200.
52. R. J. Rushdoony, *The Philosophy of the Christian Curriculum*, 149-150.
53. James Nickel, *Mathematics: Is God Silent?*, 14.
54. Johannes Kepler, *Epitome of Copernican Astronomy & Harmonies of the World*, trans. Charles Glenn Wallis (Amherst: Prometheus Books, [1618-1621, 1939]1995), 245.
55. Cited in J.J. Fahie, "The Scientific Works of Galileo," *Studies in the History and Method of Science*, ed. Charles Singer (New York: Oxford University Press, 1921), 232.
56. Galileo Galilei, *Discoveries and Opinions of Galileo*, trans. Stillman Drake (Garden City: Doubleday, 1957), 183.
57. Ibid., 182.
58. Ibid., 196.
59. Jaki, *The Road of Science and the Ways to God*, 106.
60. Newton, *The Principia*, 440.
61. Ibid., 440-442.
62. Blaise Pascal, *Pensées* (number 425).
63. "Christian Schools Angry Over Ban on Teaching Creationism," *The Sydney Morning Herald*, March 3, 2010: http://www.smh.com.au/national/education/christian-schools-angry-over-ban-on-teaching-creationism-20100302-pgjb.html accessed on 21 March, 2010.
64. Butler, Trent C. Editor. Entry for 'Education in Bible Times'. Holman Bible Dictionary. http://www.studylight.org/dictionaries/hbd/view.cgi?n=1737. 1991.
65. http://www.scrollpublishing.com/store/head-covering-history.html; http://www.faithfulgenerations.com/hc.htm; http://www.headcovering.info/articles.html accessed 25 March, 2010.
66. *Truth and Transformation* by Vishal Mangalwadi ©2009 YWAM Publishing.
67. Herod Antipas, the Tetrarch, was the son of Herod the Great (who was Arabic by descent) and Malthace, a Samaritan woman. He certainly wasn't Jewish by genealogy. Though he may have at times publically presented himself as sympathetic to Judaism,

this was for expedience, to gain the favour of the Jews. The Lord Jesus exposed him as a self-serving Gentile when he called him a fox in Luke 13:32. A fox is not only sly, but unclean according to Leviticus 11:4-8 because it neither chews the cud nor divides the hoof. (Also See Luke 3:19-20; 13:31-32; 23:11-12, Acts 4:27, Rom. 2:28-29, Josephus, Antiquities 17.20, War 1.562.)
68. Christianity can combat conservative Islam threat, The Daily Telegraph, July 30, 2010
69. *Complacency.* Dictionary.com. Dictionary.com Unabridged. Random House, Inc. http://dictionary.reference.com/browse/complacency accessed March 26, 2010.

www.ingramcontent.com/pod-product-compliance
Lightning Source LLC
Chambersburg PA
CBHW030311080526
44584CB00012B/530